Educating for the
'New World Order'

by
B. K. EAKMAN

HALCYON HOUSE
PORTLAND, OREGON

Library of Congress Catalog Card Number
91-73096

ISBN 0-89420-278-2

344100

Epilogue Revised for the
Fourth Printing — March 1992
Fifth Printing — July 1992

This book is for anyone, parent or educator, who ever ran afoul of the education bureaucracy...
or expects to.

Acknowledgements

MANY OF THE documents referred to in this book were directed to the author by researchers, interested parties, and education professionals from all over the United States. Their tireless efforts to collect information over long periods of time — as far back as 45 years — made it possible to chronicle a series of events, and to put them in a context that provides insight into the times and circumstances surrounding each event.

There are many people to thank for their painstaking work to keep the plethora of correspondences, records, and documentation straight, not the least of whom is Anita Hoge, who took the real "slings and arrows" in an attempt to make sense of a system that goes out of its way to frustrate those who, in other circumstances, would be its greatest supporters.

Accolades are also in order for Erica Kenney, who shared some ten years' worth of documentation from House and Senate records, untangled their frequently convoluted language, and provided the context in which the various pieces of legislation occurred. Her help in editing and ensuring the accuracy of the manuscript kept the task from becoming overwhelming.

Many thanks go to my publisher, Carl Salser, who once bolstered the confidence of a struggling young author and educator, without compromising the standards of excellence.

A special word of appreciation goes to Charles M. Richardson, of New York, for his reference materials and for lending still another perspective to the issue — from the business and scientific communities.

Thanks also go to Senator Arlen Specter and his staff for keeping the channels of communication open between his office and his constituents under difficult and trying circumstances.

So many others are deserving of mention that it would take many pages to thank them all. Many sources have requested anonymity. So I will list the

States these other worthy individuals represent: You know who you are, and I am deeply appreciative.

California (1)	Texas (3)	Pennsylvania (4)	Virginia (2)
Idaho (1)	Florida (2)	Maine (1)	Maryland (2)
Washington (1)	Tennessee (2)	Wisconsin (1)	Michigan (3)
Colorado (1)	Nebraska (6)	N. Carolina (1)	Indiana (2)

And, finally, a word of thanks to my husband, David, for putting up with all of this for the past four years.

Some of the excerpts in this book may be from works still in copyright. It is the author's belief and understanding that quoting isolated excerpts, with credit in a footnote, for the purpose of critical commentary, is regarded as "fair use," under the copyright laws. Because some documents were collected over years, there was no way to verify whether some were ever in copyright, thereby making it impractical to give acknowledgement to the sources in question. If any holders of copyright have been overlooked, the author offers apologies and promises correction in later editions.

Contents

Preface

ON APRIL 18, 1990, nearly five years after Anita Hoge filed a complaint against Pennsylvania's Department of Education, U.S. Senator Arlen Specter's local office in Pittsburgh called to say her complaint had been resolved. She had won. The staffer who telephoned on the Senator's behalf praised Mrs. Hoge for her incredible persistence and sacrifice of time. Not to mention money.

This is the incredible story of how one gutsy woman stood the whole education establishment on its head and forced a cabinet-level government agency to obey the law. What began as a simple citizen complaint against a local school district resulted in a massive investigation — and coverup — of irregularities in this nation's education system dating as far back as 1965. Bungling education bureaucrats in West Alexander, Pennsylvania, never dreamed they would one day be on the losing side of a fight against their Washington counterparts, whom they previously had imagined to be allies. Even less did officials in Washington dream they would be out-maneuvered into opening a Pandora's Box of white papers, position papers, working papers, official memos, appropriations, review boards, "secure" lists, and task forces that eventually would reveal one of the most unique and mind-boggling cases of misrepresentation in American history.

Anita Hoge herself did not expect to be declared winner in a case against the U.S. government — even before it went to court, and before she had had a chance to make her case public.

But, then, that was the one thing the U.S. Department of Education had sought desperately to avoid.

In the larger sense, this book addresses the ongoing debate over why it is, in this Information Age, that America's high school graduates continue to become less knowledgeable about things that ought to be, well . . . common knowledge. It attempts to explain to bewildered analysts — and to an even more bewildered public — how the Era of the Microchip can produce young people of such stunning ignorance, culturally and academically. In recounting the events of the Anita Hoge case, a major question is raised as to whether certain individuals or groups, by dint of their experience, reputation, or influence, may perform actions "in the public interest" without the public's knowledge or consent. In describing how the federal government became the transmission belt for the ills that plague American education, the book is a case study on usurpation of power in a democracy. Children entering school today are the first recipients of birth-to-death computerized dossiers built around a social security number. Included in their files are probable political leanings, personal hangups, and family financial and personal background data — all couched in terms of "demographic research" and "academic testing." For this reason, *Educating for the "New World Order"* is a frightening account. If the mood of the country should ever shift dramatically — as a result, for example, of some volatile political development — schools already set up as "clinics" and "laboratories," where youthful opinions are analyzed for defects, documented, and sent to cross-referenceable, non-secure, centralized computer banks, along with private information about family members, will be in a position to do considerably more than make state by state comparisons of educational data. Schools will, in fact, be able to help government inflict a kind of computerized slavery on every man, woman, and child in the America.

Whatever faction winds up in control of American politics in the year 2000 will inherit the new supercomputer, the Elementary and Secondary Integrated Data System, brought on line in 1988. With easy access to cross-referenceable personal information, including value judgments and political viewpoints, this faction will become powerful beyond imagining.

Moreover, *Educating for the "New World Order"* details how virtually any group or organization with enough money and influence can manipulate even the most democratic of political systems, utilize high technology to establish top-down control and coercive regulatory bodies, and in the end implement its own agenda.

List of Allegations

- storing cross-referenceable personal information in non-secure data banks in such a way as to pose a threat to national and individual security and to violate the Fourth Amendment;

- permitting the unauthorized cross-use of official records;

- using the social security number in a manner inconsistent with Section 7 of the Privacy Act of 1974;

- using taxpayers' money to amass personal data accessible as psychological profiles, on children and their families, through the use of mandated school assessment tests, fraudulently passed off as academic achievement tests;

- scoring said tests for "correct" attitudes (in violation of the pluralism ethic) and giving official seals of approval to curricula which purport to remediate incorrect attitudes (as assessed from the test), in violation of the legal prohibition against the federal government establishing curriculum for the nation's schools;

- creating a closed-loop distribution mechanism for federally approved curricular materials;

- fraudulently representing (or allowing to be fraudulently represented) corrective "remedial" programs aimed at promoting state-desired opinions and attitudes;

- abetting the obstruction of public access to documents that would truthfully explain and label attitudinal tests and programs;

- colluding with private, tax-free organizations for the purpose of creating a national test and a national curriculum in violation of federal law;

- allowing certain government agencies to be used as pawns of private organizations seeking to redefine, if not revamp, America's social and economic framework (thereby placing these government agencies in the position of conspiring to overthrow the U.S. Constitution);

- obtaining funds for one purpose and using them for another;

- inducing local educational institutions to accept federal money — for ulterior purposes and by deceptive means;

- creating and subsidizing, in effect, a legalized private education system mislabeled a "public" school;

- subsidizing a policy of practicing medicine without a license (by permitting medically unlicensed practitioners to carry out therapeutic programs); and

- violating the Competition in Contracts Act.

INTRODUCTION

"Grievance Procedure" and the Rights of a Citizen

IN THE SPRING of 1986, the first incriminating evidence against the federal government on education policy started pouring out of computer banks in Pennsylvania. It covered a wide range of information, all related to a November 1986 complaint initiated by one Anita Hoge, who had challenged the use of a test given to school children in her district. That test was known as the Educational Quality Assessment, or EQA. In the course of following up her complaint, puzzling irregularities began to surface — irregularities in the funding of the test; in the contracting; in the legal mandates implementing the test; and, most disconcertingly, irregularities in the so-called "corrective" learning programs aimed at remediating student weaknesses assessed from the test.

The gist of Anita Hoge's complaint against the state education agency was that a test requiring written parental consent had been given to her son, and to the other children in her son's class, without parents' knowledge or consent. Furthermore, what was being passed off as an academic test, she alleged, was a sophisticated psychological survey, and it violated the Protection of Pupil Rights Amendment, enacted by Congress.

The petite, 34-year-old former high school majorette and college honor student did not start out with the intention of launching a personal campaign against the state. More than anything else, she was annoyed by the arrogance of local authorities, and indignant at the conflicting responses pawned off on her by officials who were too lazy, apparently, to get their stories straight. A perfectionist by nature, Anita Hoge could not resist the temptation to point out the inconsistencies, and often outright errors, in their replies.

Anita Hoge was also a "pack rat"; she never threw anything away. As the months of correspondence wore on, she began to accumulate official handbooks, guidelines and legal documents which she quoted to patronizing bureaucrats in Pennsylvania and Washington, D.C, to prove that she knew what she was talking about. Every letter, she thought, would be her last. But each response she received — or failed to receive — brought a new taunt. It was as if education officials were sticking out their collective tongues at her.

In the course of events, Anita Hoge was put in contact with various experts, parents, activists, and just plain interested parties. To her immense surprise, others had been engaged in similar correspondence battles with authorities for years. In fact, there were networks all over the country, all dredging up documents, exchanging information and newspaper clippings, and conversing via computer.

Anita Hoge thought it was time to start pooling resources. She formed a six-person research team eventually dubbed "the Pennsylvania Group." Knowing virtually nothing about the inner workings of Washington and only bits and pieces of educational jargon, computer networking, legal argument and precedent, this group of "little old ladies in tennis shoes" (as one annoyed Education Department official later put it) rolled up their sleeves, dug in their heels, and decided they were going to learn.

Before Anita Hoge and her colleagues were through, they had plugged into activists all over the country. Together, they amassed so much incontrovertible evidence of misrepresentation that all they needed was the money for court costs.

But even if they could have gotten the money together, that was not the way the system was supposed to work. A Grievance Procedure, taken in proper sequence, was supposed to result in a fair and objective evaluation of data by officials without citizens having to invest their life savings in court costs. Taxpayers did not elect their representatives to be told, in effect, to put up or shut up every time they ran into a problem. Citizens were not supposed to be passed around from one bureaucrat to another, to be stalled, vilified and delayed until they tired of any attempt to see justice done. Their rights were clearly protected by legislation. In this case, the Protection of Pupil Rights Amendment set out how complaints should be made and the proper procedure — on the part of complainants and authorities — for resolving grievances. That "the system" did not work became an issue as important, or more important, than the original complaint. Grievance procedure policy, at least in education, turned out to be a bad joke.

Anita Hoge was a quick student. She cultivated mentors in Washington who taught her the ropes. She wasn't intimidated by criticisms like: "That letter is too long" or "sounds too housewife-ish." Anita learned to craft not only her letters but her style. She learned how to play the game; to use her supposed naiveté and "housewife-ishness" to advantage; and, in the end, she proved to be as tough as her opposition in the Washington and Pennsylvania bureaucracies.

Anita and her group of lay researchers spent nearly five years being alternately insulted, patronized, lied to, and ignored. Anita herself spent hundreds of dollars of her own money on documentation, interviews, and long trips away from home to find answers to the puzzling questions her complaint had unearthed. She and her husband had to supplement their income — by some $15,000 a year — to place their three children in a school that did not accept federal funding. Had Anita been paid by the Department of Education for the kind of work she was doing on educational research, however, she might have earned ten times the amount the couple needed — as much as $150,000 — by April of 1990.

That was when Senator Specter's staffer called to say the Deputy General Counsel's Office (the legal arm of the U.S. Department of Education) had ruled that yes, the EQA was a psychological test; that yes, federal funds had been involved; and that yes, some of the seven areas protected under the Protection of Pupil Rights Amendment, which forbade psychological testing, had been violated.

Anita Hoge, and the Pennsylvania Group, had won.

Or had they?

The Department's capitulation turned out to be a clever ploy to get Anita Hoge off the federal agency's backs.

But once again, bureaucracy-wise officials in Washington had underestimated their worthy opponent.

Arrogance is, of course, endemic to large bureaucracies — corporate and governmental — and official Washington is no exception. The assumption is frequently made that the little guy is lazy or stupid or both; that at the very least, the average citizen doesn't have time to delve into matters of complexity. To divest themselves of pesky irritants like Anita Hoge, bureaucrats employ a familiar pattern of good-riddance tactics: First, the old runaround; or, if that doesn't work, they ignore queries, provide conflicting information, convolute the wording of correspondence, create delays, and pull out the red tape. If these approaches fail to exhaust the patience of busybodies, there is always the court — where citizens can spend thousands of their own dollars.

The first time a self-satisfied bureaucrat underestimated Anita Hoge was when an official at the district education headquarters in McGuffey, to get rid of her, reluctantly permitted her a few minutes with "secure" documents. Little did the district staff imagine that a short time later, the genius with a near-photographic mind would walk out — not only with the contents in her head, but with the accompanying computer codes committed to memory, which later would enable her to order other important documentation, such as the "interpretive literature" to the Educational Quality Assessment test, from education data banks — just like the professionals do.

Some three years later, in ruling in Anita Hoge's favor, the bureaucracy was one-upped again. It had admitted, in effect, that officials at the highest levels of government were lying for more than forty months about the thrust of educational testing and the extent of federal involvement in curriculum, thereby exposing the U.S. Department of Education to multiple charges of illegal conduct, including collusion, unauthorized cross-use of official records, obtaining funds for one purpose and using them for another, violating the Competition in Contracts Act, conflict of interest, obstruction of public access, violation of Fourth Amendment rights, and more.

At that point, Anita Hoge's only problem was that the letter she got in the mail didn't match what she had been told over the phone by Senator

Specter's staffer. The letter obviously had been crafted in such a way as to avoid naming any specific violations of which the federal and state Departments of Education might be guilty. Technically, all Anita Hoge had in her hand were banalities and the promise that new policies would be implemented to prevent "future violations."

Apparently the mighty in Washington had forgotten four years' worth of letters and correspondences, written by the staffs of people like Assistant Education Secretary Bruno Manno; Emerson J. Elliott, head of the Center for Education Statistics; Hazel Fiers, Director of the Student and Family Education Rights and Privacy Office; state authorities like Pennsylvania Department of Education's Dr. William Logan, Acting Commissioner of Education (Bureau of Basic Education); McGuffey School District's Superintendent, Frank Zitto; and Dr. Robert Coldiron, Chief of the Department of Testing and Evaluation in Pennsylvania — all individuals who had performed their jobs as they saw and understood them, by denying the truth about assessment testing, its purpose, and any questionable follow-up strategies used to "improve" student performance. A few may even have been ignorant of these truths.

Anita Hoge, ever playing the disgruntled housewife, had all the while carefully tracked and dated these correspondences. So in May of 1990 she placed them into the hands of a top constitutional lawyer. She was ready to pull out her trump card.

No longer was Anita Hoge the put-upon housewife, vying uselessly for the attention of her senator or representative. In point of fact, she had been enjoying herself enormously for a year and a half!

For Anita Hoge had hit on an idea that would force the bureaucratic hands of Washington and Pennsylvania. It hinged on the government's plan to make use of the social security number in elementary and secondary testing programs — something that would allow testers to identify the opinions and attitudes not only of special groups, as in the past, but of individual children and their families, contrary to what the public was being led to believe. Because the Pennsylvania Group and its now-nationwide underground of researchers had located the working paper to the new supercomputer, the

Elementary and Secondary Integrated Data System, Anita Hoge knew it would be possible to link the test data with as many as 85 other state and federal computer networks — something that had not been possible before — and, in effect, create dossiers on every citizen in America.

In the end, the U.S. Department of Education was forced to the obvious conclusion: Anita Hoge was not going to give up — no matter if her kids had graduated, no matter whether she won a few minor battles, irrespective of whether she got any monetary settlement.

Anita Hoge was not after money. She was after justice.

As far back as 1973, officials in Pennsylvania had been dreading the day when they might be called on the carpet for failing to send parents notification of testing programs. Any parent who examined the literature too closely, after all, would see clearly enough that their children were getting a psychological test, at least in part. If enough parents were to balk and refused to allow their youngsters to participate, the validity of those tests would necessarily be compromised and the results skewed. For reasons that eventually would become apparent to Anita Hoge and others, validity had to be maintained at all costs.

But the time to elucidate those reasons to the public had not yet come.

So in 1973, Pennsylvania education authorities got their first jolt. Some parents got the American Civil Liberties Union to go to bat for them about violations of their and their children's privacy on a test. The test in question was supposed to be voluntary but, for some reason, it was mandatory and given without any prior notification. This was long before the Protection of Pupil Rights Amendment, long before Anita Hoge had children in school. The ACLU settled the case out of court in the complainants' favor, warning Dr. Robert Coldiron, Chief of Pennsylvania's Department of Testing and Evaluation, to henceforth give proper notice and see that the test was voluntary, in which case there would be "no basis" for charges of privacy violation.

But by the 1980s, Dr. Robert Coldiron apparently had decided he could ignore the warning. He never expected anyone to uncover the ACLU's admonition — certainly not Anita Hoge, the housewife.

Meanwhile, the new supercomputer — that technological marvel which would consolidate three existing computer banks of school-related data and add more — was ready ahead of schedule. Washington and Pennsylvania testing proponents did not like the new turn Anita Hoge's research was taking. It became crucial that she be stopped and her case resolved and closed.

Anita Hoge was getting too close. She had to be pacified and defused.

But the only way to close the case was to get Anita to drop it.

Again the "experts" miscalculated. By now, Anita Hoge was as good at legal maneuvering as they were, and she knew the bureaucratic mind.

The United States education system was a "house of cards." It was time to start pulling apart the deck, one card at a time.

And though education officials didn't know it, Anita Hoge's case was only the tip of the iceberg.

Part

I:
THE FEMININE
MISTAKE

CHAPTER 1

West Alexander, Pennsylvania, 1985

THE PARENTS OF three active elementary and secondary school children, a boy and two girls, Anita and Garrett Hoge were born and raised in small towns outside of Pittsburgh. The couple had never questioned their schools. When their own children reached school age in the 1970s, they deliberately moved to Washington County — specifically, to the city of West Alexander, Pennsylvania — many commuter miles from where Garrett worked as a financial planner. The couple thought a rural environment would be emotionally healthy for their youngsters. They had heard from friends that Washington County schools were particularly responsive and enthusiastic in their relationships with parents and students. The Hoges were not disappointed.

Until 1981 — when everything changed.

First, one of their daughters was forced to play out peculiar games, emotionally unsettling games — like the one where third-graders drew little red tickets, as in a card game, to decide which children would be ostracized and ridiculed by the class that day.

The purpose of the exercise? To teach compassion.

Then there was the drug-abuse prevention course for first graders. After several films on drug abuse, the Hoge's eldest daughter had nightmares for two weeks — the bad guys with needles were coming to get her.

Instead of being seated alphabetically or by achievement level, activity, or interest, the children suddenly were assigned seats on the basis of a sociogram — a device that ranks children according to popularity (technically known as "the degree of acceptance or rejection by peers"). The teacher used this teaching strategy to capitalize on the class' social relationships so that she could direct her lessons toward the most popular students and thereby (she thought) enhance her own popularity and class discipline. What the instructor was actually doing was to encourage peer pressure, precisely the thing that drug-abuse prevention courses were struggling to overcome. Worse, children were seated around long tables instead of in desks, so that they could easily see each others' papers. The Hoges' eldest daughter came home in tears one day explaining that she didn't understand "when to copy and when not to copy."

Youngsters who excelled in their work suddenly were relegated to day-long series of menial tasks — scrubbing desks and emptying trash; or they were moved to the back of the room to "help" lower achievers. This help, however, translated to giving the slower pupils the answers.

Home assignments diminished. Graded papers rarely came home. Printed lessons and exercises were distributed on mimeographed sheets, which were then collected and kept by the teacher for the next class ("to save paper"). Social studies became more social than studious.

When the students wrote anything profound, it was something morbid, like their obituary. Essay assignments were replaced by endless multiple choice and true-false exercises (again, on mimeographed "dittos"). No longer were there classes that specifically addressed penmanship, geography, or English grammar. Students now "role-played," even acting out the part of a prostitute or a drug addict. Role playing scripts consistently depicted parents as overbearing, selfish, or punitive; never loving, kind, or gentle.

Field trips were taken to cemeteries. Some assignments sounded like a collaboration between Sigmund Freud and Freddy of *Nightmare on Elm Street*. Class work increasingly reflected sociological themes: "If your town was about to come under nuclear attack and there was only room for three members of your immediate family in the bomb shelter, which ones would you leave out, and why?"

This, for eight-year-olds.

The next year, the Hoges' ninth-grade son, Garrett, Jr., changed drastically. He became sullen, argumentative. He angered easily, which was uncharacteristic, and he started displaying a generally negative attitude. His grades dropped.

Worried, the Hoges made a trip to the school to see if any of the teachers might have clues other than the usual process of adolescence. They found nothing. No suspicion of drug use, no problems with the teachers — and no samples of their son's work.

Then the boy came home with a story about a film his science teacher had shown that day. It was incredibly hard-hitting, and the child was visibly upset.

It had been a silent film, supposedly about the environment. It opened with an idyllic, rustic landscape — birds singing in the trees, mother ducks leading their young on a pleasant excursion down a creek, rabbits scampering over the ground.

The scene oozed fresh air, sunshine, and peace.

Suddenly an immense tractor-bulldozer appeared. The camera zoomed in on the word "**AMERICAN**" emblazoned on the side of the yellow tractor-bulldozer. The designation represented the name of the company, or make, of the equipment, but young children had interpreted it to mean "an American tractor." Due to camera angle, the vehicle gave the impression of a tank, and it started overturning everything in its path. Shrubs and grass were torn apart. Exhaust filled the air.

One man jumped out of the front seat and went to the embankment to drain the creek where the ducklings had been following their mother. Another man brought over a can of gasoline, poured it over portions of the surrounding area and ignited it. Flames leapt into the air. Trees caught fire; living creatures ran for cover.

Suddenly the ducklings, who by that time had emerged from the creek, were overcome by encroaching flames and burned alive in front of the children's eyes. Nests of baby birds came crashing to the ground, and the camera zoomed in on what was left. In a final close-up, the tractor-bulldozer was shown plowing under the remains of the nest, the ducklings, and the bird eggs.

As the scene receded from the screen, this sentence flashed: "Man cannot foresee or forestall. He will end by destroying the earth."

The teacher turned off the projector and divided the children into groups for a follow-up exercise. It was called "Who Shall Populate the Planet?" Young Garrett took home his "ditto" copy of the lesson sheet. The choices for populating the planet were a priest, a football player, a black minister, a microbiologist, a pregnant woman, and a teacher. The students were to select three.

When Garrett's mother, Anita Hoge, went to the school to see the film in question, it wasn't there. In fact, she didn't get to see it until three weeks later — after the film had made the rounds to dozens of schools. It was entitled "The Cry of the Marsh."

Irked, Anita started questioning Garrett more closely about his activities at school. Over a period of a couple weeks, he started opening up, and out tumbled a plethora of what the Hoges felt were inappropriate, violent, even "sick" lessons for schoolchildren.

Furthermore, Garrett had been selected to participate in a special class. He told his mother it was a "defective ed" class. Anita Hoge discovered that the class in question was called an "affective education" course.

The dictionary defines *affective* as "acting on the feelings or the emotions; having to do with or caused by the emotions rather than logical thought." The affective education class in question was not included on report cards and was billed as "a small group interaction therapy meeting" once a week. Other parents, Anita found, were not aware of the class — or that one of its purposes was to improve scores on a test called the Educational Quality Assessment.

The Hoges paid another visit to the school. But they found no sympathy there — and no explanations, either. Many of the old teachers they knew had left, and new ones had taken their places.

CHAPTER 2

The Test that Wasn't There

THE LAST STRAW occurred one year later, when the Hoges found that Garrett, Jr., had taken a "voluntary" assessment test they knew nothing about. By now, of course, young Garrett was aware that all was not well. He started bringing home more copies of the mimeographed lessons, although teachers usually tried to collect them. Garrett also began reporting to his parents class activities that seemed "weird." That was how they found out about the assessment test. The Hoges finally told their son that although he must always obey the teacher and make the best grades he could, he was under no obligation to divulge personal information about himself and his family unless he wanted to.

The following March, Garrett went through just five pages of another test before he excused himself to go to the bathroom. Instead, he called his mother. Anita Hoge asked her son if he had studied for the test he was describing. No, he said; it was a surprise. And even if he had tried, he added, there was no way anyone could study for a test like this one.

Anita Hoge knew she would never be able to make it from her home to the school in time to do any good, so she told Garrett not to make a fuss, to remember what he could, and to see if he could find out the name of the test.

Garrett did better than that. He managed to scribble down some of the test questions on scratch paper, along with the name of the test: the Educational Quality Assessment, put out by the Pennsylvania Department of Education. He took his notes home.

What the Hoges read was odd, indeed; questions like: "The prospect of working most of my adult life depresses me — Check 'yes,' 'no,' or 'sometimes.'"

And: "A person is in a large crowd on a street corner. They are protesting about something. Some people pick up rocks and start throwing them at windows. In this situation, I would ALSO THROW ROCKS when I knew: (a) there was no chance of getting caught, (b) I agreed with what they were protesting about, or (c) my closest friend decided to throw rocks."

What about the kid who *wouldn't* throw rocks? Choice *a, b,* or *c*? How many questions like this were on the test? About half, answered Garrett.

Anita Hoge marched herself to the school and demanded to see the test. She was told it wasn't there. She asked to see the teacher who had given the test, but proctors had been brought in from outside the school to administer it. Anita asked why questions like the ones Garrett brought home were being asked. In response, she was reprimanded about her son's having compromised the test results by writing down questions. Then she was told the questions measured aptitude.

"But you said it was an *assessment* test," she insisted.

Were testers measuring achievement, then, or aptitude, or what?

Anita started quizzing other parents on the matter of testing. It turned out that some three years before another angry parent had obtained a test through her then-state senator. It was an Educational Quality Assessment test — one of the first to be given in the district. Apparently, the senator had since been told the error of his ways in having allowed a test to get away, but now he was retired and there was little anyone could do to him — or to get the test back. The parent passed it on to Anita Hoge. The school district was still using it, she said.

What Anita saw confirmed that more than half the questions were blatantly attitudinal — about personal feelings, opinions, and home life. Like the other parent, Anita Hoge, too, examined the source: the Pennsylvania Department of Education, Division of Educational Quality Assessment, Harrisburg, Pennsylvania.

Armed with this information, Anita Hoge called Margaret Smith, Secretary of Education in Pennsylvania. Anita demanded to see a copy of the current test (even though she already had the set passed to her by the other parent) and also any accompanying literature. Unsurprisingly, Smith declined, but in order to pacify her irritated caller, she sent along something called the *EQA Commentary*. The *Commentary* proved very revealing. Among other things, it mentioned a set of booklets: "Educational Quality Assessment Resource Packets."

Anita petitioned her state representative, Pennsylvania Representative Roger Raymond Fischer, and told him she wanted to see the test, the Resource Packets, and any accompanying explanatory material. As usual, she was refused access to the test and foisted off on an aide. Fischer's beleaguered aide, Billie Majors, got rid of Anita by sending her a few samples of the 1981 "Educational Quality Assessment Resource Packet" booklets.

The actual title of each Educational Quality Assessment Resource Packet was "EQA Resources for Improvement." Each was an approximately 25-page compilation of curricular materials, described in detail, and developed by the staff at the Department of Education "with the aid of PDE [Pennsylvania Department of Education] curriculum specialists." Each packet had a subtitle on the cover: Work, Understanding Others, Self-Esteem, Arts and Humanities, Interest in Learning and School, Citizenship, and others. These subtitles were each followed by an asterisk, and when one looked farther down on the cover page, to the meaning of the asterisk, it was explained as referring to a particular EQA area. For example:

*EQA area Information Usage

*EQA area Career Awareness

*EQA area Citizenship

In every case, the "*EQA area" designation was followed by the name of an EQA test portion. So the curricula described in the booklets were clearly connected to the Educational Quality Assessment test, or state assessment. The booklet covers also indicated that both the test and the curricula outlined inside were connected to federal funds and to something known as "NAEP objectives." Listings in the recommended professional reading section, at the end of each booklet, often stated it as well.

At the bottom of each booklet's cover page was the designation:

Pennsylvania Department of Education
Bureau of School Improvement
Division of Educational Quality Assessment
Harrisburg, PA 17108

Thus it appeared that specific curricula were being developed and disseminated through the state education agency, which of course is funded by the federal government. The purpose of the learning programs described in the booklets, apparently, was to correct students' "inappropriate" answers on the Educational Quality Assessment test. The table of contents for each booklet listed a *goal statement, measurement rationale, scoring,* and something at the end that would later prove enormously significant — *validated projects* — the list of "selected resources," which were a list of additional curriculum titles, with two-to-five-word descriptions.

Anita Hoge was astounded at how completely each booklet sought to correct students' attitudes and "inappropriate responses" on the Educational Quality Assessment, how thoroughly and systematically the approach had been thought out. But when she examined the Resource Packet (booklet) for Citizenship, Anita noticed on page 23 a listing for a "selected resource" curriculum that she recognized as being one of the more questionable learning programs: *Community Involvement for Responsible Citizenship.* She decided to order a copy of the teachers' edition and examine it in detail. The listing in the Resource booklet described the citizenship program as "an ESEA Title IV-C project operated by Allegheny Intermediate Unit #3." Anita Hoge noticed a similar designation in another Resource Packet booklet: "ESEA, Title I." Curious, she looked up the meaning of "ESEA" — the Elementary and Secondary Education Act of 1965. There were five "titles, " or entitlement provisions, in all. Title I was the first article, or funding provision, under that law. It was for disadvantaged children. Title IV was the fourth article. It had to do with the government establishing regional Educational Research Laboratories and Centers. The "C" in Title

IV-C was a subprovision of Title IV — for "educational innovation and support". Anita Hoge looked back at the Citizenship Resource booklet, at the designation "Intermediate Unit #3." What was that? An address for the Intermediate Unit was given, in Pittsburgh.

When Anita Hoge found out what the Intermediate Unit was, and where the funding for it came from, that was a turning point in her up-to-now casual research. This knowledge, combined with the meaning of the term "validated project" implied that the federal government was conspiring with agencies at the state level to create and control curriculum, in violation of federal law.

It was merely a matter of follow-through to find out how the school district had obtained its citizenship curriculum. It came from a list of approved, or "validated" curricular programs, obtainable by computer — the R.I.S.E.[1] computer. The program was designed to correct "inappropriate" attitudes about citizenship.

With evidence of federal funding involved in the testing program and, now, the curriculum, the Hoges contacted Dr. Robert Coldiron, then Chief of the Division of Educational Testing and Evaluation in Harrisburg. They expected him to lower the boom on Washington County Schools.

Dr. Coldiron was angry, all right. But not at the schools. He insisted, first of all, that the test was neither mandated nor federally funded; secondly, that parents did *not* have to be informed in advance; and furthermore, he said, the Educational Quality Assessment was "mostly cognitive" — a term the Hoges took to mean "academic."

Anita Hoge was nonplussed. How, she wondered, could she have been so mistaken?

CHAPTER 3

Paper Chases: Part One

ANITA HOGE WAS the next-to-youngest child in a family of seven children. Despite youthful successes in her school's band, chorus, dramatics, and yearbook staff, she had always tended to be somewhat of a loner, like her Italian immigrant father, a coal-miner. When her father's family had stepped off the boat upon entering the United States, in 1914, customs officials couldn't seem to spell or remember his name, "Armando," so they wrote down "Herman."

"Herman" was an extremely intelligent, philosophical young man who, due to circumstances, never had a chance to become educated. One of 15 children, there was not enough food, and he was given to his grandparents to raise. To survive, he would walk along the railroad tracks and pick up coal to sell. The only formal education he got was up to the fifth grade. His first job was the mines.

Anita's father may have been down, but he certainly wasn't out. "Herman" eventually left the mines and started his own meat business. He not only survived, but prospered. A proud, religious man whose parents hadn't forgotten their Italian heritage, Armando/"Herman" passed it along to his own seven children.

He also passed on two personal traits — perseverance and determination (some would have said "obstinacy") — which his daughter, Anita, now exercised with a vengeance.

Anita Hoge went to her state senator in Washington, Pennsylvania: Senator Barry Stout. She repeated her demand to see the Educational Quality Assessment test (even though she still had the set given to her by the other irate parent earlier on).

Senator Stout was somewhat taken aback to discover that such a seemingly simple and reasonable request was being made so difficult for his constituent. Unable to obtain permission to review the test, he hurried to fulfill Anita Hoge's second demand: to see a R.I.S.E. printout. Anita could not get it herself, so Senator Stout paid for the printout and Anita Hoge reimbursed him.

The R.I.S.E. computer network is one of the largest regional education computers in the country — a prototype, in fact. It combines the contents of two federal data banks full of education curriculum and research data. Once one understands the computer codes and how to order, all it takes is a fee to obtain curricular materials and other documents.

The most interesting part about the whole process, Anita discovered, was that curricular programs were described one way in the printout — and another way once they reached local schools. For example, if a program was based on a teaching methodology called "values clarification"[2] it said so in the printout. But by the time it got to local school districts, any potentially objectionable descriptors were gone.

It was now 1986, and officials in Pennsylvania started to worry that Anita Hoge would take them to task for obstructing access to documents, because of the Freedom of Information Act. Today, assessment tests are exempted from the Act in most states, but at the time no one was sure — least of all officials in Anita Hoge's school district. When Anita showed up at the district headquarters to see the test, it was made clear that her presence was unwelcome, and that authorities there were humoring her to get rid of her. Reluctantly school district officials allowed Anita to see an Educational Quality Assessment test, as long as there was someone else in the room with her to make sure she didn't take or copy anything.

That, of course, proved to be Mistake Number One on the part of the local bureaucracy. For although Anita didn't take or copy anything, she did, in fact, walk out with the materials — questions and all — tucked away inside her head. Anita knew enough to recognize a computer code when she saw one. She decided to order something called "the interpretive literature" and the "scoring mechanism" to the test.

These two documents seemed to prove that what was being billed as a "cognitive," or achievement, test, was in reality a psychological profile, with only token testing of academics. Furthermore, the attitudes and opinions collected in this manner were being scored, graded, against a predetermined criterion. How could such practice be consistent with America's pluralism ethic? Anita wondered.

She also discovered from her examination of the documents in the school district office that yes, indeed, parents were supposed to have been notified in advance of the Educational Quality Assessment test so they could exempt their children if desired. She spent an afternoon on the telephone. No parent from her son's old class had received any such notice. They were prepared to swear to it.

It occurred to Anita Hoge she was no longer chasing a local issue, confined to abuse of parental rights on testing. What she had uncovered was far worse, and it looked as though not only her own state was affected, but others as well. The federally funded education establishment was bypassing parents and communities completely in an effort to control curriculum. Attitudinal testing now appeared to be merely a tool used to determine *which* curricula school districts would get. The selected programs were coming into the schools via the federally legislated ESEA entitlement provisions, or "titles," as they were called. So-called education "reformers" apparently intended to shove their approved (i.e., "selected") learning programs down the throats of unsuspecting parents. They would get around meddlesome textbook adoption committees and other local watchdog groups by bringing their materials into school districts through the back door.

Local control in education was gone, yet state and federal education agencies continued to perpetuate the myth that it wasn't. Why?

Anita quickly surmised that she had a lot to learn. If she and her husband were going to debate the likes of Dr. Robert Coldiron, the couple would have to know what they were talking about. Obviously there were technical terms and jargon she knew little about, and just as obviously, Dr. Coldiron and his colleagues would be able to take advantage of such ignorance.

Anita Hoge started with the terms she had already written down: Ten Quality Goals of Education, NAEP, non-cognitive tests, Affective Domain, EQA Resource Packet, Intermediate Unit, validated projects, and Educational Testing Service.

The computer codes that Anita Hoge had found on the R.I.S.E. network were **SEARCH** codes. Using these, she could, for a price, order related documents and materials, just like the schools did.

A little persistence. That's all it would take.

The first thing on Anita Hoge's agenda was to master educational jargon and the names of the leaders in the field — the ones who apparently had cast education policy and methodology. When a book was referred to in the literature, she ordered it and studied it. When a passage mentioned an unfamiliar term, she looked it up. Whenever a particular study was alluded to, Anita Hoge found it.

Instead of being overwhelmed by the unfamiliar terms and dry dissertations, the way most parents in her situation would have been, Anita found what she was learning utterly fascinating. The more she read, the more she wanted to know. Her college background in early childhood education helped.

This interest inevitably took her to other people, some of whom were experts in their own right, at area colleges and universities, and to those who were merely curious, like herself, and happened to be working along the same lines. Unintimidated by officialdom, Anita didn't hesitate to call on individuals in the U.S. Department of Education in Washington in order to clarify points she didn't understand. These calls often led, in turn, to other insiders and staffers, some of whom claimed to be as dismayed as she at what was going on in education.

As it happened, bureaucrats who were too free with their information found themselves transferred to other agencies. But a few sympathetic officials became valuable informants, and copies of memoranda, meeting minutes, and letters between state and federal agencies eventually were passed along to Anita which seemed to confirm what her network of lay researchers, later dubbed the Pennsylvania Group, already knew: that the federal government was colluding with certain extraordinarily wealthy, private benefactors to bankroll an audacious scheme that would re-direct educational objectives on a massive scale.

The scheme was masked under the appealing term "educational reform." And the public had taken the bait.

As Anita continued her study of educationese, it became somewhat of a mystery to her that the press never questioned terms used by education officials — like the comment from former Education Secretary Lauro Cavazos (June 1990), when he said "too much time [was being] spent on lower-order thinking skills."

"Lower order thinking skills," when one looks it up in the professional literature, implies basics — like reading, spelling, and computational skills. If schools were spending "too much time" on lower-order thinking skills, then it meant that too much time was being spent on basics — the very thing that education reform was supposed to be about. Cavazos' comment was typical, though: educational bigwigs had long been promoting "higher-order thinking skills," which meant something entirely different.

Beginning back as far as the 1940s, a whole new euphemistic vocabulary began evolving to describe psycho-behavioral techniques. By the late 1970s, the General Accounting Office had begun to investigate complaints about something called *behavior modification programs*. Already, terms like "critical thinking," "higher order skills," "reasoning skills," and "inferential learning" had become popular buzz-words for attitude-opinion molding. And for some reason, reporters didn't pick up on it.

But, then, why should they have?

When a publication like *Education Week* comes out with a headline such as "NAEP Finds Basic Skills Up; Higher Order Skills Lacking,"[3] the finished article is usually taken from an official press release — mailed or given to the publication's department head by the organization or government agency that writes it. Little or no actual research is done by the publication staff to write the report. Terms like "higher order skills" are rarely defined in releases. When pressed, officials may rephrase the term as "values" or even "non-cognitive learning," which, again, vaguely resembles English but otherwise means little to the lay person. The real substance of the words tends to be found only in technical papers that circulate among professionals.

Fortunately for Anita Hoge and her colleagues, academics live in a publish-or-perish world, and many, if not most, of their technical papers wind up in the Educational Resource and Information Center network (nicknamed ERIC) — a federal computer bank which houses theoretical and technical materials on education. There, a persistent researcher can locate specific education terminologies, even obtain whole dissertations detailing the rationales and their supporting sources — providing one knows what to look for.

Anita Hoge learned how to use these data searches. And she knew exactly what she was looking for. Thus went the 47-month campaign of Anita Hoge, which took her from her local school to the district superintendent; to her state senator; to the state education agency in Harrisburg; to the U.S. Department of Education in Washington; and, finally, to Capitol Hill with a suitcase full of documentation for Senator Arlen Specter and the Education Appropriations Subcommittees.

Part
II:
A TALE OF TWO PRINTOUTS

CHAPTER 4

Fuel for the Fire

GARRETT HOGE, SR., soon tired of the battle. Not to mention the phone bills and documents.

"You can't change the world, you know," Garrett reminded his wife. But he nevertheless was convinced of the wisdom of sending their three youngsters to a school which did not accept federal funding.

The handsome, lean six-foot blond, was surprised, though. He had never seen his wife so consumed with a project. It wasn't as though Garrett didn't consider himself a committed person, after all. But when you've nothing whatever to gain from a thing; when all you get is a runaround — and you're in the hopeless situation of being one person against an army of bureaucrats...where's the sense of spending one's time like that? he wanted to know. Wasn't life tough enough?

Anita was surprised, too. She hadn't expected to get so caught up in the issue. She wasn't the type, really. Anita was outdoorsy, not bookish; artsy and creative, not a paper-pusher; interested in motherhood, not in a full-time desk job — especially an unpaid one.

As she sat alone one February morning in 1986 at the kitchen table, after the kids had gone off to school, Anita thought back to her own childhood in rural Burgetstown, when she used to take long walks in the woods and sit by herself and contemplate. Just like she was contemplating now.

Anita sighed. Maybe it was just the timing. Her mother had died recently of a stroke. Perhaps she just needed something new to do.

But deep down Anita Hoge knew that wasn't it. Ever since the day her son had called home about "that weird test," she'd had a sinking feeling in her gut — a sense of something having gone terribly wrong. Her family, her children, had been violated. Some people in high places had gotten carried away with their own importance and decided they didn't need to share their plans with those on whom they would experiment. And nobody was doing anything about it. Oh, there were parents and their lawyers who challenged all sorts of idiotic things: dress codes, for instance, or hair-length codes, or coed football teams. They spent thousands of dollars on such trivia. But here was something really important, and practically no one was taking the slightest notice.

Then there was the matter of the way she had been treated by local and state officials. They were so condescending, so aloof. They treated her like a...like a...woman?

Now there was a new thought. She had never thought of herself as a feminist. But there it was. No ..."woman" wasn't quite the right word, either. Like a little girl. That was it. Like a *child-woman,* the stereotype bubblehead.

Well, if such treatment demoralized some and made them slink away like chastened puppies, it certainly had the opposite effect on her. It made her angry.

She snatched a folder from a nearby shelf.

Well, Anita thought. Perhaps she was reading too much into things. And it wasn't like her to do that. How did that poem go? "If you can keep your head when all about you, are losing theirs and blaming it on you. If you can trust yourself when all men doubt you, but make allowance for their doubting, too." Rudyard Kipling. Seventh-grade English. Strange that that poem should come to mind now. She wondered fleetingly if kids still had to memorize it. Doubtful, she decided.

In any case, there was no point pretending. If her suspicions, and now those of other people, were groundless, she would find out soon enough. But until that fact was clear, she would simply have to keep at it.

Anita finished off her coffee and returned to the folder of documents in her lap.

Along with the interpretive literature and scoring mechanism to the EQA test, which proved to be the two key documents, Anita Hoge found two more eye-openers: first, a copy of a 1975 memo to Pennsylvania's Senate Education Committee from Galen Godbey, Majority Staff and second, Basic Education Circular 8-80. In them were some amazing revelations:

According to the 1975 memo, two groups in 1973 had already protested both the Educational Quality Assessment test and something known as Pennsylvania's Ten Goals of Quality Education. The test, the memo claimed, was based on these goals. The American Civil Liberties Union (ACLU) had been asked to handle the case, and apparently it supported the charges of the two groups.

The 1975 memo outlined each of the charges and reported what had been done about them. Described, among other things, was the way the Educational Quality Assessment test had come into being and what it was intended to measure:

It was Pennsylvania's General Assembly that in the late 1960s had ordered the state's education agency, the Pennsylvania Department of Education, to formulate the Ten Goals on which testing eventually would be based. But the result was not at all to the Assembly's liking. All but two of the goals, the Assembly complained, were purely attitudinal. The other eight, it said, "fail[ed] to conform to legislative intent."

Ditto the Educational Quality Assessment test. In essence, the General Assembly agreed with the complainants.

More earth-shaking, however, was the news that the test was required. The memo stated that a Citizens' Committee on Basic Education in Pennsylvania had called for "mandatory district participation." This echoed the words of Anita's second find, Basic Education Circular 8-80, which stated that every school district in Pennsylvania "must" participate in the assessment at least once every five years. In other words, the test was voluntary so long as the school districts agreed to participate. The memo went on to state that students did not, in fact, have to take the test because on May 7, 1975, none other than Dr. Robert Coldiron had met with representatives of the ACLU and had agreed "to insure that each student is informed in writing that he or she may refuse to take the Educational Quality Assessment exam without stigma."

If Dr. Coldiron would assure in the future that students were made aware that their participation was optional, stated the ACLU, charges of "invasion of privacy" would then "have no basis."

Thus it appeared that Dr. Coldiron had lied to Anita and her husband about the test being mandatory. *Why?*

Anita determined to investigate further. She moved from the assessment test to the curriculum — specifically, to the citizenship curriculum her son had studied, the same one she had ordered from the Educational Quality Assessment Resource booklet — *Community Involvement for Responsible Citizenship.* Here was the teachers' guide, with the designation "ESEA, Title IV-C" on the cover.

The introduction to the curriculum made no bones about the EQA being essentially an examination of attitudes, or that similar data was being compared around the state. Nor did it mince any words about the curriculum's primary objective: to discourage transmittal of certain attitudes held by *parents.* A selling point for the curriculum, according to page 8, was that it made use of something called "intervention strategies."

Intervention into what?

The answer appeared to be "the home."

Anita Hoge read on. The goal for the citizenship curriculum was that "the pupil should be encouraged to assume responsibility for the actions of the group, to cooperate and work toward *group* goals, and to support *group* efforts. This sounded like education for conformity, not "citizenship" in the sense of patriotism, loyalty, understanding the Constitution, or any of the things commonly associated with the term "citizenship." Further on, on page 69, the guide alluded to some school districts' "highly moralistic tone" and noted that the "patriotic programs [were] designed to reinforce a predetermined value." The implication from the context seemed to be that this made it all right to inculcate *any* predetermined value.

Values and attitudes would be assessed using surveys, intervention strategies, and, finally, "moral reasoning [techniques] . . . based on the work of Swiss psychologist Jean Piaget and . . . Lawrence Kohlberg." Both Piaget and Kohlberg, Anita later learned, were well-known moral relativists and are required reading for college education majors. But Anita knew nothing as yet of the heated debate surrounding these, and other, educational philosophers. She was more concerned with how the citizenship curriculum was related to the Educational Quality Assessment test and how it would be evaluated — how its creators would know whether the curriculum had succeeded or failed.

Anita picked up the section on scoring.[4] "To assess citizenship," Anita read, "a behavior-referenced model incorporating elements related to the psychological notion of *threshold* is used . . . in reference to citizenship, threshold refers to that set of conditions necessary to bring about the desired responses. Thus by varying the situation, introducing conditions of reward and punishment, we are able to determine the cut-off levels at which a student will exhibit positive behavior."

What exactly was *threshold?* What did they mean by "conditions of reward and punishment"? What rewards? What punishments? Who determined what "positive behavior" was?

Anita went back to the first section. Apparently experts were using "experimental control groups" and "measurement . . . as determined by instruments of the Pennsylvania Department of Education's Educational Quality Assessment" — the EQA.

No wonder Dr. Coldiron didn't want parents to know about the test! If too many kids opted out, testers wouldn't know whether their programs were effective or not.

But did that also mean schoolchildren would keep getting curricula that "corrected" their weaknesses until the EQA results said they had it right? And suppose a child was exempted from taking the EQA. Would he *still* get the EQA-based curriculum, like the rest of his class?

Yes, and yes.

The teachers' edition alluded once again to the Ten Quality Goals of Education—something Anita had seen before. Those were the goals which, according to the 1975 ACLU memo had "fail[ed] to conform to legislative intent." Here, the teachers' edition of the citizenship curriculum was stating that the citizenship goals were aligned with the Ten Quality Goals of Education — and that these, furthermore, reflected NAEP objectives. What was NAEP?

CHAPTER 5

Looking for Clues in all the Wrong Places

THE PUBLIC ACTUALLY knows precious little about how the Education Department's nearly $50 billion annual education budget[5] is spent. Complaints are aimed variously at local, state, and federal governments. But complainants generally have tended to zero in on what they consider unethical rather than what can be proved illegal. And while the opinion is frequently voiced that this great abstract thing called "federal aid" is somehow responsible for American schools having become virtually learning-proof over the past two decades, such opinion has failed to identify a single unifying thread that runs through the numerous individual complaints so that either government, or its dollars, can be nailed down as a causative agent.

It is easy to get bogged down in motives and ethical questions. But it is legal technicalities, even the small ones, which eventually bring the house down.

What Anita Hoge and her husband stumbled into — and were smart enough to recognize — was the elusive thread that runs through the majority of complaints about American education: the assessment test. Or, as it was known in Pennsylvania, "the Educational Quality Assessment." Nearly every state has its version of the test, and it is given at three grade levels, such as third, fifth, and tenth, depending on the state.

This test is connected to still another test at the federal level, called the **National Assessment of Educational Progress (NAEP)**. It turns out that the word this acronym rhymes with is an apt description of what happens to education in general and the taxpayer's wallet in particular when the two tests are combined, which they usually are. For the NAEP is also given at three grade levels, different ones from the state assessment. So, between the state test and the national test, every child gets tested as many as six times by the senior year.

Were these truly academic tests, and were the government legally sanctioned to use a "national test" and produce a "national curriculum," perhaps the whole business would fly — the only complaint being, perhaps, redundancy, or overkill. But if tests are primarily, or even half, attitudinal in nature, set up in such a way as to bring in psychologically manipulative curricula to correct "wrong" answers, then a question of legality arises. Federal law specifically forbids the government from involving itself in curriculum *at all*, much less nationalizing it. Assessment testing, therefore, appears to depart significantly from the legislation, which is described below.

It is Public Law 92-318, Section 432 that expressly forbids the federal government establishing or developing curriculum. In addition, Public Law 96-88, Title I, Section 101, no. 3 states: "The primary responsibility for a child's education belongs to parents." To presume to remediate children's beliefs and values without parents' knowledge or consent, using materials that bypass parental and community approval, can arguably be called a usurping of parental rights. In 1970 Congress placed an amendment in the General Education Provisions Act to specifically include, again, a "Prohibition Against Federal Control of Education." This prohibits the federal government from exercising:

> direction, supervision, or control over the curriculum, program of instruction, administration or personnel of any educational institution, school, or school system, or over the selection of library resources, textbooks, or other printed or published instructional materials by any educational institution or school system....

The thing could hardly be stated more clearly. Furthermore, the Education Amendments of 1976 extend provisions forbidding federal control of education to programs in the Education division of the Department of Health, Education and Welfare (HEW). That was back when the Office of Education was a part of HEW, before the U.S. Department of Education became a cabinet-level agency.

It was the 1975 memo about Dr. Coldiron's run-in with the ACLU, plus a 1974 document out of the Pennsylvania Bureau of Planning and Evaluation that turned the Pennsylvania Group on to the connection between the state and national assessments. The latter document stated plainly that assessment tests are "a legislative mandate, directed by the State Board of Education, and administered by the Department of Education . . . [based on] the national assessment, funded by the federal government . . . ." This information changed the direction of the Group's research. Anita Hoge and her colleagues recognized that by sticking to local and state sources of information they might be looking in the wrong places for answers.

One of the first findings to come out of this realization was that the creators of the National Assessment were among the same people who created the EQA in Pennsylvania. Later they turned up in Florida and other states, creating assessment tests right and left — always, conveniently, under separate contracts, apparently so as to avoid being charged at some point with conflict of interest.

An enormously important 1981 working paper out of the U.S. Department of Education's National Institute of Education, "Measuring the Quality of Education," by Willard Wirtz and Archie LaPointe, clarifies the fact that the states were supposed to use — and did use — the NAEP. Page 27 of the paper details the "extensive use of NAEP materials in conducting a state-wide survey (Texas Assessment Project — TAP)" and explains how "extensive comparisons were made between the Texas results and available NAEP data". The following page describes a ten-year relationship between the Connecticut assessment and the NAEP: "A State Board Report notes that 'the CAEP [the Connecticut Assessment of Educational Progress] program is modeled after the National Assessment of Educational Progress (NAEP) in its basic goals, design, and implementation.' "

Twelve other states are listed as having "closely replicated the National Assessment model"; another fourteen as having "used NAEP materials to complement their own assessment model"; and twelve more as "having drawn on NAEP for technical and consultive advice."

And this was only 1981.

Who were these people going all over the country creating tests? People like behavioral psychologist Ralph Tyler — renowned author, lecturer...and past president of the Carnegie Foundation for the Advancement of Teaching. Under what contract was the test being created? Answer: the Educational Testing Service, in Princeton, New Jersey.

Who else was bidding on these contracts? Virtually no one, said a spokesman at the Education Commission of the States in Denver, Colorado. And when another firm did bid, added the spokesman, "everyone knew there was no chance at all anyone would get it but ETS."[6]

This, of course, led to more questions — like who scores the test? Where do the results go? Who analyzes the results? Who makes decisions based on the results?

The answers kept coming back: ETS.

Finally, someone thought to ask: Who's behind ETS?

The answer was the Carnegie Foundation for the Advancement of Teaching.

But the Carnegie Foundation wasn't just *behind* the test. They virtually owned it. The organization also had created and owned the college boards — the Scholastic Aptitude Tests (SATs) — and the National Teachers' Examination. Now it appeared the organization was behind the NAEP, too.

Anita Hoge and her group got hold of ETS' annual reports, beginning with 1984. The amount of money the organization was raking in from their various tests was phenomenal. And there was little question that ETS was trying to ease out the competition. Just how much clout ETS had to monopolize testing in the United States could be inferred from the number of ETS board members who also sat at the top of the Carnegie Foundation leadership. These were the individuals who frequently appeared on state testing contracts as well as federal ones — doing essentially the same job for both.

Through their research, the Pennsylvania Group found that in 1964, the Pennsylvania Department of Education — that's the state arm of the U.S.

Department of Education — went into contract with ETS to form a testing program. A committee of unelected officials came up with what became known as the Ten Quality Goals of Education. This committee decided that any education program would be inadequate unless it took into account the development of the *total* child. Obviously, this meant more than the three R's. It meant that the whole personality—the social, emotional, intellectual, and psychomotor areas — of each child needed to be addressed in the curriculum.

Eight of the top behavioral psychologists in the country — several, such as Edward L. Thorndike and Ralph Tyler, were renowned internationally — sat on the committee that came up with the Ten Quality Goals. These are the ones who developed what became known as "the whole child" concept.

The whole child theory takes in how the child thinks, feels, and acts. If one wishes to change the way a child acts (that is, the child's *behavior*), he must change the way that child thinks and feels. The three are inseparable. To understand how children — or, for that matter, how adults — think, it is necessary to get into what is known as the individual's belief *system*. This can be done any number of ways—through a test or survey, journal-writing or diary-keeping, role-playing, and discussion groups: whatever will bring the child's innermost feelings and thoughts out into the open. To do this, the child's whole personality must be involved — the ego, the will, and so on. Behavior is merely the psychomotor manifestation — the visible result — of whatever is going on inside the mind. And unless a person changes his mind, so to speak, there is little chance that he will change his actions. Thus, for the brain to accept and/or demonstrate change, it is necessary first to reach the subconscious mind.

This, then, is the rationale for educating the whole child: the idea that it isn't real, lasting education unless it results in a change of behavior and, therefore, involves the feelings and emotions. The committee that wrote the Ten Quality Goals wanted most of all to induce children to behave, and therefore think, differently. So the goals had to be written in a particular way, so as to allow for an inductive approach to learning: one that could target the belief system and induce change. The big question became: Was the

Educational Quality Assessment a model for the larger-scale National Assessment, NAEP? Or was NAEP adapted for the EQA? It was the old chicken-or-egg question.

The Educational Testing Service (thus the Carnegie Foundation) conducted a survey in 1967 to find out what kinds of state testing programs were going on. They found some 74 state testing programs in 42 states, most of which "were not in any sense mandatory" and indicated little about the level and progress of education in the state as a whole. In short, a void existed, one that could be exploited.

A 1974 publication entitled *Crucial Issues in Testing,*[7] coedited by Ralph Tyler and Richard M. Wolf solves the chicken-or-egg question about the NAEP and the state assessments. The book is a compendium of articles and essays on then-current educational issues written by various experts in the field, among them several from ETS.

Under "Some Current State Assessment Programs," editor Ralph Tyler includes a review of state-level educational assessment that appeared in a NAEP newsletter February 1973. "By using some of the same exercises and survey techniques pioneered by NAEP, states can obtain educational assessment results comparable with those obtained on a regional and national basis by NAEP," said J. Stanley Ahmann, NAEP staff director. The newsletter also indicated that in Maine, private, as well as public, schools were, even then, using a testing program that paralleled NAEP. The newsletter went on to quote Joe Natale, project director of Maine's assessment, as saying that one of the best things about the "NAEP methodology" was that it explored children's feelings. On pages 130 and 131, specific states are listed as having used NAEP exercises, NAEP criteria for scoring and analysis, or were at that time (1973) in the process of "consulting with NAEP as they develop assessment programs" (under separate contract, of course): Massachussetts, Colorado, Iowa, Maryland, Louisiana, Wyoming, Minnesota, Illinois, Missouri, Arizona, Wisconsin, and Alabama.

Still another survey of state officials was conducted in 1970, this one a joint enterprise of the Education Commission of the States (another Carnegie-inspired organization), the Educational Testing Service (the brainchild of the

Carnegie Foundation), and the ERIC Clearinghouse on Tests, Measurement, and Evaluation. The purpose of the survey, as described by Henry S. Dyer and Elsa Rosenthal of ETS,[8] was to find out as much as possible about what the states planned to do with regard to statewide educational testing, what kinds of problems they were having, and how they were coping with these problems. The goal of the survey was to obtain detailed information about educational assessment from all 50 states and the District of Columbia. The first step, say Dyer and Rosenthal, was to identify in each state two or three persons — generally officials in the state education departments — who were most likely to supply information. The Education Commission of the States, which the Carnegie organization launched earlier on, "assumed responsibility for assembling a list of state personnel to serve as contacts," who could be counted on for cooperation. ETS then assigned 21 people from ETS' various field offices to conduct in-depth interviews with those state contacts identified by ECS. Thus did CFAT secure its top helpmates in the states — people they knew they could trust. This was the first step toward filling the void in educational testing.

What followed was a series of statewide and regional conferences in 1970-71, involving varying numbers of laymen and professionals to "rework goals and collect opinions on priorities." Dyer and Rosenthal explain how ETS managed to "achieve a workable consensus" while retaining the perception of input from laypersons. The Delphi Technique, alluded to below, is a very unethical method of achieving "agreement" on a controversial topic in a group setting. It requires a well-trained professional who deliberately escalates tension among group members, pitting one faction against the other so as to make one viewpoint appear ridiculous and the other sensible, whether such is warranted or not.

> The mingling of laymen and professionals...occasioned a search for ways to ...achieve a workable consensus within practical time limits. The survey reveals that some state educational agencies...plan[ned] to train their staffs in the use of the Delphi Technique, a process that may prove particularly useful in the goal-setting process. The Delphi technique was originally conceived as a way to obtain the opinions of experts without necessarily bringing them together face to face.... If the trend toward community delib-

eration on state policy matters continues, there will need to be further adaptations of the Delphi Technique in large-scale settings.[9]

The point is, all through the writings of Carnegie Foundation and ETS leaders — from Dyer and Rosenthal to Wirtz and LaPointe — one finds over and over references made to preserving the illusion of lay, or community, participation while lay citizens were, in fact, being squeezed out.

CHAPTER 6

Getting Inside the EQA

BY THE TIME the bureaucracy closed in the first time, in early 1987, the Pennsylvania Group had managed to obtain and forward to fellow researchers in Washington enough hard evidence to interest legal experts. One such piece was an "embargoed" (not-for-publication) release from the Office of Technology Assessment (OTA) concerning the lack of security at the Center for Education Statistics. Another paper emanating from the OTA, by staff person Lawrence P. Grayson,[10] made clear in 1978 the kinds of data being collected at the Center — as if the Pennsylvania Group hadn't found more than enough already to substantiate the allegation that the EQA and other assessments in Pennsylvania were psychoanalyzing children. Clinical psychologists to whom the Group showed the tests agreed they were looking at sophisticated personality profiles. An Iowa psychiatrist, a Veterans Hospital psychologist in Kansas, and other experts all indicated they used many of the same questions in their initial sessions with troubled patients.

In the experimental literature used as a basis for Pennsylvania's *Teaching for Essential Literacy Skills* (TELS — an ideal test title for public relations purposes[11]), behavioral research aide Norman Wallen writes in the Foreword that the test "measures gullibility or one's ability to see through attempts to mislead" and, then that "[t]he test also appears to measure knowledge to some extent . . . ." Wallen adds that students must have "at least a passing acquaintance with the Judeo-Christian tradition" in order for certain test questions *"to function as an indicator of gullibility."*

So-called "basic skills" tests, therefore, may ask children, on the reading portion, for example, not who the characters were or what the setting of a selection was. Instead they may assess the child's feelings about the piece. To take a hypothetical example, a test question might ask "How did you feel when the emperor executed the man in the flying machine [from, say, a Ray Bradbury story]?" The choices would range from anger to amusement. Or, perhaps a word is taken from the selection and turned into what looks like a vocabulary question: "You would be *incensed* if your parents … ." The choices would contain some things parents might do to intensely irritate their offspring. Some of the choices would be "appropriate" causes for anger, others would not be. The point is, what is being tested is called the ***belief system*** of a child, not academic knowledge, not what the average parent would call "skills."

One of the best documents to be dredged up by the Pennsylvania Group was a booklet alluded to in a Resource Packet listing — a 1984 pamphlet called *Getting Inside the EQA Inventory*. This manual left little doubt that children were being scored for "preferred" attitudes — that is, each child, unbeknownst to his parents or himself, was being judged on opinions and personality traits. "Unacceptable" and "nonproductive" attitudes, stated the manual, would be changed through remediation. Since the terms "remedial" and "remediate" have virtually no negative connotations in the public eye, neither parents nor the press asked questions.

"Re-education" might have been, however, the more appropriate term.

Getting Inside the EQA Inventory explains every aspect of the Educational Quality Assessment test, from the rationale to the way it works in practice. It explains, for example, that each school district's tests are analyzed by test creators at ETS for areas of "weakness." The clincher, however, is what it claims analysts are looking for. It is not, as is sometimes implied, for "pre-suicidal" children or "sexually abused" youngsters.

Basically, analysts are seeking answers to just six questions:

- What is the student's "locus of control"?

- Is the student "externally or intrinsically motivated"?

- How amenable is the student to change (i.e., "willingness to receive stimuli")?

- Will the student conform to group goals?

- To what extent will students be willing to comply with directives from authority figures?

- Finally, what situations/factors will cause a child to change his behavior or attitudes?

"Locus of control" means the controlling influence in a person's life. The test literature cites three possibilities: the child's authority figure (teacher, parent, policeman, etc . . .), his peers, or the child himself.

"Intrinsic" or "external" motivation is what causes a person to behave in accordance with certain predictable patterns; more specifically, do forces outside oneself motivate behavior, or is the person internally driven?

The degree of "willingness to receive stimuli" will indicate open-mindedness, tolerance of new ideas — or their opposites. Responses also serve as indicators of how firmly held, or entrenched, are beliefs and attitudes. If an individual is highly principled, that could be interpreted by test analysts as "dogmatic" or "closed-minded," characteristics which apparently are considered negatives on the testers' balance sheets. (Never mind that many school drug-abuse prevention programs encourage values of principle, including absolutes of right and wrong.)

Willingness to conform to group goals is, obviously, an individual*ity* indicator. But individual*ism* doesn't seem to rate very highly. Getting along with everyone, fitting in, appears to be paramount. Thus the parent who admonishes a child by saying, "I don't care what everybody else is doing ..." is going to be undercut by schools that view individual*ity* as a plus, but individual*ism* as a minus — as a "weakness" that needs to be remediated.

It is true that the term "individuality" frequently is spoken of in glowing terms by school authorities, particularly in public relations messages promulgated by the education establishment. But the connotation, if one listens closely, is not "individual*ism*." What they are saying does not equate to self-sufficiency, personal autonomy, or independent thinking. The "individuality" of educationese is limited to the *worth* or *value* of the individual (in other words, human life is precious, not cheap), and the liberty, therefore, to dress or look differently, to have tastes, proclivities, and interests different from one's neighbor.

That is fine in itself, but it is not the meaning of "individualism."

What behaviorists apparently want to see is an attitude of "interdependence" — the "we all need each other" philosophy. However, behaviorists take the idea a step farther, to encourage consensus and conformity of thought. Nonconformity is permissible in areas like dress, sexual proclivity, or taste (decor and food, for example) — but not in larger issues that require a deeper, more profound level of thought. As will be described in one *Resources for Improvement* booklet further on, that is what remedial programs — those lessons aimed at *overcoming* the tendency toward individualism — will emphasize: consensus and conformity, always wrapped in the "we all need each other" package.

These are not distinctions easily grasped by the parent casually leafing through his or her child's textbook. What happens is that over time, parents tend to get an increasingly uncomfortable feeling about their children's education through a variety of incidents — vague things that busy mothers and fathers can't quite put their fingers on. Then one day they see a textbook or experience some incident that sets off the alarm bells, as in the case of Anita and Garrett Hoge.

But as soon as these parents try to express their concerns to authorities, they are likely to find educators smiling reassuringly and repeating pat expressions like "relevant," "meaningful," and "child-centered curriculum." The fact is that unless parents gain a command of educational jargon and are willing to devote many months to studying educational philosophy and curriculum with a critical eye, they will not be able to present their cases to authorities who have been "prepped" in advance for complaints.

As for what factors cause a child — or for that matter, a person of any age — to change attitudes or behaviors, that is the crux of what testers want to learn. Thus test questions are constructed in such a way as to introduce hypothetical situations involving **reward and punishment** so that educational testers, like psychiatrists, can find out what makes kids tick.

The questions utilize sophisticated inductive techniques, in large part pioneered by the late Hilda Taba, who immigrated to the United States from Estonia in the 1930s. She had long specialized in designing questions to elicit information people don't want to divulge and continued her work when she got to this country. Accounts published in the official record of a 1958 California Senate Investigating Committee hearing reveal that Taba was a much-disputed figure, even then, and there was an uproar over her techniques being used in an educational, as opposed to a clinical, setting.

Taba's professional life after immigration included UNESCO professor in Brazil; Director of Research of Teaching Strategies and Cognitive Functioning; Chairman of the Board of a child guidance clinic in San Mateo, California; and high-level office-holder in several psychological research organizations.

After the California Senate investigated her activities in American education, references to her work faded out for a time, but by the mid-60s there was renewed interest. Credits to Taba's psychological treatises[12] suddenly started surfacing in the fine print of teaching texts and other instructional materials: in the November 1965 issue of Social Education, "Techniques of Inservice Training"; in a footnote explaining Office of Education grants given to Taba to "help pupils think"; in an article in the Contra-Costa Times (a California newspaper) naming Taba as consultant on a curriculum project. And so on.

Taba's method, as well as that of her prolific protégé at the Carnegie Foundation for the Advancement of Teaching (hereafter referred to as CFAT), Ralph Tyler, utilizes a combination of word-association techniques, passed off as vocabulary quizzes, and negatively worded multiple-choice questions from which the child selects responses to match what he would do or would not do in various high- and low-stress situations — conditions involving reward and punishment, as per Edward Thorndike's theories in behavioral psychology. Take the following question, noting in particular the wording of choice (c):

> There is a secret club at school called the Midnight Artists. They go out late at night and paint funny sayings and pictures on buildings. A student is asked

to join the club. In this situation, I would **JOIN THE CLUB** when I knew: (a) my best friend asked me to join, (b) the most popular students were in the club (c) my parents would ground me if they found out I joined.

The assumption is made that the child would join the organization under *some* circumstance. It is the duty of the testers to find out what that circumstance might be. The questions are fun, like a game of "Scruples."

What is more significant, however, is that there is a pre-determined, correct answer for each choice — and it's probably not the one the average parent would expect. The possible responses to each of the choices above are "yes," "no," or "maybe." For choice *a*, the state-desired response is a surprising "yes." The reason for an affirmative answer here, according to the scoring mechanism booklet, is that it demonstrates a "willingness to honor self-made commitments to individuals or groups." Thus the student gets one point for an affirmative answer and a zero for "no" — the answer that supports an ethic against vandalism.

For the situation *b* — *I would join the organization if the most popular students are in the club* — the state-desired response is "yes" again. The kid is not a lone wolf, which would have been deemed undesirable. A "yes" answer demonstrates conformity to group goals, a bowing to group consensus, and that makes it the preferred response.

The oddly phrased choice *c* is an attempt to find out whether the child will obey if punishment is expected to result from disobedience. In other words, can this child be controlled through reward and punishment? If punishment from any authority figure (including the state) is incurred, will the child obey? That may sound positive, but put in the context of the other test questions, a somewhat troubling picture emerges.

The responses of all the children in the district to the test questions are tallied and compared with the state desired responses. From this will be determined the areas of "weakness" for each school district, and curriculum will be adjusted accordingly. That test results may interpret as a weakness the entire Judeo-Christian ethic is of no importance, since separation of church and state precludes taking religious doctrine into account. After all, the children may be Moslems or Hindus for all the test analysts know!

Some questions are glorified true-false tests. A statement is given followed by three or four choices for response: I agree strongly, I agree somewhat, I disagree, I disagree strongly; or perhaps just "yes, no, or maybe." Frequently, the catch is that the test-taker often cannot opt for "none of the above." In any case, the test literature makes a selling point of the fact that the same questions are asked in a variety of ways so that students will not be able to fool analysts by responding the way they *think* they are supposed to, but, rather, will give themselves away as to what they really believe (or, more accurately, the way they have been brought up to believe).[13]

It is fairly easy for the lay person to pick out the attitudinal questions using the format described above. That, no doubt, is one reason tests have been so carefully secured from an inquisitive public. But since 1984 the formats and construction of questions have improved. To pick out the attitudinal questions today, one must be familiar with leading experts and papers in the field. Too, state assessment tests are not the only vehicles for collecting this psycho-behavioral data. Health questionnaires and various writing samples[14] are used, too.

But the state assessment test is the favored gauge, mainly because so many students take it. These are the vehicles for determining just which attitudes need to be corrected, or, in the jargon of educators, "made appropriate."

CHAPTER 7

How Attitudes are Made "Appropriate"

ANITA HOGE GOT hold of her district's Five Year Long-Range Plan, which confirmed that the EQA test was being used as a basis for curriculum decision-making. Other states that have their assessment tests in place do pretty much the same thing.

She also discovered that teachers, who are expected to remediate students' attitude-value "weaknesses," can do so by obtaining learning programs through either of two federally owned computer networks: the Educational Resource and Information Center network (ERIC, referred to previously) and the National Diffusion Network (or NDN). Graduate students in education also use these data banks for their research. The ERIC contains the most technical, professional literature, while the NDN carries more in the way of curricular programs. Access to these computers is made available through regional terminals like R.I.S.E. and through local curriculum libraries (usually it is the subject-area department heads in a school who do the ordering).

Because curricular programs are considered "supplementary," teachers can integrate them into any course they teach — English, social studies, home economics, or whatever. That is the meaning of the all-important buzz-term, "interdisciplinary use." *Interdisciplinary learning,* particularly when it applies to attitudes or values, is served up in minicourses — courses within a course — technically known as *"strands."* Understanding this procedure is crucial to comprehending how the rest of the education system works.

In Pennsylvania, the city of King of Prussia houses the R.I.S.E.. As indicated earlier, it is one of the largest in the country. Anita Hoge used this terminal to locate the curricular programs that correct, or "remediate," student weaknesses on the EQA test. As Anita discovered, printouts of "Resources for Improvement" packets between 1979 and 1986 reveal that many programs — or "strands" — are labeled and described one way for professionals who use the computer and another way for classroom consumption.

For example, in the computer printout, titles and descriptions of "validated" (federally approved) learning programs are clearly labeled as "behavior modification" and, getting even more specific, "values clarification exercises." Other revealing descriptors, such as "intervention curriculum" are placed beside some curriculum titles, "social adjustment exercise" by others, and a few even carry the label "psychological therapy." Bible Belters would be amazed to see printouts of curriculum labeled "situation ethics" and "humanistic exercises."[15]

A computer list of recommended, "validated" programs, therefore, may look like this in an NDN computer printout:

Mainstreaming/Social Adjustment 278-3-79

Ethnic Education Curriculum & Models 289-3-78

Global Education 301-3-78

Behavioral Objectives in the Affective Domain 429-1-74

Youth and Older Adults Issues for Dialogue 102-3-79

Racial Attitudes of Elementary School children 634-3-80

Bibliotherapy Elementary 602-3-80

Bibliotherapy Secondary 480-3-78

If one ever wonders why graduating students do not have a command of fundamental subjects and are culturally illiterate, the above list of courses might provide some insight. Of the entries above, the last two are probably the most questionable in terms of legality. "Therapy" can be construed as a medical term requiring licensed practitioners like psychiatrists. No matter how many inservice workshops teachers attend, they generally do not have such a license. For them to make use of psychological therapy is akin to practicing medicine without a license. The problem, of course, with pursuing something like this is that even if the course's creators are taken to task, the course will simply appear under another name later on, with the objectionable terms removed. That is one reason why the ERIC and NDN computer printouts are valuable tools in the battle against what is termed "psycho-behavioral programming"; they provide a truthful description of courses along with codes (the numbers at the right in the example above) that permit a researcher to find out more.

It is not just paranoia that causes parents to feel that educators are being less than forthright about the purposes of their programs. Take a look at this excerpt promoting death education from the May 1977 issue of *The School Counselor,* a magazine aimed at professional counselors:

> As in the case of many other problems, many Americans believe that educa- tion can initiate change. . . . [D]eath education will play as important a part in changing attitudes toward death as sex education played in changing attitudes toward sex information and wider acceptance of *various sexual practices.*[16]

Is the "wider acceptance of various sexual practices" (italicized above for emphasis) what parents are told these classes are for? And in light of what has happened since this article was written — particularly the AIDS epidemic — this commentary on the true purpose of sex education is really an insult to the responsible parent.

Another way to nail the use of unlicensed therapy by schools is to get hold of invoices (preferably ones that show federal or state funds) used to purchase therapeutic programs. Take, for example, an invoice forwarded to Pennsylvania Group researchers by a knowledgeable purchasing depart- ment in Tacoma, Washington. The Tacoma School District ordered six programs from Academy Therapy Publications on April 15, 1986, amount- ing to a total of $66.00. The materials were shipped to Stadium High School. On the invoice, next to the subtotal, is a federal identification number.

Many, if not most, of these psycho-behavioral programs were researched and developed at the Department of Education's official regional research Laboratories and Centers, thanks to the Title IV in the Elementary and Secondary Education Act of 1965 (that's the ESEA) and private foundation grants. One of the craziest programs to come out of the "Labs," as they are called, is The World Core Curriculum of the Robert Muller School, which is the basis for Robert Muller's (former United Nations kingpin)[17] School of Ageless Wisdom in Arlington, Texas. The "Ageless Wisdom" curriculum's quasi-religious overtones must have been missed by the U.S. Department of Education-funded Mid-Continent Regional Education Lab. This Lab has served seven states since 1978; thus, many youngsters got the World Core Curriculum.

Behavioral colleges also play an important role. There are four major ones in the United States: the Institute for Applied Behavioral Sciences, the Midwest Center for Human Potential, the Western Behavioral Sciences Institute, and Esalen Institute. Computer printouts of curricula and professional papers make frequent reference or give credit to these institutions.

Of the private benefactors, CFAT of course is the primary player, but other foundations have also provided generous grants for behavioral R&D efforts, most notably the Rockefeller Foundation, the Danforth Foundation, the Spencer Foundation, the Charles F. Kettering Foundation, the Ford Foundation, and the Aspen Institute for Humanistic Studies. (Keep in mind, tax-exempt foundations typically are funded by still other tax-exempt foundations, as well as by corporations. Atlantic Richfield (ARCO), the big oil conglomerate, for example, is the primary funding mechanism for the Aspen Institute for Humanistic Studies. ARCO's president and Chairman of the Board, Robert O. Anderson, is also Aspen's president and CEO.)

Now comes that all-important term "validation." On the first page of the "Resources for Improvement" booklets (the Resource Packets) is a notice that each curricular program therein has been "validated" by a body known as the Joint Dissemination Review Panel (JDRP), a government-appointed review board. The JDRP is under the auspices of the U.S. Department of Education and its former government affiliate, the National Institute of Education.[18] "Validation" means that the program(s) contained in the booklet have been reviewed and approved for use in the school by the panel, which in this case represents the federal government. So validation is, in essence, a seal of approval. If a learning program is deemed exceptional, it may even be tagged "exemplary."

All validated programs, exemplary or not, are entered into one or both national curriculum computer networks, the NDN and/or the ERIC.

It is by means of a circulation process known as the ***Intermediate Unit*** that supplementary materials for these approved learning programs make their way into the classroom carrying innocuous labels like "Home and Family Living," "Working," or "The Cry of the Marsh" (the film on the environment shown in young Garrett Hoge's science class). The most popular method of disseminating materials, like books and films, that complement affective, or psycho-behavioral curricula, is by van, routed through a regional curriculum or distribution center, which serves as a centralized repository for educational materials. In Pennsylvania, these regional repositories are called Intermediate Units, paid for by the state education agencies out of federal block grants.

Originally, the Intermediate Units (or IUs) were to serve as mobile units for learning disabled and emotionally handicapped students.[19] But they evolved, apparently, into something considerably different.

There are some twenty IUs in Pennsylvania. Their vans go from school district to school district loaning films and other "supplemental" teaching aids. The Pennsylvania Group claims it has even seen these vans parked outside a few private and parochial schools that receive federal funds. Parents can be assured that by the time they get around to asking about a controversial film like the one in Garrett Hoge's class, it will have disappeared to another school and maybe to another county.

The citizenship curriculum that originally piqued the interest of Anita Hoge and her husband came to the school via the IU. Recall the curriculum cover, where it stated, along with the federal funding source, "Allegheny Intermediate Unit." Allegheny is another school district in Pennsylvania. The Hoges' school district was McGuffey, in Washington County. Thus, the Allegheny unit loaned its citizenship curriculum to McGuffey.

States use different terms to describe Intermediate Units, which made it difficult for lay researchers to locate them nationally. But once they found the IU counterparts in Nebraska (Educational Service Units, or ESUs), others were located quickly. Moreover, between the testing, the funding, government "validation," and the Intermediate Units, there is little doubt that curriculum is being created by government-sponsored groups with government funds and targeted to groups of students whose tests results indicate "inappropriate" attitudinal/value responses.

Anita and the Pennsylvania Group also found clear evidence that the federal government had been actively engaged in such activity for a very long time. Indeed, it had been piloting curriculum even before the official start of the National Assessment, NAEP, in 1969.

It was discovered, for example, that the *objectives* for the controversial Pennsylvania citizenship curriculum actually were written in 1964, using the Ten Quality Goals. That's five years before the official start of NAEP. This could only have happened if the EQA had been planned as the *national* validating system representing equal partnership with the NAEP in the area of citizenship.

As it turned out, an old annual report from the Educational Testing Service (ETS) provided evidence that the research for creating the Educational Quality Assessment actually *predated* the National Assessment, NAEP. Work on the EQA began in 1964, when a fellow by the name of Henry Dyer, president of ETS and Project Director of EQA, headed the advisory committee that developed the test. Both NAEP and EQA officially got off the ground in 1969-70. The last page of the report even names the advisory committee members — eleven of whom (that's almost all of them) came from ETS. Thus it was crucial that every child in Pennsylvania participate in the EQA test; it's why the test could not be made purely voluntary. The Educational Quality Assessment appears to be a pilot, a first draft, if you will, for what would become the first national test, the National Assessment of Educational Progress (NAEP).

The "Ten Quality Goals," meanwhile, were passed off to the public as a term applying to Pennsylvania and developed by the community. Not so. The term was the brainchild of that first committee of unelected officials, primarily behavioral psychologists, who came together in 1964. The intent, apparently, was to make the goals generic for the entire country. In other words, if they worked in Pennsylvania, they should work anywhere.

In 1975, after the Pennsylvania goals had been in place awhile, ETS worked with the man who would become the first Secretary of Education, Terrel H. Bell, to get the whole business moving according to a specific timetable. The plan was called the Cooperative Accountability Project (CAP). It coordinated testing-programming in seven states and launched the model for testing and collection of data nationwide. CAP will be described in more detail later on. For the time being, it will suffice to say that today assessments all over the United States monitor the same citizenship objectives that were "validated" and "proved effective" under the "Resources for Improvement" booklet in Pennsylvania's "*EQA area Citizenship." If the EQA test was the model for assessment, then so were many of the remedial programs aimed at correcting lagging scores. These curricular programs, eventually "validated" by the JDRP, used the same criteria established under EQA in the 1960s, before it was ever known as the EQA.

As if the case against the federal government in the matter of curriculum control wasn't enough, another computer search turned up two more documents: first, a 1982 paper from the U.S. Department of Education out of the National Diffusion Network stating that *only* programs which are *federally funded* could be validated by the JDRP for insertion into the NDN. This is one of the documents which, as will be shown, eventually served as Anita Hoge's trump card when Deputy Counsel at the Education Department tried to close her case.

A second watershed document explains how a deal was cut between the federal government and a marketing firm called LINC, out of Columbus, Ohio, in the early 1970s — to link "approved" curriculum developers and textbook writers to the NDN computer bank, thus ensuring that their programs would be "validated" by the JDRP. The government accomplished this questionable feat through Titles I through IV-C of the ESEA law.

The implicating document is "Dissemination for School Improvement, Volume I: A Study of Dissemination Efforts Supporting School Improvement," published by The Network Inc. and produced by Glenn Shive (Oct. 1981). All the sections point to a federal scheme to control curriculum — and, in particular, to implement programs under the label of basics which "are not typically considered 'basic'." The best sections, quoted here, speak for themselves (key in particularly on the words italicized for emphasis):[20]

> In 1974, Title III was consolidated with six other federal programs and renamed Title IV-C. One of the few things that Title III shared with the six other consolidated programs was a *political constituency* that was too weak to spring programs free of the network . . . . In the bureaucratic shuffle that followed, the staff who had managed the federal Title III office [Title III was for "innovative programs" funding] . . . broke away from the program and started the National Diffusion Network. Meanwhile the staff who managed Title V State Strengthening Programs *took over* the local innovative programs as part of the new Title IV-C. Title V managers had dealt primarily with state education agencies and administered the programs as an extension of their relations with the SEAs [i.e., took local and state innovative programs under their federal wing]. They became most involved in . . . the administration of *consolidated federal programs*. . . . Rather than giving $300,000 to three [school] districts for local development . . . an SEA could [now] get $10,000 for 90 districts for *adopting disseminated programs*. The NDN disseminated many of these programs. Indeed the incentive of Adoption/Adaptation grants funded by Title IV-C offices of the SEAs became a valuable asset to the NDN network. . . . In 1977 the Bureau of Education of the Handicapped (BEH) [in the U.S. Office of Education] contracted LINC Resources, Inc., of Columbus, Ohio, for $250,000 to facilitate the publication and distribution of special education materials developed with support from BEH. LINC set up a five-step process of getting BEH materials to market: (1) LINC prepared a profile on each product it received from BEH; (2) the Marketing Task Force reviewed each product for suitability for commercial publication [remember they are under contract to the federal government]; (3) products approved are announced to all publishers through a Product Alert . . . ; (4) LINC *negotiates a license* for each product with the publisher . . . then puts the publisher in touch with the developer [that's the author or group, such as at a Lab or Center, who got the federal grant to create the program]; (5) LINC *monitors the publication and distribution efforts* and reports to BEH [i.e., the federal government].

The paper goes on to describe how LINC licensing and JDRP validation, together, will result eventually in a regulated approval-distribution mechanism. The process will become a closed loop. Creators of curricula (called "curriculum planners," in the vernacular) along with publishers who are *not* in the loop will not be able to sell or disseminate their wares to anything but a tiny few local — usually private — schools. No one will be in the loop who is not "validated," and no one's work will be "validated" who is not already in the loop (that is, receiving federal funds or foundation grants to create instructional programs). So anyone out there who comes up with a good curriculum, and finds an unlicensed publisher for it, will not likely see that curriculum in tax-supported schools. This has already happened with an excellent mathematics text, by John Saxon. *60 Minutes* recently aired a segment on it. But since the *60 Minutes* staff didn't know about the LINC deal, or validation, they really didn't have a clue as to why the book didn't make it. All they knew was that the text was successful, yet stodgy school officials wouldn't have it.

The bottom line is that the U.S. Department of Education's Labs and Centers decide who and what gets published for classroom consumption. The term "basics" becomes a misnomer used to deceive taxpayers. Proof of the latter is found in still another line from the same "Dissemination for School Improvement" paper: Under the Title I Right to Read Program, the term "basics" is described as an obstacle that must be gotten around so that instructional programs can be disseminated "in areas that are not usually considered basic" by the public.

Thus when officials dubbed LINC as "the contractor for the 'Basic Skills' Improvement Program" they were promoting mislabeled goods.

Moreover, scores of non-cognitive, psycho-behavioral instructional programs were disseminated under the banner of "Basic Skills Projects" under Title I, and other ESEA titles, by going through the JDRP and LINC. The purpose was to "correct" any student's attitudes and opinions considered inappropriate by the state — *ergo,* by the behavioral theorists controlling education from their vantage point at the U.S. Department of Education's Labs and Centers.

CHAPTER 8

Performing Parent-Bypass Surgery

CORRECTING ATTITUDE-OPINION-VALUE "weaknesses" of students is basically a matter of presenting increasingly hard-hitting *affective* minicourses — "strands" — until a psychological condition known as *threshold* is reached. (Remember that "*affective*" is defined as "geared to the emotions.") Threshold is defined by psychologists as "the severity of stimulus tolerated before a change of behavior occurs." It is the psychological level beyond which a program cannot be continued. Recall the literature[21] which explained how the psychological notion of threshold was used to assess citizenship.

> Threshold refers to that set of conditions necessary to bring about desirable responses. Thus by introducing conditions of reward and punishment we are able to determine the cutoff levels at which the student will display positive behavior. In this way it is possible to assess not only the students' predisposition to behave . . . but also to provide some measure of the intensity of that predisposition across a wide spectrum of situations.

Three pages later, in the same literature, under "Health Habits Testing" the scaling technique is described as:

> similar to the psychophysical method of limits. This method holds the behavior constant while systematically allowing the stimuli to vary. The strength of the stimulus . . . which is required to cause a change in behavior is used to define the threshold of that behavior. . .

> . . . the student is asked to decide whether he or she would take a given health-related action. . . The health-behavior threshold is defined in terms of the severity of the stimulus contexts tolerated before changing *from a good to a poor health behavior*.

From a good to a poor behavior (emphasis added)? Just what kind of behavior change is being sought here?

Further on, the same booklet explains how test information is organized so that "student target groups" for the EQA strands can be identified. This becomes crucial to the privacy issue.

> Even though individual profiles are unavailable, it is possible to organize data in ways that . . . identify general student groups that demonstrate needs in a particular goal area. This is done by summarizing data for various groups of students formed from selected student characteristics. The characteristics defining subgroups are achievement level, sex, and father's occupational status.

That was 1975. As indicated earlier on, analysts do the job of identification more accurately today. Testers were more interested in group trends, but as time went on, targeting individual students and teachers became both possible and desirable. Tests measuring "the intensity" of a predisposition to behave a certain way are getting very much into the fine points of personality. The environmental film that the Hoge boy saw in his science class was undoubtedly a threshold-level film. Thus it was designed to be the most severe film that children could be expected to tolerate before they changed their attitudes. It can fairly be asked whether *all* the children who saw that film needed to have their attitudes changed. It could be asked whether watching living creatures being burned alive was sensitizing or de-sensitizing. Indeed, it could even be asked whether the film was actually about the environment, or whether there was another, subliminal topic. Go back to the story of the film again. Was it anti-science? Was it a statement on American greed? Was it about saving the animals?

A competent psychologist would say that any of these messages could be read into the film, that the message is in the eye of the beholder. Which is precisely the case against psychological manipulation in the classroom. It is poorly controlled experimentation. It is a methodology easily abused. (Indeed, if it turns out that this film was staged, which it appears to have been, it could well violate laws relating to the humane treatment of animals.)

In any case, the film in question came into the classroom in the usual way — as "supplementary (or resource) material." This is where the procedure of parent-bypass surgery begins. The Intermediate Unit is just one technique used to bring psycho-behavioral programs in through the back door.

Another popular vehicle for getting behavioral programs into local schools is "university experimental research." Psychological games like the "magic circle" (a popular spill-your-guts encounter-group exercise passed off to parents as "communication skills") come into the school as *pilot projects*. Parents generally know nothing of any intended experimentation, and children usually view it as a break in their routine.

The encounter-group format and other techniques are designed, say experts, to "break down" formed ideas and defenses so that the child will be influenceable and amenable to something new. Whether or not one agrees with this concept, when it is practiced by trained and licensed practitioners, the experiments and strategies are carefully controlled. Carried out by teachers schooled in one-day workshops plus, perhaps, a single pilot class, even one headed by a trained professional, the same techniques can become not only mismanaged, but emotionally brutal exercises.

"Group dynamics" is a term often used to describe encounter-type fare. Journal-keeping, diaries, and open-ended discussion games (known also as problem-solving or social adjustment exercises) are just a few of the methodologies used to encourage self-disclosure. The *Washington Post,* Feb. 21, 1984, reported on the use of journals and diaries ("Dear Journal ..."), which teachers keep track of, and turn over to school counselors or psychiatrists any time they encounter what they believe to be emotional and/or family problems. For obvious reasons, diaries and journals generally are not allowed to be taken home. That a child can write something very misleading is an issue that does not make most parents comfortable.

According to the literature out of ERIC on the subject (which is voluminous) the idea behind such approaches is to cause the subject to "trust" the group or individual to whom he has disclosed intimate information. In so doing, the child will supposedly become receptive to any new values or ideas this trusted group or individual might suggest. Independent thinking is replaced with group consensus.

Whether the new values "stick" depends upon how well and how often they are "reinforced." Continual exposure to testing and "remediation" is termed *"recycling"* in the professional literature, and that is why an interdisciplinary approach to psycho-behavioral programming is necessary — so that the same manipulative lessons can be presented discreetly, again and again.

Parents will discover that a good many "strands" come through the *counseling program* (in large part initiated using federal monies from the ESEA, added to Title III in 1973).[22] School counselors can launch all kinds of psycho/socio-behavioral programs in local schools and even take them into the classroom. Sometimes the strands are 20-to-30 minute fixed, regular sessions so many times every week, as in young Garrett Hoge's "defective ed class," or counselors can train teachers through inservice workshops (during the late summer and on those days when children are inexplicably excused from school but teachers report for duty, between two and four days a year). Teachers then use the "strand" or activity whenever an appropriate incident occurs in the classroom, or when there is a lull in a class period with nothing to do. Educational researchers Gumaer, Bleck, and Loesch write: "Psychological education has become an important part of the school counselor's function."[23]

Moreover, just because a child hasn't gone to see the school counselor or been enrolled in a guidance program does not mean he or she won't be assigned a behavioral program from that source.

One of the most audacious uses of the *"university research"* approach to psychological probing in elementary and secondary schools occurred in 1986, when Professor W. Grant Dahlstrom of the University of North Carolina at Chapel Hill allowed representatives of his psychology department to visit the local Orange High School campus and offer ten dollars to any student (grade 9 - 12) who would show up on Saturday to take a three-hour test. Induced by the money, some 400 youngsters showed up. Two consecutive Saturdays had to be scheduled.

Students had no idea what kind of test they were taking. It turned out to be the Minnesota Multiphasic Personality Inventory (MMPI) — perhaps the best known psychological test, containing some 700 extremely personal questions in a True-False format. Questions related to bodily functions, religious beliefs, sexual behavior and fantasies, parents' method of reward and punishment, sexual abuse, and more:

I have had no difficulty in starting or holding my bowels or urine.	True/False
A minister or priest can cure diseases by praying and putting a hand on your head.	True/False
My soul sometimes leaves my body.	True/False
I am a special agent of God.	True/False
I believe I am being followed.	True/False
I am being plotted against.	True/False
I hear strange things when I am alone.	True/False
I enjoy being hurt by people I love.	True/False

Legal experts Sherrer and Roston[24] note that

> ...[w]hile there are theoretically no correct or incorrect answers... , if the person being tested gives certain answers he might be admitting factual data that constitutes a felony.... With our present computers [in 1971], it would be relatively easy for the specific responses of millions of individuals to an MMPI, or other test, to be stored on magnetic tapes or discs in a National Data Center. Practically all college graduates and a substantial number of high school students have taken the MMPI or a comparable test. The idea that data revealing supposedly confidential thoughts and feelings of millions of individuals could be assembled in one spot is abhorrent to those Americans who believe they have rights.... We can be certain that science will conceive more exotic and less expensive methods of storing, retrieving, and manipulating data....

> The extent to which the tests administered in the public schools today discriminate against members of minority groups, the poor, the physically handicapped, and other disadvantaged groups, should be of considerable concern to the Bar.

Of course, Sherrer and Roston predicted exactly what did, in fact, happen in the field of data manipulation when the supercomputer, the Elementary and Secondary Integrated Data System, went through in 1988.

The domestic privacy implications are enormous — particularly in light of the mercenary nature of education-related datatrafficking. The National Institute of Education's technology expert Lawrence P. Grayson's paper, "Education, Technology, and Individual Privacy,"[25] the landmark document alluded to earlier on, which questions the wisdom of amassing student opinions and other affective data in centralized computer banks, gets to the crux of the matter when it asks whether a child's attitudes at 15 years of age will be dredged up to haunt him at age 45; and whether information divulged about family matters will be misconstrued when reviewed ten or twenty years down the road. Moreover, can officials today ensure that this information will not be used politically or for job-screening purposes? Will colleges and universities receive "integrated" data on prospective applicants (and their families) as part of the selection process? Grayson points out that a child has a right to make mistakes and to form ideas over time without the pressure of their being recorded for posterity.

In any case, by the second Saturday at Orange High, parents of the young test-takers had gotten wind of what was going on and found out who was responsible. Officials took a beating in the local press.

But this was blatant. Had the culprits at the University of North Carolina used one of the subtler, more sophisticated attitude tests being passed off today as "cognitive" (explained in the following chapter), they might have gotten away with it unscathed.

The potential for abuse is not debatable. The threat is there and it is real. The Bar, no doubt, will become more concerned as complainants increasingly are in a financial position — and mood — to press charges.

CHAPTER 9

"Cognitive" versus "Academic": A Critical Distinction

IF ONE HAS the stamina to plow through such weighty treatises as *Basic Principles of Curriculum and Instruction* and *Improving Educational Assessment and an Inventory of Measures of Affective Behavior*, both by ETS and CFAT bigwig Ralph Tyler, or James P. Shaver's "National Assessment of Values and Attitudes for Social Studies" (see chapter 6); or the Dupuis and Mitzels (eds.) piece, "The Place of Psychology in a National Institute of Education" (discussed further on), no doubt whatever will be left as to either the thrust or intent of the National Assessment (NAEP) and the state versions of assessment testing.

Dry though these documents may be, they are worth perusing, primarily for the technical terminology. In the Shaver document, for example, one learns the rationale behind defining the term *cognitive* as "belief system," rather than as "academics" — a very important distinction that is frequently lost on the public at large. On pages 5 and 6 of his paper, Shaver explains how attitudes and opinions are assessed using a "cognitive" basis. Notice that it is the so-called "*intellectual component*" of values which permits psychologically manipulative curricula to be passed off as "basic" subject matter:

> Values are, in educational parlance, both cognitive and affective. That is, despite a tendency for people to think of values as being "only feelings", they have an intellectual as well as an emotional aspect. Persons can define what they mean by a value such as "honesty", argue about whether one another's definitions are appropriate and functional, and debate whether a person has applied the value appropriately in making a decision about how to behave ... or in judging the behavior of someone else. In doing so people are using intellectual processes to deal with the intellectually knowable; that is they are attending to the cognitive aspects of values.

Shaver goes on to explain in this 1986 document that an attitude, in technical terms, is "a predisposition to a referent" (e.g., an attitude toward an object, person, group of people, or idea) based on one's values and beliefs. So our values and beliefs determine our attitudes toward everything from foreign automobiles to the President. Since values shape our attitudes, it's important for testers to find out what they are. On page 8, Shaver takes the example of citizenship education in discussing the importance of values:

> From the "social studies as citizenship education" point of view, values take on a different significance. Values, particularly moral values, are seen as important because they are an essential ingredient in political dialogue and reasoning. They are fundamental elements in an adequate framework for arguing about and justifying our decisions to support or oppose proposed or enacted public policies.... Interest in that aspect of values...is primarily cognitive in orientation.
>
> ...common commitments to values provide a context for meaningful conversation and debate about societal issues. If people lack common value commitments . . . there is little basis for agreement or even productive disagreement and there will not be direct and meaningful confrontation and discourse on issues of mutual significance.
>
> ...commitment to values is the "cement" that holds the society together....

Shaver describes why moral values "defy easy definition" and "conflict with one another." He cites as examples the promotion of freedom of speech at the expense of peace and orderliness; freedom of the press "at the expense of national security as in the Pentagon Papers case." Not only do the values conflict, he says, but when used as criteria, they result in different decisions. On page 10 he points out significantly that "certain values are given precedence over others."

Few people will argue with Shaver's logic on these points, but his examples — as in the Pentagon Papers case, an event that was highly politicized at the time — raise serious concerns about the rest of his thesis; namely, about the wisdom of educators and testers getting into the attitude-molding business. Is it right and proper that the NAEP and its state clones should test what they are testing with a view, perhaps, to changing "inappropriate" political attitudes (passed off, perhaps, as solely moral issues)? Even if doing so isn't a big concern today, how about ten years from now? Who or what will be the dominating political landscape then?

The point is this: If "commitment to values" is, in fact, the " 'cement' that holds the society together," as Shaver claims, then it can be argued that teaching strategies aimed at holding the cement together can be used just as well to tear the cement apart.

If the "ability to apply basic democratic values and affective commitment to those values are crucial ingredients of democratic citizenship", as Shaver insists, then it doesn't take a far leap of imagination to see behaviorist educators viewing their role as "straightening out" children's concepts about "democracy," as well as all the underlying values connected to that term, along lines that could undermine the nation's cohesiveness. Behaviorists may protest "that's not what we're doing!" Maybe not. And maybe so. But with the kinds of psychological probing, cross-referencing of data, and psychological manipulation that is being promoted and practiced, the undeniable fact remains that a mechanism for abuse is being created.

Terms like "democratic," after all, are constantly being redefined, along with the terms *cognitive, value,* and *moral.* Experts like Shaver constantly remind their audiences of the importance of defining terms, of analyzing their appropriateness in the context of usage. These experts are quite right. Terms and concepts we take for granted, like "democratic" and "free flow of information" can be reinterpreted, or given new connotations as time goes on.

For example, the New World Information Order (NWIO), the organization that purports to speak for the interests of many Third World emerging nations, doesn't interpret as "democratic" the United States beaming television and radio broadcasts by satellite to these countries, no matter how much time American programmers say they expend to reflect the cultural differences between Western and Third World countries. The NWIO calls America's broadcasts "cultural imperialism" — not "free flow of information," not "democracy."

In point of fact, today the term *nationalism* happens not to be viewed by behaviorist educators as a positive or appropriate attitude. That is because, says the literature, nationalism assumes superiority of some nations over others. Therefore, the values that underlie the attitude of nationalism are in need of change.

This view of the term *nationalism* undoubtedly will surprise many readers, regardless of whether they think America is a good place to live or not. The popular view is that when a nation's people take pride in, or honor, the special traditions, customs, history, and culture of their country, *that* is nationalism and *that* is appropriate. Ideas about relative superiority are generally thought to be another, separate, matter — an extreme version of patriotism, perhaps.

Thus behaviorists, particularly test creators, can be victims of their own biases just like everybody else. But "everybody else" isn't constructing test questions, or manipulating the attitudes and ideas of little children, whose basic allegiances are still, for the most part, to home and family. When "certain values are given precedence over others," as Shaver puts it, whose values are reflected in tests created and analyzed for "inappropriate" responses? The behaviorists who create the tests and the analysts who examine them. That persons close to the home and local communities have little or no say about which "values are given precedence over others" is confirmed by Ralph Tyler, in his 1986 paper "The Governance of the National Assessment of Educational Progress." Tyler's paper points out that the governing board of the NAEP is composed primarily of "policymakers" and a *minority* representing practitioners, teachers, and school administrators. No mention of community parents.[26]

Ralph Tyler told the education establishment where he was coming from way back in 1949, when he was being groomed by his mentor, Hilda Taba. It was then that Tyler first defined education as "a process of changing behavior patterns." As president of CFAT, writer, and test creator — all since that time — he never once changed his mind about the purpose of education. With this viewpoint, Tyler undertook the major part of the NAEP's designing, and was a principal designer of the Pennsylvania assessment, Educational Quality Assessment.

Perhaps it is not possible, then, to construct a psychological-attitudinal survey that is entirely free of bias. In that case, maybe children are best left to formulate their values on the basis of knowledge (facts) and life experience rather than on the basis of psycho-behavioral programming.

But that is an ethical issue.

The technical, legal issue hinges on the fact that psycho-behavioral assessment tests and corrective learning programs, like the EQA-based materials, are testing and remediating children on the basis of what they *believe* (cognitive), not on the basis of what they *know* (academics). This is why terminology is so very important to understanding what is going on in education, for such distinctions become key to the way school curriculum is selected.

CHAPTER 10

How to Create a Psychological Conflict

THE INTERPRETIVE LITERATURE to the Educational Quality Assessment is still one of the best sources of information available on the purposes and strategies of behavioral testing and programming. It explains what experts are expected to accomplish and how the assessment test serves as a temperature-taking device for the school district. In this way the computer can be used to zero in on attitudinal, as well as academic, "weaknesses," which, in turn, will be used to determine what sort of curriculum is selected for the district.

Following up footnotes, names of experts, and other data, Pennsylvania researchers went to the ERIC computer bank and ordered related technical materials, and even a few case studies.

It was noticed that a number of the behavioral experts mentioned inducing a psychological condition they called *cognitive dissonance.* Keeping in mind the educational definition of "cognitive," one should not be surprised that *Webster's New Collegiate Dictionary* defines *cognitive dissonance* as "a psychological conflict resulting from incongruous beliefs and attitudes held simultaneously." Technical dictionaries say much the same thing, in expanded form.

The "Resources for Improvement" booklets substantiate this view. Apparently students are to be presented with enough learning experiences, passed off as factual knowledge, or "basics," so that the values inculcated by the usual sources, like family or religious institutions, are brought into question. Many corrective ("remedial") programs — the "strands" — produce the desired psychological conflict by forcing immature minds to make a choice between opposing "authorities."

Assessment tests, like the Educational Quality Assessment, seem to be establishing the degree to which psycho-behavioral curricula have either (1) set up this conflict, or (2) caused a change in the child's attitude or behavior. Apparently it is assumed that once cognitive dissonance is achieved, a change in attitude or behavior will follow, or at least will be made more likely.

The purpose, then, of the assessment test is, first of all, to establish what youngsters' attitudes already are (and, by extension, what their parents' attitudes are likely to be), and secondly, to demonstrate whether corrective programs are succeeding or failing in their dual objective of first, inducing, then resolving *cognitive dissonance.*

It is interesting that among dissenting experts, cognitive dissonance is frequently cited as one of the most "dangerous teaching strategies" known. But the rationale behind its continued use in the classroom is even more disturbing.

For example, in 1971 an "Affectivity Assessment Device" (continue to keep in mind the definition of the technical term "affective") was developed and given to first graders in a pilot project in order to gain information on how the child feels about himself and others. The assessment, described in the *Journal of Educational Research,* would determine whether a behavioral curriculum called "Developing Understanding of Self and Others" had been successful. In the administrative literature, teachers were asked "to rank the children in your classroom from highest to lowest in terms of your opinion of their noncognitive or affective development."

Clearly, behavioral experts did not want teachers assessing any "intellectual component," or factual knowledge. They wanted only teacher opinions about the subject's emotional development.

The technical note at the end of the article, however, is the real revelation. It speaks volumes about the thrust and intention of psycho-behavioral education, and as such may well be the most devastating indictment against behaviorist educators ever to surface. The context of the note centers on a behavioral strategy called "contracting," which researcher Joe H. Brown (University of Louisville) promotes in the article. He states:

> ...contracting is most effective in situations which arouse cognitive dissonance. That is, a person is likely to feel greater dissonance if he publicly

commits himself to a contract or goal than if he privately commits himself to it. . . . Furthermore, when the subject can choose the persons to whom he makes his commitment public, the dissonance is likely to be greater and will subsequently produce more behavior change.

This quotation from Brown nails the case against behavioral programming. Regardless of what one may think about students making a public commitment (probably in front of the class) to a behavioral change or goal — which in itself may not be a bad idea — the passage above rationalizes a *deliberate* intent to induce a dangerous psychological conflict called cognitive dissonance.

In rationalizing this intention, Brown also reveals that group pressure figures heavily in the scheme: The other children are going to be used to get a particular child to change his behavior. The almighty Group will form a consensus, and that, Brown hopes, will determine the future direction of the child's behavior. Peer pressure, rather than being diminished, is intentionally heightened to get a child to do what behaviorist educators want him to do and, more importantly perhaps, to think what behavioral educators want him to think.

Later, of course, other educators will work to get the child to *avoid* peer, or group, pressure. But the child has already been led to believe that the Group is Alpha. Here, then, is still another opportunity to induce cognitive dissonance: Because the Group at the same time is Alpha and *not* Alpha, the child once again will experience "a psychological conflict resulting from incongruous beliefs and attitudes held simultaneously."

In case one is tempted to think Brown and his cohorts are lone wolves advocating weird approaches to education, a look at another document entitled "The Place of Psychology in a National Institute of Education"[27] confirms that the approach not only is considered valid at the highest levels of government, but explains plainly what the purpose is. The importance of the following passage can scarcely be overstated:

A form of reinforcement . . . particularly appropriate in an educational context is "dissonance reduction." If a student can be led to recognize that two previously unrelated beliefs, both of which he holds, are in fact contradictory, he can be motivated to resolve this discrepancy and should be particularly receptive to instruction that helps him reduce this cognitive dissonance.

The ramifications of this admission are so repugnant that even the researchers who uncovered the document could not believe it was reflective of majority thinking among the education establishment. The key terms in the passage are "motivated to resolve" and "receptive to instruction." Are behaviorists saying they are deliberately inducing a psychological conflict of major proportions so that they can then "cure" it? What possible justification could there be in propelling a child to such a point of confusion that he will do anything, believe anything, that relieves his emotional misery? Suppose the "two contradictory beliefs" in question involve the values of the child's parents, church or synagogue? What does all the hype about parental involvement in education mean then?

CHAPTER 11

Experts and the Dissenters Among Them

IF BEHAVIORIST PROPONENTS and education policymakers seem blind to the discomfiture of the general populace about psychologically manipulative testing and programming in schools, or anywhere else for that matter, there are scores of reputable psychologists, lawyers and educators who are not. In the bowels of the ERIC computer are not only the "pro" arguments, but, lo and behold, dissenting views as well. Many of these dissenters have troubled themselves to publish their work in the popular press because they felt ignored in professional circles.

Take Dr. Melvin Anchell, eminent psychologist in Los Angeles, California. He is so well thought of that the state government has repeatedly called on him as an expert witness, particularly in sexual abuse cases. Anchell wrote *Sex and Insanity* to publicly document his objection to explicit pre-teenage, "value-free" sex education and surveys. He gives parents high marks who instill in their children values of modesty, and low marks to behaviorist educators who "catapult the child into a world of authoritative sexual knowledge." Early sex education, states Anchell, bypasses the well-established "latency period" of child development, when sensual pleasures normally are repressed and children typically learn compassion — between the ages of roughly six and twelve. Compassion for one's fellow man, he says, is "a relatively weak instinct" and "marks a notable step forward in removing civilized man from the savage." Compassion is first felt for parents or guardian, then transferred to others. The instinct toward compassion is seriously jeopardized, Anchell points out, by sexually stimulating children in latency and, particularly, by presenting sex and sexual feelings as something other than private. "If movie producers portrayed sex realistically, they would show lovers on the screen becoming impotent when performing sex before an audience."

Graphic, early sex education, says Anchell, also:

> shatters normal fantasy satisfactions. The resultant frustrations tend to fix the child in these early stages of growth. Later in life, drugs and pornography are used to recapture the pleasures of thwarted childhood fantasies that had not been allowed to resolve naturally.

Self-disclosure techniques, encounter-group methods, and values clarification exercises are not the only types of psychological education that are harshly criticized by professionals in the field. "Acting out" games, or "role playing," as it is frequently called, also come under attack. These are not the "let's pretend" games of childhood they are cracked up to be for public relations purposes. If they were, there wouldn't be any particular problem with them. The "role playing" of the classroom setting is "sociodrama" — a social adjustment exercise conceived by the late Dr. Jacob Moreno, who pioneered the use of the strategy with severely disturbed mental patients in the 1950s.[28] The "games" are *supposed* to make the participants uncomfortable. They are intended to deliver an emotional jolt.

Elementary and secondary schools have been experimenting with something called humanistic psychology for more than 15 years. It is based primarily on the theories of the late Drs. Abraham H. Maslow and Carl R. Rogers, although elements of Lawrence Kohlberg, Jean Piaget, Gordon Allport, Kurt Goldstein, and B. F. Skinner can be found today as well. Maslow, however, is considered the prime mover of humanistic psychology, while Carl Rogers' 1951 book, *Client-Centered Therapy,* and his non-judgmental method of working with troubled patients, known as *non-directive therapy,* are the basis for many, if not most, elementary and secondary behavioral programs today. In fact, today's primary values-teaching technique, "values clarification," is based on Rogers' non-directive therapy. In the non-directive therapeutic method, a disturbed patient never gets an answer to any question he or she might pose to the therapist, especially if it has to do with rightness or wrongness. Rather the therapist responds to the patient's every statement or question with a leading comment or another question. In the end, the patient supposedly will solve his own problem, answer his own quandary, by having what amounts to a conversation with himself.

It was Maslow who coined the terms *humanistic psychology* and *self-actu-alization.* He based his theories on a positive image of mankind instead of the prevailing negative image — the criminal, the psychotic, the neurotic, and so forth — of the Freudian era. Maslow felt that a model for the study of mental health should be the mentally healthy individual, not the mentally sick. Too much time, he felt, had been expended by earlier behaviorists focusing on the demented and insane until all perspective had been lost. To understand mental illness, he said, one first had to understand mental health. Maslow viewed health as the norm and sickness as the aberration, while his predecessors, he claimed, seemed to view mental (and for that matter, physical) illness as the normal state and treated health as the oddity. He went on to describe as "self-actualizers" those individuals who, in his view, were mentally stable, and with the help of Dr. Rogers, he sought to teach those who were not stable to attain that happy state — through a conscious change of behavior and attitude. "The Third Force" was the name Maslow gave to his theory as the means whereby mental health is achieved, and his ideas eventually became popularized under the label "Third Force Psychology."

So far, so good. One can accept or reject Maslow's ideas about which is more normal: health or sickness. In one sense, Maslow was simply reviving the old Calvinist debate of ecclesiastical circles: Are human beings basically all sinners, evil beings redeemable only from outside themselves? Or is each individual born basically good — a blank sheet of paper, so to speak, with a conscience, that enables the individual to decide in any given situation which he shall be, evil or good? Maslow opted for the blank sheet of paper.

Maslow was an admitted atheist, but he was no admirer of the value-free, or value-neutral, life. He claimed, in fact, that the ultimate disease was "valuelessness." A unique aspect of his Third Force theory was that there exist values, or moral principles, which are common to the entire human race, and that this can be scientifically confirmed. He rejected some of his behaviorist colleagues' contention that values have no scientific basis and that concepts of right and wrong should be ignored.

"The casting out of values by psychology," Maslow wrote, "not only weakens it, and prevents it from reaching its full growth, but also abandons mankind either to supernaturalism or to ethical relativism."[29] He exemplified the dangers of value-free science in the person of infamous Nazi Adolf Eichmann. "Instead of cultural relativity, I am implying that there are basic, underlying, human standards that are cross-cultural — which transcend cultures and are broadly human . . . ," wrote Maslow in the same text.

The problem many people have had with Maslow is not that he was a proponent of the so-called neutral value system. He wasn't. Where Maslow got into trouble was when he went on to affirm that universal values do not rest upon "blind faith," and that rather than looking for principles of right and wrong *outside* oneself — that is, "outside of mankind to a god, to some sort of sacred book, perhaps, or to a ruling class" — individuals ought instead to be "digging into the best people in depth . . . [to] find the ultimate values which are right for mankind." In other words, Maslow thought that people would find the best values by observing the best people.[30]

The "self-actualizing," healthy and normal person, Maslow explained, tells us all we need to know about what is good and what is bad. Human beings are capable of "scientific decision-making," by going through a multi-step process of arriving at their values. Good behavior, he claimed, is natural to man, and the only reasons why bad behavior is so prevalent is that, first, man's natural instincts often are weaker than cultural forces, and second, the innate drive toward growth is sometimes overruled by a simultaneous tendency to retreat toward safety. This, in essence, was Maslow's basis for the so-called "*naturalistic* value system."

While Maslow's case against cultural relativism sat well with many people in and out of professional circles, his implication that Man is his own absurd little god did not. Many questioned the assertion that human beings are perfectly capable of figuring out what is right and what is wrong, what is bad or good, simply on the basis of observing people who seemed to be healthy and normal. The greatest problem with this view, of course, was that it allowed for all sorts of definitions about what is and is not "normal" and "healthy" behavior.

Maslow developed a list, or hierarchy, of human needs and values — beauty, goodness, honesty, and so forth — which were not particularly eyebrow-raising, but many of his disciples formulated quite a different list and attributed it to the Maslovian method. Various sexual behaviors, for example, could, under Maslow's definition, be called normal and healthy, as well as a wide range of counter-culture beliefs. If there was no God to monitor things, no commandments that one must, or even should, follow, then people were assumed to have pretty much a blank check to formulate their own set of standards and values as they went along.

The so-called father of modern education, John Dewey, took his own version of Maslow's theories into the schools. Dewey believed that children are capable of becoming scientific decision-makers, and furthermore that the decisions reached by children — when they go through a multi-step process similar to Maslow's — are as valid as those made by their parents. This idea evolved into the notion that in a democratic society parents have no right to make decisions *for* their children because children can make decisions for themselves. That is why parenting how-to books since about 1950 encourage parents not to assume such authority. The writers claim that it is bad psychology to follow the biblical injunction about "train[ing] up a child in the way he should go." Furthermore, they imply that this argument is more than mere theory, that it has been proved.

The result, by the 1970s, was the popular wisdom: "If it feels good, do it." According to counter-culture logic, which formed the lion's share of pop psychology of the seventies and eighties, if "it" felt good, "it" must be healthy and normal and, therefore, right. This went somewhat beyond Maslow's theories.

There was, of course, the sticky problem that arises when something that "feels good" to one person hurts somebody else. That's where tolerance and education entered the picture. Maslow's theory was reinterpreted by behaviorist extremists to imply that people only get hurt because they *think* something is going to be harmful. Maybe it is one's culture or parents or church which teaches that certain behaviors are harmful. If so, this inflicts a needless and intolerable guilt upon the individual and compromises his right to choose. In a new twist on Maslow's logic, extremists came up with the idea that if children are educated to believe a thing is not harmful, the potential for harm is eliminated. They took this idea into the schools.

So the humanistic movement took another turn. It combined atheism and the scientific method into a cult having all the characteristics of . . . well, a religion, complete with its own creed and doctrine. This was later confirmed by the Supreme Court, and this humanism-as-a-religion stance would later carry enormous implications for separation of church and state arguments as they applied to education.

Some time during the upheavals of the mid-1960s, Dr. Maslow started having second thoughts about his and Dr. Rogers' humanistic psychology. He could see that it was being twisted by extremists and used in a way he had never intended. Soon after his granddaughter was born, Maslow did a 180-degree about-face, and he spent the rest of his life in vain attempts to retract his earlier contentions and to set the record straight.

"Self-actualization does not occur in young people," Maslow wrote. He explained that children have not yet achieved identity or autonomy, that they haven't had time to experience such things as a long, enduring love relationship, that they do not realize their own mortality, and so forth, all of which, taken together, Maslow insisted, make youngsters vulnerable to exploitation. Maslow spent some 1350 pages — two volumes in all — in regrets and retractions, repeating frequently that he had never meant his theories to be applied to children and insisting that his methodology was appropriate only for some two percent of the population. He died at the age of 62 — from overwork and exhaustion.

Carl Rogers did a turnaround, too, though not so blatantly. His grandchildren were twelve years older than Maslow's granddaughter and so did not get the full brunt of the new theories as they came to be used in the classroom. But in the last piece of work he wrote before he died, "Freedom to Learn for the Eighties," in 1983, Rogers described the experiments he had been involved in with Maslow as "a pattern of failure." An exceptionally reliable, stable man, Rogers chronicled in his later years his own emotional deterioration — due, he claimed, to some twelve years of enduring "feeling experiments." Rogers recognized, apparently, that as these experiments increased, so did his vulnerability and the trigger on his emotions. He described his feelings — which ran the gamut from elation to depression — as increasingly "volatile." This is confirmed by Rogers' prize graduate student and, later, colleague, Dr. William Coulson, who is today the only voice still left to speak for the late Maslow and Rogers.

Coulson met Rogers in 1963 as a graduate student at the University of Wisconsin. The two hit it off splendidly. So fascinated was young Coulson by Rogers' ideas that in 1964 Coulson took his wife and relocated to California with Dr. and Mrs. Rogers, where the two psychologists worked together for eighteen years.

Today Coulson is the Director of the Research Council on Ethnopsychology — and a hot item on the lecture circuit. He describes for stunned audiences how he and Rogers and Maslow, beginning in 1963, "hatched a scheme," as Coulson puts it, at the Western Behavioral Sciences Institute in La Jolla, California, to bring the methods of non-directive psychotherapy into classrooms across the nation. Children would be encouraged, he says, to turn inward to find the answers to life's moral questions.

Coulson also confirms the fact of Rogers' emotional deterioration as the experiments went on and on. Like Rogers and Maslow, Coulson, too, began to have second thoughts about the Frankenstein they had co-created. Today, he travels all over the United States explaining the theories behind humanistic psychology and its subsequent uses in the schools. He has appeared on numerous radio and television talk shows, most recently television's popular *20/20*, and *Phil Donahue,* and continues to be a source of considerable embarrassment to modern proponents and purveyors of so-called "values education" materials. Most school boards, kowtowing to behaviorist extremists, deny parents the right to bring Coulson in to speak, even if the parent groups pay Coulson's expenses.

The later attempts by Maslow and Rogers to set the record straight, Coulson insists, were hushed up, relegated to the ramblings of old men. If these later writings are included at all in modern anthologies, they are placed obscurely behind their former writings. Coulson explains how the opportunistic faction of behaviorists and publishers scrambled to create a market for the "new" psychology. Their most profitable market, of course, was the education establishment, where eventually the theories of self-actualization, non-directive therapy, and humanistic psychology took on a life of their own, frequently with political overtones.

Coulson cites reams of statistics and studies showing that the teaching method evolved from Rogers' non-directive therapy called values-clarification results in an increase in experimentation when it is applied to "family life" and drug-education courses among teenagers. In telling parents not to preach to their youngsters, Coulson says, what extremists are really saying is "leave the preaching to us." This preaching is accomplished subtly, as with advertising. Notice how billboards don't merely *suggest* that you do something, says Coulson, they tell you — using the imperative tone, as in "Come to where the flavor is," as if it were a command. "Don't defer to children's uninformed intelligence," he warns parents. "Tell them confidently and with authority about the wrongness of experimenting with drugs and premarital sex."

Coulson is careful to remind parents that children are not miniature adults, that they think differently. By way of example, Coulson notes that while educators do not imply there is a "choice" as to whether youngsters shall attend school or steal the principal's automobile, they do lead youngsters to explore the "alternatives," or options, when it comes to drug experimentation and premarital sex. Because they don't think like adults, young students, Coulson says, interpret this mixed message to mean that attending school is more important in the scheme of things than whether kids fool around with life or death matters like drugs and sex. Furthermore, youngsters are led to believe they don't *have* to follow their parents' admonitions, that they are ready to "be their own person," having arrived at their conclusions about right and wrong through a supposedly scientific process. What actually happens in the free-discussion, humanistic setting of the classroom, however, is that the experienced youngsters — those who have already experimented with drugs or sex, for example — teach the inexperienced ones, who are naturally somewhat reluctant to talk about the subject. "It doesn't seem to work the other way around," says Coulson.

Anyone interested in what the term "humanism" means today as applied to education — and, indeed, to life — can obtain a copy of the 17-point humanist creed by writing to the American Humanist Association (AHA) for a copy of *Humanist Manifestos I* (1933) and *II* (1973). Prometheus Books also sells them. The 1973 document is an update of the first and was written by the editor of *The Humanist* magazine, Paul Kurtz, and his colleague Edwin Wilson, past director of AHA.

Humanist Manifesto II gets about as close as one can to a general agreement among all those who call themselves humanists on matters of religion, freedom, economics, and education. The document contains several out-and-out statements specifically condemning religion, protesting that "traditional theism, especially faith in the prayer-hearing God, assumed to love and care for persons, to hear and understand their prayers, and to be able to do something about them, is an unproved and outmoded faith." Nothing wishy-washy in that.

The document goes on to describe religious bodies variously as "obstacles to human progress" and "a disservice to the human species." The writers (and some 200 signatories) claim there is "insufficient evidence for belief in the existence of a supernatural" and charge that "promises of salvation are both illusory and harmful." Moral values, the document continues, "derive their source from human experience. Ethics are autonomous and situational, needing no theological or ideological sanction." And so on.

The view that humanists hold of themselves is probably best expressed in a highly technical book by Albert Ellis, *Humanistic Psychotherapy*, in 1973.

Ellis echoes the primary claim of all humanists when he asserts on page 2 that humanism "goes hand in hand with the scientific method."

"[U]ntil someone definitely proves otherwise," he says, "there is nothing beyond human existence; and . . . any hypothesis [to substantiate the existence of a Supreme Being] must be backed by some form of data which are . . . observable and reproducible." He goes on to insist that any hypothesis for a deity which "cannot be backed by evidence that ordinary humans can observe and replicate is deemed to be theological, supernatural or magical . . ." and generally unsuited to the field of either "general or psychological science." Moreover, humanists view themselves as the ultimate pragmatists — the true, or "pure," scientists.

Unfortunately, the same extremist faction of behaviorists, often called "futurists," which won control of education and its purse strings, seized upon the humanist credo and began implementing it in earnest in the schools beginning about the time Maslow died, shortly after something known as the Behavioral Science Teacher Education Program (B-STEP, described later) came out. This one-thousand-plus page document, as will be shown, completely revamped teacher education courses across the country. Up to that time, there were sporadic attempts to introduce elements of humanistic psychology — à la Maslow and Rogers — into course work, but nothing like the massive inundation that occurred in the late 1970s and into the 80s, when behaviorist extremists sought to merge school psychologists, counselors, pupil tests and profiles, as well as curriculum into one gigantic experimental laboratory, using Dr. Maslow's early theories as their bible and Dr. Rogers' "client-centered therapy" as their model for school structure. Teachers, believing they were learning to be "relevant" and "meaningful" in "relating to students" became pawns in a game they didn't understand. With the demise of scholarship and excellence, the wrath of the public fell on teachers instead of on the perpetrators of the crime. If it had been a military campaign that was at issue, the public would have blamed the generals, not the front-line troops.

But the strategy of behaviorist extremism in education was well-planned and coordinated: The perpetrators diverted attention away from themselves and their helpmates in government and focused it instead on teachers and their supposed shortcomings. Predictably, teachers took a defensive posture. They voted to consolidate the heretofore independent national, state, and local teacher organizations into two enormous labor unions and empowered their leaders to call strikes, make demands, and lobby for political non-education-related issues, thus further alienating the public, particularly the professional classes. Understandably, teachers bristled at charges of incompetence and resisted moves toward accountability and credentialing. As the profession continued to change, many good teachers left for other careers, and less able, Karen Valentine and Kotter types, who were more interested in "relating" than teaching, took their places.

Moreover, teachers played right into the hands of behaviorist extremists, whose motives were sometimes earnest and sometimes political, and purveyors of humanistic teaching materials, who by now were raking in a fortune from sales to educators.

To teachers' great satisfaction, their union heads, as well as the popular press, were taking their side against "unreasonable" parents, even as academic scores declined further and illiteracy and school violence soared. What neither teachers, parents, nor, apparently, the press realized was that all the time, for at least 20 years, teachers were being set up. They were the Expendables: the perfect foils for the behaviorist establishment.

Had anybody followed carefully what government and university officials were saying during this period, they might have become suspicious: Nobody thought to ask, for example, just how it was that teachers trained under government-subsidized programs (that is, programs funded in one way or another with tax dollars, under government grant or contract), could be graduating "incompetents" in need of *re*training. Who was on whose side? Who was it that was training teachers, and then turning around and calling them "incompetent"?

Fundamentalist Christian conservatives eventually tagged the term "secular" (meaning outside and independent of religion) onto the word "humanism" to describe what they saw as a deliberate move away from traditional values in the schools. Soon parents outside of Fundamentalist, and even Christian, circles took up the battle cry, too, because they didn't like their authority being undermined any more than the Christian Fundamentalists did.

The behaviorist extremists quickly seized upon this new term, "secular humanism," laughed heartily, and challenged anybody to find reference to it anywhere except in Christian Fundamentalist literature. Sure enough, the term, worded that way, could not be found to exist in scientific or official circles, and efforts at dictionary definitions of "humanism," "humanist," "humanize" produced only "human interests, values, and ideals; to make human or humane."

Who could object to that? Didn't everyone want education to be humane?

Thanks to a well-planned media strategy (also found in that landmark treatise on teacher education, B-STEP), behaviorist extremists succeeded in focusing public attention on Christian Fundamentalism and the term "secular humanism," thereby again deflecting criticism and ignoring references to Maslow; Rogers; the Humanist Manifesto documents and their signatories; the American Humanist Association; and one huge, enormously rich, international quasi-political organization known as the Aspen Institute for Humanistic Studies. The public (including some Christian Fundamentalists), for the most part, still has no idea where the term "humanism" originated or how it came to be linked to a psychological tool aimed at school children. They couldn't tell you Maslow from a mastiff, much less what role humanistic psychology plays in teaching techniques like Moreno's psychodrama, or role-playing, values clarification, encounter groups, and other affective exercises.

Dr. Coulson tries to fill the void by explaining to audiences exactly how programs like *Quest, The New Model Me, Project Charlie, Here's Looking at You* (and *Here's Looking at You 2000*), *Growing Healthy, Omsbudsman, Meology,* and *Decide and Dare* employ the Maslow-Rogers models. He outlines the decision-making process taught to children in these courses, which tell youngsters to "look within themselves for answers which truly do not lie there." Coulson explains how children sit in a circle, or some other group-discussion mode, and are led through essentially five steps by a "facilitator," the new term for "teacher." First children identify a problem, and then they are asked to "examine the alternatives." To the childish mind, which has been taught, for example, abstention from drugs or pre-marital sex or stealing, the word "alternative" is a real grabber. The child suddenly has the power to choose in an atmosphere free of admonishments and guidance from family and church or synagogue.

What is the alternative to abstention, then? Well, participation in these activities, of course.

Meanwhile, real, substantive learning takes a back seat to self-analysis games; yet it will be the failure to acquire basic knowledge and learn basic skills which will lead to the kind of low self-esteem that is so prevalent among young drug users, dropouts, delinquents, and the unemployed. But behaviorist extremists do not see self-esteem in these terms. It has nothing to do with loyalty to principle or special talent or knowledge. The self-esteem exercises of affective educators are little more than exercises in conformity and narcissism, or, in the words of ethnopsychologist Dr. Coulson, "unearned applause." The bottom line is: If the group likes you, your self-esteem ought to be high. If it doesn't, for any reason, then you are doing something wrong and need to make a major behavior change.

Moreover, humanistic teaching methodologies have evolved over the past few years into other, even more hair-raising, consciousness-expanding techniques, including self-hypnosis and "guided imagery," which promise a heightened learning capability — while delivering a marked rise in suggestibility and an exaggerated emotionality. These newest techniques are called Fourth Force Psychology, sometimes popularly referred to as New Age, although this latter term also has other meanings.

In 1987, a program called *Tactics for Thinking* appeared in Indiana. It was billed as a "critical thinking" curriculum — the latest euphemism used to describe psycho-behavioral programming. (It is somehow never asked whether children have any factual knowledge to think about.) The senior author, Robert J. Marzano, was found to be the Director of Research at the Mid-Continent Regional Educational Laboratory in Aurora, Colorado — one of the U.S. Department of Education's official Labs. *Tactics* wasn't published by the Lab directly, but through the Association for Supervision and Curriculum Development, a National Education Association spinoff organization. So Marzano got federal funding for the research, if not for the publication of his material.

In any case, Marzano's manual describes the program as a concentration-enhancement curriculum, featuring a technique called "deep processing" to achieve "attention control." Marzano was interviewed by an uncritical Barbara Walters on the television program *20/20,* and Marzano minced no words in describing his work as a mind-control technique to teach children to concentrate better, the purpose of which is supposedly to help youngsters make better use of their own innate learning capabilities.

Again: So far, so good. But if one looks a little more closely — say, at Marzano's references, such as behavioral psychologists Peter Lindsey and David Norman, authors of *Human Information Processing* — there is a lot more going on here than a concentration-enhancement exercise. What the pair describe is a type of self-hypnosis, in which the subject learns to induce a trance-like, semi-aware state of consciousness. This is a very popular subject among behaviorists right now. Experts call the technique "altered states of awareness."

The idea is to lay bare the subconscious mind so that it becomes responsive to suggestion or stimuli. Many behaviorists blame failure to learn largely on mental blocks, fear, and other psychological hangups. The rationale for introducing the "altered states" technique into the classroom is that it gets the conscious mind — the part with the hangups — out of the way so it will not impede the free flow, as it were, of information into the brain. The subconscious mind then is supposed to get on with the job of taking in information and remembering it.

But once the conscious mind is out of the way, another interesting thing happens. The individual becomes highly suggestible and easily influenced. He may not even be aware of who or what is the source of the information he is getting.

Another of Marzano's references, a Russian psychologist who spent some years working at Moscow's experimental institute, explains in his book, *The Working Brain,* that the condition Marzano calls "involuntary attention" reflects an increase in alpha waves, which negates the brain's conscious reasoning ability and enhances the feelings and emotions.

Marzano's method may be considered a breakthrough by some, a disaster by others. Used with the understanding and consent of adults who wish to expand their learning potential, maybe it's worth a try. But the unrestricted use of such techniques with children in the captive classroom carries an intolerable potential for abuse.

Marzano is hardly the only educator to emphasize consciousness-raising psychological techniques. Innovative programs have been known to come into the schools from such research centers as the Lozanov Learning Institute of Silver Spring, Maryland. Its learning strategies are unorthodox, to say the least, and are characterized as "suggestopedic or superlearning methods." Lozanov, founder and mentor of the organization, advises teachers, among other things, that since "hypnosis" has a bad connotation, the term "suggestology" ought to be used instead. His techniques are applied, for example, by the Society for Accelerative Learning and Teaching in Ames, Iowa. Its Compendium of Enhanced Learning Techniques includes some 3,000 "time-distortion techniques" and other experimental approaches. A newsletter in 1986 asks members to contact the organization about any "special techniques you know of, hear of, or care to invent and try out in your classroom." That some of these brain-related research experiments may not be appropriate for all children, and even damaging to the impressionable, does not appear to be a concern. Would these and other innovations qualify for a program's inclusion in the National Diffusion Network? Based on what is already in the computer and the manner in which it gets there, the answer would have to be "yes."

Dr. Coulson isn't the only dissenter in the professional community, but he is one of the most knowledgeable since he helped launch the use of psychological techniques. Other dissenters include Dr. Kathleen Gow, renowned sociologist and international researcher, winner of numerous awards for clinical research in England, Scandinavia, and the Middle East. She wrote *Yes, Virginia, There is a Right and Wrong* to protest the kind of "value education" perpetrated by behaviorist extremists. Her book did not get the hype that is reserved for behaviorist fare, but it was so well researched, documented, and written, that big-name organizations and individuals in the psychiatric community publicly endorsed her work.

Dr. Karl Menninger of the well-known Menninger Foundation wrote *Whatever Became of Sin?*, a title that speaks for itself, and Cornell's Richard A.

Baer spoke out in the January 1977 issue of *The Education Forum*, describing certain popular behavioral approaches as "too traumatic" and "potentially damaging."

Educational researchers E. R. Gerler, Jr., and C.W. Pepperman reported on "Children's Reactions to Small Group Psychological Education" in 1976. At the end of it all, they questioned "whether all children should be unquestioningly exposed to . . . psychological education."

Researchers Robert W. Day and Robert E. Griffin wrote "Children's Attitudes Toward the Magic Circle [Encounter Game]," for the December 1980 issue of *Elementary School and Guidance Counseling*. At the end, they asked: "Can psychological education be required of all students if the possibility of detrimental effects is as distinct as these results [described in their article] suggest?"

Carl W. Salser, long-time executive director of the National Book Company, Educational Research Associates, and a member of President Reagan's National Council on Educational Research (NCER), as well as his eminent colleague at NCER, Donald Barr, former headmaster of top-notch Hackley School, have each written books outlining their objections to psycho/behavior-based education.

Elucidating the legal perspective are lawyers Charles W. Sherrer and Ronald A. Roston, who itemized their concerns in the Spring 1971 issue of the *Federal Bar Journal* under the title "Some Legal and Psychological Concerns About Personality Testing in the Public Schools." They explain that

> [a]ny personality test constitutes an invasion of privacy to some degree, as the person tested rarely understands the implications of all the questions ...or the significance of the responses. The tests may not only reveal the thoughts and feelings which the student desires to withhold from others but those he is trying to keep from his own consciousness. The courts have recognized a common law action for invasion of privacy.

The authors cite *Pearson v. Dodd, Olmstead v. the United States*, and *Griswold v. Connecticut*, and the rationales behind these decisions.

On the issue of parental consent, Sherrer and Roston[31] say: "It is unlikely that the average parent knows to what he is consenting when he signs a piece of paper stating that the school psychologist can examine his child."

One might also ask whether the average parent knows what he's "consenting to" when he isn't aware that any psychological exam has taken place.

In 1975, Reed Martin was sufficiently alarmed about the legal ramifications of psychological probing that he wrote a book directed to behaviorist experts themselves, entitled *Legal Challenges to Behavior Modification: Trends in Schools, Corrections, and Mental Health.* He was warning behaviorists about their vulnerabilities in promoting psycho-behavioral programming. They didn't listen.

They didn't have to; they were already way ahead of Reed Martin. Behaviorist leaders had crossed that bridge two years earlier and decided how they were going to handle it. The proof, once again, is found in *Critical Issues in Testing,* the book co-edited by Ralph Tyler and Richard Wolf. On page 120, in a section subtitled "Some Emerging Problems," behaviorists started anticipating the kinds of flak they were going to run into. Remember as you read that this was published in 1974 and written, therefore, at least a year before that. Key in especially on numbers 3 and 4 below:

> ...The problems fall into four categories: 1) lack of communication and coordination, 2) the relation of assessment data to financial incentives, 3) the handling of sensitive data, and 4) confusion and conflict about goals.

The section goes on to address these problems one at a time. They take on "The Handling of Sensitive Data" on page 123, and it is clear from the following that behaviorists understood exactly where they were vulnerable (see italicized portions) and what kinds of legal challenges they could face.

> ...The fear is that data of this sort will be misinterpreted by the public....

> The problem is further exacerbated when pupils and/or their teachers are asked to supply information about their ethnicity, their economic and social backgrounds, their behavior tendencies, and their social attitudes. *Hard questions are raised not only concerning the propriety of using such information once it is in hand,* but also concerning the possible deleterious effects on

children of merely asking for such information in the first place. . . . ; it can also be regarded as *invading privacy.*

Furthermore, there is always doubt whether the responses to such questions can be taken at face value...[T]he respondent may be "faking good" or "faking bad" and not representing his true feelings.

Co-editor Richard M. Wolf does the honors himself on page 159, where he discusses "Invasion of Privacy." Quoting Bernard Berelson in the *Journal of Educational Measurement,*[32] he writes:

. . . "[G]reat society" programs have heightened the demand on behavioral scientists to work on social problems . . . . [G]reatly increased financial resources for research have not only increased the level of activity but have also made large projects possible. Being highly visible, the large research project is more subject to public criticism . . . . And there are recent indications that the involvement of public funds evokes a special public concern for privacy.

. . . the concerns are greatly heightened by the advent of computer technology. . . . The danger lies in gradual erosion of the individual's right to decide to whom he wishes to disclose personal information.

Wolf goes on to address five major aspects of the privacy issue. Note the second one, in boldface: "(1) respecting the dignity of the person tested, (2) *permissibility of deception,* (3) the rights of an institution to obtain information necessary for achieving its goals, (4) the special status of school children, and (5) limits on the freedom of scientific inquiry."

The furor which developed over the ethics of obtaining and using personal information could not possibly have come as a surprise to these people. When the Protection of Pupil Rights Amendment was passed, and when articles started appearing regularly from the professional community and the public condemning psycho-behavioral testing and programming, the behaviorist establishment pretended shock. But from these accounts it is plain that from 1974 onward, behaviorists systematically shrugged off protests as the ravings of little old ladies, bored housewives, and religious zealots who presumably had nothing better to do with their time than make trouble for educators. The behaviorist extremists stacked the deck against their opposition well in advance, using ridicule as their primary strategy and a dollar-conscious press to help them de-legitimize other professionals in the field who balked. Of the concerns itemized above, behaviorist extremists decided that number 3 was the most important and that number 4 was merely convenient.

On the thorny issue of "permissibility of deception," Wolf admits that

> [t]here are many occasions in which the test constructor tries to outwit the subject so that he cannot guess what information he is revealing. From the test constructor's point of view this is necessary since he wishes to ascertain information that the individual might not be able to furnish if it were sought directly. A number of personality inventories fall into this category....

> ...Educators and psychologists who are involved in the development and use of tests often justify the use of deception on the grounds that it is necessary in order to obtain information for worthwhile purposes . . . . However, if the results of a testing situation in which deception was employed are used in making a decision which the individual considers adverse, such as denial of admission to a particular program or institution, there are potential serious legal and ethical questions. *Entrapment is an explicitly illegal procedure in the United States. To what extent the use of deception in testing can be considered a form of entrapment has yet to be determined.*

Wolf asks whether the school has a right to withhold test information from the student and his parents, and whether students and their parents have a right to know what information the school possesses about them. He should have referred these question to lawyers Sherrer and Roston, who understood Concern Number 4, the "Special Status of School Children" — the captive audience — better than anybody.

Finally, under Concern Number 5, "Limits on Freedom of Scientific Inquiry," Wolf concludes that "fundamental constitutional issues could be involved." He cites L. J. Cronbach, who writes in *Essentials of Scientific Testing*[33]: "Coding of records is not a full safeguard. Identity can be detected by matching facts from the coded questionnaire with other facts that are openly recorded."

Anybody who believes in 1991 that behaviorists don't understand their opponents or the charges being made against them has not read their papers from the 1970s.

The fact is, students are not the only ones today filling out affective surveys. Job-seekers increasingly are asked to do the same. In a piece that appeared May 7, 1990, in the popular Sunday magazine, *Parade,* entitled "Should You Tell All?" Bernard Gavzer wrote about an employee test to predict whether a prospective applicant might lie, steal, or become involved with illegal drugs. Some twenty questions from a 704-item test for job applicants were reprinted in the article. Some questions were sexual and personal.

An applicant for a plainclothes position at Target Stores in California had the audacity to ask whether this sort of thing was legal. He was hired anyway, then terminated some ten days later. He became a key figure in a class-action suit against Target Stores.[34]

I have insecurities and feelings of inferiority.	True or False
It would be nice to have enough money to never have to work again.	True or False
I would enjoy being seen dining or talking with important people.	True or False
As a child, there were times I hated my mother and father.	True or False

How often do you insist on having things your own way?

How often are you embarrassed?

How many people cheat on their income taxes?

Do you agree that most accidents and injuries at work cannot be avoided?

Have you ever done anything you feel guilty about?

Guess wrong on any of these questions and one can be denied the means of earning a living. Stated Harvard law professor Alan M. Dershowitz for the *Parade* article: "On the basis of such a test, which claims to predict whether you might steal something, . . . you can be penalized simply because a test says you may have a proclivity to be dishonest. In other words, you are guilty without a trial. . . . Truly honest people, reveal proclivities, [and] have to fail the test."[35]

The Office of Technology Assessment is doing a review of the tests. They may be banned. The ACLU national director, Lewis Maltby, says "[t]he worker has a legitimate concern that his privacy be respected . . . ."

The author of the article in question discusses some of the other "personality-based" tests, like the Minnesota Multiphasic[36] and attitude tests. The political persuasion of company leaders who use these tests does not appear to be a factor. The Parade article mentions the ultra-conservative Coors Brewing Company[37] using attitude tests to screen employees as well as more liberal trade unions. This may explain why both conservative and liberal, Republican and Democratic, administrations have taken a *laissez-faire* view of psychological testing and manipulation in education.

Depending on the outcome of OTA's review of employee tests, the use of psychological tests and surveys in educational settings may be challenged again. But even if OTA's review is negative on psychological testing of prospective employees, it is highly likely that educational institutions will be exempted from any bans on attitude-personality probing, particularly if behaviorist extremists in education and their cohorts in government have anything to say about it. For example, unlike in 1973, the ACLU today won't touch this issue if it applies to education, but it will if the charge is against business.

Moreover, affective education destabilizes good kids — mainly because its use is based on the assumption that most children are brought up improperly. All the affective methods discussed in this chapter are founded on a kind of therapy that is used with troubled people, not healthy ones. It is even contrary to Maslow's earliest contention — the one that made him famous — that treatment ought to be based on the healthy, not on the sick. Consequently, the children who are well brought up are traumatized for the sake of those few who are not.

The examples of professional dissenting opinion on psychologically manipulative strategies are voluminous. As has been shown, these are not the ramblings of pop psychologists found in grocery checkout stands, but the well-documented evidence of thoughtful, highly regarded experts, speaking out in respected technical publications.

Yet, by some strange coincidence the dissident views of these men and women, although sometimes politely heard, have at no time been seriously heeded, even at the highest levels of government.

CHAPTER 12

What Constitutes a "Captive Audience"?

IN A 1973 court case, *Kamowitz v. the Department of Mental Health*, a legal precedent was set that dealt with the rights of individuals in a captive environment with regard to their personal thoughts and feelings. The ruling went thus:

> Intrusion into one's intellect when one is involuntarily detained and subject to the control of institutional authorities, is an intrusion into one's constitutionally protected right of privacy. If one is not protected in his thoughts, behavior, personality, and identity, then the right of privacy becomes meaningless.

With this in mind, a word should be said here, perhaps, concerning certain well-known psychological inventories — for example, the popular Myer-Briggs Type Indicator (MBTI), developed during World War II — that are given primarily for aptitude purposes to students and adults on a purely voluntary basis.

The MBTI is one of those psychological evaluators of war-time vintage, the use of which probably was spurred by the need for Intelligence gathering among prisoners of war. The legal and ethical differences in their use lie, first, in the "voluntary" nature of the exercise and, second, in where the data is going. If tests are going to be administered, analyzed, and reviewed in a closed setting — say, at a private school or private career counseling center — and both the results and the questions are going to be available for perusal by test-takers (or, in the case of juveniles, by their parents), then that is "informed consent" and there is nothing wrong with it. Many people would like insight into their personality type, to know how they might perform better, given their attitudes and other characteristics, and to get an idea generally about what makes them tick. Even though such tests are far from perfect, they can provide indicators that might be valuable in career selection and other matters.

Such devices become fraudulent when they are passed off as something other than what they are. Affective testing devices become intrusive when the test-taker does not know where the data is going and has no control over who sees the data. When psychological testing devices become downright abusive is when test-takers become unwilling laboratory "subjects," when they (or their guardians) are refused access either to the questions or the results. The worst form of abuse is to presume to "remediate" psychological tendencies and attitudes that test-takers, held in a captive environment (like the school), are not even aware were assessed in the first place.

This form of abuse also may be illegal. On October 31, 1975, the National Commission for the Protection of Human Subjects of Biomedical and Behavioral Research released a staff paper, "Prisoners as Research Subjects." On page 32, this paper alludes to individuals placed in "a captive environment" — particularly those institutions receiving federal funds. They were, stated the paper, protected against experiments that intruded into their private thoughts and feelings or which sought to alter their personalities. Another law, P.L. 93-348 (January 13, 1978), "Research Involving Children," also touches on this issue, as does page 5 of an April 1, 1977 document, also entitled "Protection of Human Subjects."

But oddly, educational institutions and children are either specifically *exempted* from the captive-environment protection, or they fail to be named. It was the late Senator Sam Ervin (D-N.C.) who sought to amend the regulations so as to include children in a classroom setting along with instructional techniques.

The use of such experimental techniques by the *medically* unlicensed, such as teachers, becomes, again, a valid concern. Given the sophistication of today's psychological techniques and the fact that psychiatrists are supposed to be medically licensed, the U.S. Department of Education would appear to be on thin legal ice by promoting, even indirectly, personality-altering methodologies in a "captive" setting. Moreover, if consenting adults want to invest their time and money into courses that have them "expanding their consciousness," "acting out," pouring out their most personal experiences and feelings to strangers, rolling around on the floor, and hypnotizing themselves, that is their right and no one should interfere with it. What Senator Ervin (and at least two other members of Congress) wanted to establish is whether children, as a captive audience, are legally bound to accept this sort of thing. Are taxpayers, who think they are supporting education and teachers, legally obliged to pay for mismarked or unlabeled goods?

CHAPTER 13

The Slippery Slope

THE MOST IMPORTANT message of behavioral programs — regardless of the stated purpose of any particular "strand" — seems to be that the group is Alpha. Parents are not Alpha. The individual is not Alpha. Authority figures — teachers or the police, for example — are not Alpha. Certainly a Divine Creator is not Alpha. The Group is Alpha.

When parents complain that they are being undermined by the school, their complaint — however it may be expressed — generally boils down to the feeling that in matters of curriculum and education policy they are being squeezed out. "You are the only parent who has ever complained," becomes a standard response. Oh, there is always talk about parental involvement, parental participation, getting the community behind programs (particularly if they happen to require more money). But these platitudes refer to parents as a *group*. What an *individual* parent *thinks* is not important. The parent is not Alpha.

As the years go by, parents frequently talk about feeling manipulated — into positions they don't really want to be in; into accepting educational principles and policies that in reality they question. When parents try to teach their children right from wrong and something about integrity, morality, and standards, they find educators underscoring the "gray zones" before parents have had an opportunity to explain what the black and the white zones look like. Later, after their youngsters are in trouble and estranged from them, parents are blamed for failing to teach standards.

Caring, responsible parents seem to be lumped by educators and education policymakers with that minority which is irresponsible, neglectful, and abusive. Even parents who agree with some of the behavioral thrusts to education eventually feel the weight of the education establishment looking at them as though they are incompetent and remiss. Only in their professional fields of expertise, if they happen to have any, do the ideas of average parents count. Parenthood is not a "field" — unless your name is Dr. Spock or Dr. Brothers, or some other Ph.D. who has made child psychology his "field." It becomes an act of audacity to insinuate that one's own child is of any special importance. Children (plural) are important, "the younger generation" is important, "the leaders of tomorrow" are important — but an individual child is not considered important. The individual child's parents, and their concerns, are not treated as important.

The Group is Alpha.

In opposing psycho-behavioral education, the ethical issue is only part of the problem. Of equal, or greater, concern is the potential for abuse inherent in the whole operation. However much one may dislike a particular curriculum or thrust, there is no law against promoting, say, particular political beliefs in the classroom — socialism, fascism, capitalism, or globalism or what-have-you.

The point is that schools set up as behavioral psychology laboratories — particularly when results can be documented and sent to cross-reference-able, internationally accessible, centralized computer banks, as will be shown further on — are in a position to inflict any sort of indoctrination, political or moral, that they choose upon the population at large — racial hatred, Ayatollah-style Islamic fundamentalism, atheism; a fear of science; a distaste for Democrats or Republicans; a hostility towards one's own parents.

Schoolchildren, as indicated in the previous chapter, are mandated by law to be there. Parents are not welcome in the classroom as day-long spectators, nor would most have the time if they were. If they stayed around, however, they would see that the system as it stands today — without any further embellishment on the part of behaviorists or the federal government — can be used to get children to spy (and report) on their parents, without youngsters being aware they are doing so.

This means, for one thing, that there is a huge potential political weapon available for use against regional/geographic groups. Candidates running for public office, or interest groups attempting to drum up support for legislative proposals, can have their survey research done essentially for nothing using the attitude surveys of children. They will be able to use this attitudinal information to construct regional profiles on parents, using the survey information to build their political campaigns and sidestep any issue they don't want locals to hear. Children can misread questions, too, and lead authorities to believe a parent is abusive or neglectful, that a child is suicidal or psychotic, or any number of other things that may not be even remotely true. Thus attitude surveys and tests can violate intimate family relationships and private thoughts and feelings, and be used as a means to harass parents and other groups.

Did American soldiers lie in their blood on foreign soil in World War II so that policymakers at home could perpetrate an Americanized version of Hitler's Youth?

If this seems an outrageous charge, consider one teachers' edition of a health curriculum approved for Tennessee schools. Every few pages there is a drawing in the top margin of a child holding his finger to his lips in a "Sh!" pose. These pages contain sexual or other intimate information relating to students' family members. In checking on the meaning of this drawing, it was found that "Sh!" did not mean the subject was private; it meant that the student was to be admonished not to discuss the material with his parents. The rationale was that the material was intended to create an awareness of sexual abuse.

Of course there are parents who sexually abuse their children. It is a heinous crime. But if it is acceptable to give children the impression that their parents are as likely to be cruel and abusive as not, that it is in the interest of the child to keep secrets from his parents, then what kinds of "secrets" will youngsters be asked to keep from their parents in ten years? In twenty years? When government authorities (which, in essence includes the school) begin intruding into the family, pitting one faction against the other, it is the beginning of a very slippery slope.

Parents consider it a violation of trust, at the very least, when they are not given the facts about innovative learning programs — experiments — used in the classroom. That is why, in Indiana, some 250 parents armed with

1600 signatures on a petition stormed a school board meeting in 1988 to protest a teacher-inservice education program that promoted the use of *Tactics* program, described in Chapter 11. It is why angry parents in Wisconsin in 1986 went to the ACLU for help in halting the use of a sex/drug quiz (under the innocuous-sounding title Student Assistance Program). These parents claimed the quiz advocated turning their children into spies. Violation of public trust was also the reason why, in 1987, hundreds of parents picketed outside the state capitol building in Austin, Texas, to protest the use of behavioral curricula in general, and why another 400 parents did the same thing outside Michigan's state capitol building the year before that.

Somehow these revolts by parents never make headlines. It is almost as if the word goes out to the media ahead of time that the demonstration in question "won't be any big deal." So why cover it?

Part
III:
SENATOR ZORINSKY AND THE ILL-FATED LITERACY CAMPAIGN

CHAPTER 14

Taking On the Education Subcommittees

WHILE ANITA HOGE was doing battle with the education bureaucracy in Pennsylvania, Erica Kenney, legislative assistant to Senator Edward Zorinsky (D-Neb.), was waging a similar war on Capitol Hill. As a mother of four, she had had first-hand experience with the use of psychological techniques in her children's classrooms both in the Maryland and Virginia suburbs of Washington, D.C. In 1977, she was assigned to work with a group of Omaha parents who had met with the Senator after being stonewalled by their local school board. She was amazed to hear about the same manipulative strategies being used in Nebraska.

The Omaha group was very concerned about the psychological direction their "local" curriculum was taking. The point of contention that year was a federally funded program they thought had come down too hard against parental authority and the family unit — repeatedly portraying parents as irrational, fanatical, unreasonable, misguided, and so on. It also seemed to single out religion and patriotism as the major culprits in children's social adjustment problems.

The group eventually succeeded in getting the objectionable program removed, but soon it appeared in other places around the country.

To get a handle on the issue, Erica Kenney started doing some research. By 1978, the Senator was expressing alarm about the schools becoming more concerned with children's attitudes and personal beliefs than with providing a basic education. His comments were sent to the Senate Education Subcommittee but drew little attention for the most part. However, a few of Zorinsky's colleagues were quite interested, among them Senator Orrin Hatch (R-Utah), who placed Zorinsky's remarks in the Congressional Record. Senator Hatch subsequently introduced the Protection of Pupil

Rights Amendment (PPRA), and it was passed as part of the Education Amendments of 1978.

Five years later, *A Nation at Risk* was published. It was the first serious attack on the quality of American education. Senator Zorinsky subsequently introduced a bill to establish a commission on teacher education, with special emphasis on how teachers were trained in the use of psychological techniques and what strategies were being used to teach reading. He zeroed in on these two points because of the evidence in *A Nation at Risk,* which showed deficiencies in teacher training. Subsequent research by Erica Kenney revealed the greatest deficiency to be in the area of reading instruction.

If teachers weren't learning something as basic as how to teach reading in their college training, what *were* they learning?

It has been said that the alphabet ranks alongside fire and the wheel as a basic tool of civilization, fostering giant leaps beyond picture-writing by expanding the capability to express abstract ideas such as hope and freedom. The alphabet, of course, was invented for only one purpose: to encode the *sounds* of language. With knowledge of an alphabetic code, a person could be taught to read virtually any written material. This is not to disparage cultures that use a different writing system, but the advent of the alphabetic system definitely permitted a wider range of written expression and a means other than sheer memorization for figuring out the pronunciation and spelling of unfamiliar words. In the mid-1800s a man by the name of Thomas Gallaudet (for whom a college for the deaf, Gallaudet University in Washington, D.C., is named) began experimenting with a sight-memory method of teaching deaf persons to read. Since deaf individuals cannot recognize sounds in the usual way, Gallaudet ignored the sounds of language altogether, in the mistaken belief that the concept of sound was not useful to them. More recent research has shown this assumption to be wrong, and Gallaudet's original reading primer is gone. But the first line of that primer took on a life of its own: "Frank had a dog. His name was Spot."

Renowned educator and author Samuel L. Blumenfeld has traced reading instruction methods since our Colonial period. He and other experts have chronicled how Spot had his ups and downs through the rest of the 1800s, then remained mostly dormant until 1931, when the friendly pooch was suddenly revived and launched into America's so-called progressive schools via the Scott Foresman series by William S. Gray and the Macmillan series by Arthur I. Gates. These were the familiar "Oh! Oh! Look! Look! Dick and Jane see Spot run!" beginning ("basal") readers that discouraged sounding out words in favor of memorizing whole words strictly by their appearance. This was a task of visual memory. It allowed children no supportive connections to spoken language. But it was the new, progressive way, and the phonetic approach to reading was suddenly out.

The absurdity and non-effectiveness of sight-memorization, points out Blumenfeld, is obvious when one examines the escalating repetitiveness in reading pre-primers over the next few years: In 1931, 68 sight words were taught in 39 pages of story text, with one illustration per page and 565 words total. The word "look" was repeated eight times, "oh" 12 times, and "see" 27 times. But by 1951, the same reading pre-primer had been expanded to three books totaling 172 pages, 184 illustrations, 2,316 words. The word "look" was repeated 110 times, "oh" 138 times, and "see" 176 times — all to teach a sight vocabulary that was now down to a mere 58 words, ten words less than in the 1931 pre-primer! This teaching method became known as "look-say."

The books were boring; the task required of children ridiculous. Why did the education establishment stick with it?

They stuck with a pedagogic flop because certain unscrupulous members of the publishing and education community had stumbled into a financial gold mine. Charles M. Richardson, a former electrical engineer-turned educator, columnist, and director of a learning clinic in New York, describes how these publishers and professors worked together to turn out a plethora of remedial texts for the new "special education" market — a market founded on an artificially created illiteracy. Not only that, there emerged an even larger market for ever-simpler texts in the basic subjects — texts "dumbed down" for youngsters whose only fault may have been the inability to memorize the appearance of every single word in the English language!

Senator Zorinsky cited a typical example of "dumbing down" in a testimony before a joint hearing of House and Senate education subcommittees:

> 'Tap, tap, tap. I make good things. See the red one. See the blue one. See the yellow one. No, no, no, I do not want red ones. I do not want blue ones. I want green ones.'

> This is an adaptation of the fairy tale 'The Shoemaker and the Elves.' But it does not use the words shoemaker or elves because readability formulas limit sentence and word length and delete unfamiliar words.

Ridiculous though the material may have been, the markets for such "dumbed down" texts became so lucrative that those less principled among the education and publishing community saw advantage to controlling what prospective teachers were taught about reading methodology. "Look-say" was touted despite all the negative evidence against it until it became an article of faith.

The ink was barely dry on Rudolf Flesch's landmark exposé, *Why Johnny Can't Read,* hailed by *Time* magazine in 1955, when the education establishment, which by now was virtually run by these opportunists, closed ranks and created the International Reading Association (IRA). It was founded by those with close ties to educational publishing (for example, Dr. John Manning, former IRA president, was a paid consultant to Scott Foresman Company, megabook publisher of education texts), and from 1956 to this day the organization controls most of what prospective teachers are taught about reading methodology and what Congress gets told about the reading problem. Flesch and his book were crucified in the IRA journals, and the establishment continued on with look-say despite criticism from parents and professionals in the field. The label "look-say," however, was changed frequently to avoid appearing old-fashioned — first, to "meaning-emphasis," then to "comprehension-oriented," "holistic" (meaning "universal" and "comprehensive"), "psycholinguistics" (which means "guessing"), and finally to "whole language," which is the buzz-word for it today.

Throughout the 1960s and 70s, many studies were funded to investigate the escalating illiteracy problem. The results continued to report what a growing cadre of education manipulators did not want to hear — the superiority of phonics (that is, code-emphasis methods) over primarily non-alphabetic, sight methods. One of the most widely acclaimed of these studies was Dr. Jeane Chall's *Learning to Read — The Great Debate* in 1967.

Chall's credentials were unassailable — Director of Reading for the Harvard Graduate School of Education, a bastion of establishment credibility in the field. All the more reason, then, to discredit her. How dare she! thought the education-publishing hierarchy. "The teacher, not the method, is what counts," screamed an IRA journal. After that, serious researchers began to shy away from the subject of reading instruction altogether.

Throughout the 1970s the Department of Health, Education and Welfare (HEW) showed the illiteracy rate rising from 18 million to 23 million in just five years. They soon stopped printing statistics. More recent figures on illiteracy generally come from sources outside government. The money tree had been sprouting new branches as ever more individuals and organizations began cashing in on remediation and dumbing down.

By the time Senator Zorinsky seized upon the illiteracy issue, remedial reading and "special ed" classes had become a way of life from elementary school through college. The Reading Reform Foundation and other dissident groups made attempts to inform the public and Congress about what was really happening, but they didn't have the by now enormous monetary resources of the "look-say" faction. Senator Zorinsky and his able assistant, Erica Kenney, worked to make the point that it costs less to do things right the first time. But it was too late. Bureaucrats were engaged in their favorite pastime: manipulating tax dollars to "improve" educational quality — despite mounds of statistics showing that educational quality does not necessarily correlate with expenditures. It wasn't the children, after all, who were reading, multiplying, and eating dollars. Those functions were left to the bureaucracy.

The Senator dead-ended. Zorinsky's proposal to establish a commission on teacher education was found unacceptable to the Senate Education Subcommittee, which only held a hearing on the bill because the state of Vermont happened to be interested in a completely unrelated issue that had come before the Agriculture Committee, on which Senator Zorinsky also served, along with Vermont's junior senator, Patrick Leahy. Zorinsky told Leahy that since Robert Stafford, the senior Senator from that state and Chairman of the Senate Education Subcommittee, had not seen fit to call a hearing on his education bill, he, Zorinsky, would not support Vermont's agriculture initiative.

After a phone call from Leahy, Stafford quickly agreed to a hearing.

———————

SENATOR STAFFORD WAS the only member of the Senate Education Subcommittee who managed to make it to the hearing that day — because he *had* to be there to chair it. Although much of the testimony was explosive and the hearing room was packed, it didn't earn so much as a line in the mainstream press. What's more, the education establishment—particularly the National Council of Colleges for Teacher Education — strongly *opposed* Zorinsky's bill to investigate teacher training, on the weak grounds that no such commission was necessary.

The following year a commission similar to the one Zorinsky had asked for was formed — by guess who: the same National Council of Colleges for Teacher Education that had opposed it. Consequently the commission was set up so that it addressed none of the issues the Senator had raised.

Senator Zorinsky continued to follow education issues, and he became increasingly concerned, not only because of the ongoing complaints from his constituents, but because of parallels he saw in complaints around the country. In April of 1985 he began introducing legislation—this time limiting the issue to illiteracy, which he thought surely had a chance of being heard in the Subcommittee and passed by Congress.

He wanted to get to the bottom of allegations that there are inexpensive, effective methods of teaching reading, but they are being brushed aside in favor of more expensive, ineffective methods. Zorinsky's new bill would have established a national commission on illiteracy, with emphasis on how teachers are trained to teach reading. Since by this time there was a good deal of support for such a measure around the nation and in the Senate — the bill had over 30 co-sponsors — it should have passed speedily.

But once again, Zorinsky encountered stiff resistance from the Education Subcommittees—this time in both the House and the Senate.

A sympathetic Armed Service Committee briefly came to the rescue, adding Zorinsky's proposal to its Defense Authorization Bill—for they recognized that literacy was in some measure related to the nation's defense. The bill passed the Senate, then went to conference in the House, where Senator Stafford's congressional counterpart, Congressman Augustus Hawkins (D-Ca.), chaired the House Committee on Education and Labor.

Hawkins proved as obstinate as Stafford. Hawkins opposed the bill so vigorously that an astonished Armed Services Committee dropped its support. It couldn't afford to jeopardize its own measure over one small provision on illiteracy.

Later in 1985, Hawkins and Stafford decided to hold a series of joint hearings on illiteracy. In his testimony at the second hearing on October 1, Senator Zorinsky stated that any discussion of illiteracy must address prevention as well as remediation and that any discussion of *prevention* must take into consideration methods of teaching reading. He noted that the top reading professionals in the country had concluded that teaching phonics is essential in the early years but that most schools were not using it and most teachers had not learned it.

Zorinsky also made mention of the fact that the previous hearing had been one-sided with no mention made of teaching methods. In a magnanimous gesture, Hawkins indicated that Zorinsky could recommend witnesses for a future hearing. Zorinsky took him at his word and quickly followed up.

On March 20, 1986, the House Subcommittee held another hearing — this time with witnesses selected by Senator Zorinsky. Their testimony was astounding. Charles Micciche, then-Superintendent of Schools in Groveton, New Hampshire, for example, noted that when his district switched to phonics, the per-pupil cost went from $16 a year to just $2.25, and the reading scores dramatically increased and remained consistently above state and national figures — and this from one of the poorest districts in the country!

Witness after witness presented proof of the superiority of phonics instruction and the lack of teacher training in the method, but the three subcommittee members who showed up were not swayed. In fact, the general hostility to phonics was demonstrated by Congressman Goodling, the ranking Republican and a former educator. He came over to the staff sitting behind the podium and told them to come up with some non-phonetic words (that is, words which are not spelled the way they sound) — ignoring the fact that one doesn't throw out the rule just because there happen to be some exceptions to it.

When this action by Goodling was brought up later in the hearing, Charles M. Richardson, alluded to earlier on, responded that "irregular words [non-phonetic words] comprise less than 15 percent of our language. If the student is initially taught the rules which apply to the other 85 percent, then he can learn this 15 percent . . . which is a much more efficient system than learning 100 percent of the language by sight memorization . . . ."

Completely baffled by the vehemence of the opposition, and indignant over the erstwhile appropriation of a sum identical to what his legislation would have cost ($1 million) for the study of salmon in the Pacific Northwest, which was passed without any discussion whatsoever by Congress, Senator Zorinsky started digging in his heels. But every time he or his staff pried into education, they were thwarted by the same people who were supposed to be overseeing such matters. It was almost eerie. Whenever a point was brought up by Zorinsky during the hearings, words would come out of the other members' mouths that sounded like agreement and genuine concern. But even as they were speaking one could tell that they had no intention of following up. It was all rhetoric — for the benefit of the record and any listeners from the public who were in the room.

Senator Zorinsky's final effort passed the Senate in 1986, shortly before he died. It was an amendment to the Human Services Reauthorization Act, P.L. 99-425, Title IX, Sec. 901, which called on the U.S. Department of Education to compile a list of beginning reading instruction programs and methods, indicating the average cost per pupil and whether they did or did not meet the recommendations of the Commission on Reading in its 1985 report, *Becoming a Nation of Readers*. This report recommended, among other things, that "teachers of beginning reading should present well-designed phonics instruction." The purpose of this legislation was to provide parents and educators with specific information to help them, at least, determine whether their schools were using the most effective reading programs. Even this proposal, however, was opposed by Congressman Hawkins, who finally relented over the objections of his staff.

But that did not mean the law was carried out. The U.S. Department of Education subsequently claimed that it did not have to carry out this mandate because there was no appropriation for it. Erica Kenney, Zorinsky's chief staffer on education issues, who all the while had been guiding Zorinsky's bills through the legislative process, including negotiations with other staff, argued that this was a ridiculous position since the amendment was not an authorization of appropriations. It was a clear-cut *directive* to the Department, which had already agreed to compile a list with *existing* funds.

Whereupon the Department of Education hooted its contempt, and refused to carry out the law as it was enacted.

Today, the Department is still working to sidestep Zorinsky's reading legislation, even though numerous senators, representatives, and private citizens have written (and are still writing) to the Education Secretary asking that it be implemented. A study has been done, but it does not meet the requirements of the law. The Department's answer to public inquiries about the Zorinsky legislation is confusing, too, because responding officials always claim they are meeting the intent of the law. But it is important to remember that there is a difference between basal reading programs, which may claim to use phonics but in reality contain only a smattering, and that poorly conceived, and truly worthwhile programs which, according to *Becoming a Nation of Readers*, teach children to decode, by having them hear the sounds of letters both in isolation and in entire words and having them blend the sounds together in order to identify the words. Only experts can make these distinctions, which is why Senator Zorinsky, in his legislation, asked for a simple listing of reading programs "written in such a way as to be understandable to the general public."

Despite the President and Mrs. Bush's War on Illiteracy — or, more accurately, Hype on Illiteracy — the U.S. Department of Education continues to air excuses as to why it cannot disseminate a simple list describing the content of reading programs. Two of the most infuriating excuses came from John Sununu, White House Chief of Staff, on April 11, 1990, and from the Department itself on May 4, 1990.

When questioned at a briefing about why, in light of the President's interest in eradicating illiteracy, the Department of Education had not carried out the P.L. 99-425 legislation, Sununu cited, of all things, the prohibition against the federal government becoming involved in curriculum. That the Department had been *involved* to the hilt since 1965 in psychological, and other, curriculum through its various programs disseminated through various government agencies, not to mention the National Diffusion Network, did not seem to occur to him.

On May 4 a representative of the Department echoed Sununu's remark by arguing that the directive to compile a list had a "questionable requirement that calls for the Department to pass judgment on particular texts and programs."

Somehow that never came up, either, when the issue was psycho-behavioral tests or government-validated attitudinal programs.

The fact is, the Education Department is charged *by law* with the task of disseminating information on what works — passing along proven research in a field or subject area. That was a provision of the legislation which created the Department as a cabinet-level agency, and it was the reason given for creating the ERIC and the NDN networks.

Since the ability to read is fundamental to all subject areas, and no further education can proceed without it, failure to disseminate the research on reading methodology flies in the face of Administration rhetoric about eradicating illiteracy; it is tantamount, in fact, to *promoting* illiteracy, not eliminating it. Although the President and Mrs. Bush's goal of eliminating adult illiteracy is laudable, they apparently do not realize it is unachievable as long as schools continue to graduate students who cannot read.

Congress has never followed up on any of the concerns expressed by Senator Zorinsky and all the money for illiteracy programs is still targeted toward remediation. The 1990 omnibus education authorization bill would have added to an ever-growing illiteracy bureaucracy by creating, among other expensive initiatives, an interagency task force on literacy and even a National Institute for Literacy with its own Governing Board. However, the final version of the $800 million education bill died in the Senate because of other provisions opposed by some Republicans. Even so, there is no reason to believe that Congress will not continue to spend billions of dollars for remediation — and nothing for prevention. In fact at this writing a 1991 version of the same has been introduced and is on the fast track through the legislative process.

CHAPTER 15

Education Issues: No Trespassing

JUST WHO, OR what, was paralyzing every effort aimed at investigating the particulars of educational methods and practices? Why was no serious official investigation permitted?

This became the proverbial 64-thousand-dollar question, and Senator Zorinsky's efforts, though mostly unsuccessful legislatively, made him something of a point-man for education issues with the public. Hundreds of citizens around the country, it turned out, had taken on the education establishment in their states, to no avail. Because of Zorinsky's apparently sincere interest, those citizens who were following education issues brought to his office their queries, complaints, and concerns—most of which, eventually, fell into the hands of Erica Kenney.

Kenney and the Senator discovered that following up education issues was like trying to nail "jello" to the wall. Every time Kenney tried to track a citizen complaint, she ran afoul of endless channels of bureaucracy and overwhelming oppositionist forces. It didn't matter what the complaint was about. The subject was clearly off limits to anyone but the House and Senate Education subcommittees — and they never did anything.

Curious and put-out, Zorinsky's able staffer made it a point to become extremely knowledgeable about education theory, methodology, and legislative issues. By 1986, Kenney was a familiar face at education-related conferences and forums on Capitol Hill and around the country. Frequently she was a speaker. It was at just one such forum, held in the Russell Senate Office Building in Washington, D.C., where she met another by now well-informed source in her own right, who was seated in the audience.

Her name was Anita Hoge.

The three years Anita Hoge had spent thus far to resolve her complaint had made her something of a celebrity. Already, she was in demand as a speaker in Pennsylvania and was a frequent guest on radio talk shows.

Official reactions to the documentation she had brought to Washington ranged from shock to disbelief — or seemed to. Discomfort intensified when Anita presented staffers on Capitol Hill with a stack of corrective learning booklets called "Resources for Improvement" together with the teachers' guide on citizenship, all of which pointed to a psychologically manipulative emphasis, with links to EQA and to federal funds. But Anita Hoge had only begun to learn about government. Until she was initiated into the rites of bureaucratic process that year, the feisty meat-packer's daughter from Burgeltstown was still under the odd impression that men and women are elected to Congress so they can get to the bottom of complicated puzzles and investigate allegations.

None of the Capitol Hill officials Anita Hoge went to see in Washington, however, had any idea where to begin. They knew nothing about it. Most claimed they did not like what they were seeing, but other matters pressed. So they sent the nice young woman with waist-long brown hair, suitcase in tow, to the U.S. Department of Education, which made the monumental error of sending her back to Pennsylvania — to the state education agency in Harrisburg.

And it was the Pennsylvania Department of Education's singular misfortune to underestimate the resourcefulness of the one person they would least have wanted snooping into curriculum changes in McGuffey School District — a computer whiz with a near-photographic memory, who was by now a very angry woman.

ERICA KENNEY RECOGNIZED that the story she was hearing from the Hoge woman was considerably more detailed and specific than most. Indeed, here was a citizen who had actually documented the grass-roots version of what Zorinsky and his staff had been battling at the federal level for five years. So Kenney sent Anita Hoge to a hand-picked group of experts in Washington who would take it again from the beginning — this time putting it down in bureaucratic language.

With a little experience and some good advice from mentors in Washington, Anita Hoge and her Pennsylvania Group started getting more aggressive about pooling resources. She and her cadre of researchers traced information by mail, telephone, and computer through universities, professional libraries, and located still other networks of individuals around the country — in Michigan, Maine, Florida, Texas, California, Arizona, and elsewhere — to help them. These people, in turn, used graduate students, "headhunters," and small business executives to obtain documents and materials.

A mere teacher, after all, didn't rate access to certain educational information.

And neither, discovered Erica Kenney, did a United States Senator.

Part

IV:
THE SCIENCE
OF "PLANNED
CHANGE"

CHAPTER 16

Uncovering the How-to Manual of Behavioral Programming

IT WAS IN 1986, then, that Pennsylvania Group researchers — who included, by this time, people in Washington, D.C. — felt like they had entered the Twilight Zone. They were looking for proof that the idea of inducing psychological conflicts in order to "cure" them did not represent establishment thinking, or at least did not have the blessing and endorsement of the federal government.

What Group researchers expected to find was evidence to support the contention that the U.S. Department of Education and its colleagues in other government agencies really had no idea what was going on in education; that they neither endorsed nor disapproved behavioral teaching strategies because they didn't understand what they were; that officials had allowed a branch of experimental research to be pursued at the Labs and Centers and to be promulgated in the nation's tax-supported (and even private) schools because the bureaucracy was out of control and, essentially, doing its own thing.

What Pennsylvania Group researchers did *not* expect to find was a how-to manual with a 1971 U.S. Office of Education contract number on it entitled *Training for Change Agents;* or seven volumes of "change agent studies" commissioned by the U.S. Office of Education to the Rand Corporation in 1973-74; or scores of other papers submitted by behaviorist researchers who had obtained grants from the U.S. Office of Education for the purpose of exploring ways to "freeze" and "unfreeze" values, " to implement change," and to turn potentially hostile groups and committees into acquiescent, rubber-stamp bodies by means of such strategies as "the Delphi Technique."

No longer was it mere speculation that federal funds for education were being used to pursue behavioral objectives instead of academic ones; here were official texts and documents, solicited by the U.S. government, saying so specifically. With the training manual in hand, it was learned also for the first time precisely how sophisticated psychological manipulation techniques were being used to defuse potentially hostile elements — like parent groups (PTAs), teachers, and community watchdog organizations — so that they are maneuvered into accepting programs and strategies of which they really do not approve.

To say that the Group was shocked by this find would fail to capture the essence of the moment. The room that first examined *Training for Change Agents* looked like a mass dental examination — every mouth was open.

Change agent training was launched with federal funding under the Education Professions Development Act (1967). The original purpose of the Act was to provide funds to *local* education agencies to attract and train teachers because of the then-critical shortage. But by the early seventies, these funds were being used by the U.S. Office of Education, under the Department of Health, Education and Welfare, *"to award grants to colleges and universities for the training of change agents."* The Office of Education even ran one elementary school in Gary, Indiana, jointly with the Behavioral Research Labs to test change agent theories! It is not known whether parents knew anything about it.

By following up references on "behavioral strategies," Pennsylvania Group researchers stumbled onto a series of documents about "how to gain social acceptance for an innovation." In these documents, schools repeatedly were referred to as "experimental laboratories." Each time researchers ran across terms like this, they tried using it to gain access to additional reference material, by author and title, from the ERIC computer system. Thus, terms like *"laboratory," "behavior," "operant conditioning," "social reinforcement," "internal-external control,"* when linked with the word *education(al)*, eventually turned up listings for "change agents" and "educational change." Subtitles were found on "training change agents," "the role of the state facilitator," and so forth. A less obvious subheading, "performance contracts" revealed even more change agent documents.

One of the first papers the team read was Clyde Hall's[38] 21-page "How to Implement Change." In it, he explained "the science of planned change," which translates to *legislated and managed change*. In one passage the reader learns that

> [i]n a managed change process an outside agent is usually involved which is referred to as a 'change agent' and the population with which it works is called the 'client system.'

The Hall paper goes on to discuss the techniques of "freezing" and "unfreezing" attitudes — today called "programming" and "de-programming." But he was not talking about students' attitudes; he was talking about teachers' attitudes being changed — through teacher workshops, inservice education, and revised college/university teacher education programs.[39] The change agent, he states, would only be withdrawn when "the new attitudes are stabilized."

It turned out that Ronald G. and Mary C. Havelock were the major sources of research and information on change agents for the federal government. Four lengthy papers of theirs, including case studies of change agent *teams* in three schools, were uncovered in addition to another text, *The Change Agent's Guide to Innovation in Education* — all paid for, in whole or in part, under government contract.

But the *Training for Change Agents* text was the researchers' gold mine. It sought to justify, among other things, deceiving the public about learning programs and their intended usages. The strategy for doing this is called, appropriately, the *fait accompli.* The Havelocks say that in certain cases it is best not to tell the truth about the substance of an educational program until after the fact (the *fait accompli*), when the "profound results" supposedly will render its merits obvious.

It is worth mentioning here the results of one change agent program on drug education that used peer pressure to resist drugs. According to Havelock's 1973 "Guide to Innovation in Education" (Handbook II, page 24) the program actually increased students' tolerance toward marijuana use and promiscuous sex. The change agent in charge, as well as the program's supporters, were baffled. School authorities, of course, had gone to a lot of trouble to garner community support for the class (billed, again, as a "pilot program"), so this result wasn't advertised. Nevertheless, the change agent continued to garner support for the program until it was placed in the curriculum over the objections of parents and the community.

Another problem with this particular project, states the change agent recounting the incident, was that because he had failed to make a formal survey of parent reactions to the course concept, a furor erupted when he announced that "teaching morals" was being avoided. The program was to help students "make responsible value judgments" — a goal which, he says, he had "been intentionally sliding over...in...discussions with the public." In any case, his noble objective backfired according to the results, since the students became more permissive of drug use and promiscuous sex according to follow-up surveys. To minimize the damage to the program, then, the opposition was labeled "extremists" and the course, despite its disappointing results, was continued.

A typical chapter subtitle (page 44) in the Havelock text, *Training for Change Agents*, reads "Extinguishing Existing Attitudes, Knowledge and Behavior." An excerpt from page 151 states:

> The first role [of the change agent] is that of advocate-organizer-agitator...who clarifies and defines the problem...by helping it to surface or escalate.

Again, the idea gets back to inducing a conflict and exploiting the results.

The Rand Corporation's change agent studies — full of statistical data and very hard to obtain — are essentially a set of feasibility studies. Apparently, the federal government wanted to know how difficult and costly it would be to move forward with a national version of the change-agent program. Volumes II and IV, respectively, of the Rand series are entitled *Factors Affecting Change Agent Projects* and *Factors Affecting Implementation and Continuation*. Without going into depth on these lengthy statistical studies, the titles here give a pretty good idea what the thrust of the work was. As with the other change agent documents, the federal contract number is emblazoned plainly on the front cover of each Rand volume.

Training of change agents apparently is done through the behavioral colleges — alluded to earlier. Change agentry is not a subject one majors in, exactly; it is something one more or less works his or her way into as a result of clinical and/or theoretical work performed in behavioral science. In other words, it appears that the kingpins in the behavioral field — CFAT people and others who already have made a name for themselves — scout out individuals/colleagues whom they believe will make good change agents.

What happens is that local education agencies (LEAs) discover at some point that they need help in promoting or implementing certain programs and policies. It may be a pilot program (one of those "innovative programs" department heads can access through the NDN computer), or a new guidance program, or some new policy they think parents won't like. So they call on the state, the curriculum creators, or even the federal agency (if the program concerns a federal initiative or policy) to request "technical assistance." The "help" local schools may receive from the state or federal agency will come in the form of a "change agent" — sometimes called a "technical assistant" or a "facilitator."

To implement a curriculum, the change agent will instruct the teacher by launching the pilot program.

To gain community and/or parental support for a policy, mandate, or curriculum, the change agent will form a committee comprised of the people from whom support is sought. He or she will serve as a lightning rod to draw out the objections (and, more important, the object*ors*) so that the target group can be manipulated toward an affirmative consensus.

This is why the change agent must be an "advocate-organizer-agitator," as described in the Havelock quote earlier.

As an "advocate," the change agent gets the target group to trust him (or her), by making the group believe he/she is on their side, a "good guy," someone who really cares what each individual in the group thinks. If the group is composed of teachers, the change agent will say: "I know how much time you spend on paperwork." If the group is parents, the change agent will commiserate: "It's so hard to get kids to want to learn, isn't it."

The change agent goes through the motions, acting as an "organizer," getting each person in the target group to voice concerns about the policy, project, or program in question. He listens attentively, forms task forces, urges everyone to make lists, and so on. While he is doing this, the change agent is learning something about each member of the target group. He is learning who the "leaders" are, who the loudmouths are, which persons seem weak or noncommittal, which ones frequently change sides in an argument.

Suddenly, Mr./Ms. Nice Guy change agent becomes Devil's Advocate. He dons his professional agitator hat and pits one group against the other. He knows exactly what he is doing, who to pit against whom. If the change agent has done his homework, he has everybody's number, as the saying goes. He deftly turns the "pro" group against the "con" group by helping to make the latter seem ridiculous, or unknowledgeable, or dogmatic, or inarticulate — whatever works. He wants certain members of the group to get mad; he is forcing tensions "to escalate." The change agent is well-trained in psychological techniques; he can fairly well predict who will respond to what. The individuals against the policy or program will be shut out.

This is called the Delphi Technique. A specialized application of this technique applied specifically to teachers is called the Alinsky Method. The setting doesn't make a lot of difference except for the fact that specific groups of people tend to share certain characteristics and knowledge, which means using a specialized application of the basic technique.

The method works. It works with adults. With teachers. With schoolchildren. Even church groups. And the targets rarely, if ever, know they are being manipulated. Or, if they suspect it, they don't know how.

Eventually, certain trusted teachers, sometimes department heads, are made change agents in their own right. They conduct inservice workshops and generally get other teachers behind a program — enough to implement it, in any case.

CHAPTER 17

CFAT and the "Education Reform" Gambit

MOST LOCAL SCHOOL districts will not admit they are following a federal mandate when they give a state assessment test. Many local officials, in fact, may not know. The state education agencies (called SEAs for short), however, do know, and people there don't ever admit anything in writing if they can help it.

The state education agencies today are the state arms of the U.S. Department of Education. In fact, many of them are called *state departments of education*.

It wasn't always that way.

"State education agency" is a term that was used before there was such a thing as a U.S. Department of Education, before 1976, which is the year President Carter fulfilled a campaign promise by handing the education establishment (the Carnegie Foundation, the Educational Testing Service, the National Education Association, and the rest of the behaviorist faction) its own Cabinet-level agency. Before that date, the federal body handling education was, as indicated earlier on, the Department of Health, Education and Welfare (HEW). The Education part of HEW was called the Office of Education. Much of the preliminary planning for the federal takeover of education — including assessment testing, computerization of records, and closing of the curriculum-publishing loop — was begun at the old Office of Education, under HEW. Apparently, once education reached such a state that public attention was being focused on the problem in the media, that was the signal for the behaviorist establishment to make its move for a Cabinet-level agency, which would enable them to "reform" education. Whether it was all a set-up, only history can judge for sure, but the number of coincidences, as shall be seen, do strain credulity.

The Carnegie Foundation for the Advancement of Teaching (CFAT) was established in 1905 as a pension fund for college professors. It was, of course, one of the philanthropic trusts created by steel magnate Andrew Carnegie. One year after it was organized, the organization obtained a Congressional charter that allowed it not only "to provide retiring pensions . . . for the teachers of universities, colleges and technical schools" in this country and Canada, but "in general, to do and perform all things necessary to encourage, uphold and dignify the profession of the teacher and the cause of higher education." This charter permitted the Foundation to sponsor educational surveys and policy reviews, many of which eventually would decide the direction and organization of American education at elementary and secondary levels as well as at the university level.

CFAT began in earnest its control over American education in 1965 by crafting that endless piece of legislation called the Elementary and Secondary Education Act (ESEA). It was almost solely high-level CFAT people (men like Francis Keppel and John Gardner, and Ralph Tyler, all past presidents of CFAT) who comprised the Task Force on Education under President John F. Kennedy, passed on to President Lyndon B. Johnson in 1963 when Kennedy was assassinated. Keppel, who also conceived the National Assessment idea, wrote a book, *The Necessary Revolution in American Education,* describing how and why the ESEA was created. Gardner served as HEW Secretary, with another Carnegie man, Wilbur Cohen, as his undersecretary. Tyler was founder and Director of the Center for Advanced Study in the Behavioral Sciences.

It was by dominating the Task Force, however, that CFAT accomplished what no other group, public or private, has been able to do in the history of the United States — *namely, to legally gain access to the private lives and thoughts of a majority of American citizens, and to do so in such a way as to be able to manipulate and influence future events.*

Francis Keppel was U.S. Commissioner of Education 1962-65. Keppel discovered that, in the original charter of the U.S. Office of Education (1867), a charge was given to the U.S. Commissioner to determine the progress of education. This provided the impetus for the National Assessment [NAEP].

> After a number of conferences and discussions initiated by Commissioner Keppel, John W. Gardner, then president of Carnegie Corporation, asked a distinguished group of Americans to form the Committee on Assessing the Progress of Education under the chairmanship of Ralph W. Tyler (then director of the Center for Advanced Study in the Behavioral Sciences, Stanford, California). . . . Specifically, they were to:
>
> 1. Determine how a national assessment of educational progress could be designed;
>
> 2. Develop and test instruments and procedures for the assessment; and
>
> 3. Develop a plan for conducting the assessment.
>
> Four years of work, financed by the Carnegie Corporation of New York and the Fund for the Advancement of Education of the Ford Foundation, went into defining goals and developing measuring instruments . . . .[40]

Every American President, from Kennedy and Johnson to Reagan, inadvertently helped this organization and its allies achieve significant gains in educational policy-setting. As indicated, Presidents Kennedy and Johnson provided the initial Task Force which led to the enabling legislation; President Nixon appointed top Foundation men to head a special education policy-making group. It was during this period that the education blueprints were forged.

President Nixon appointed Alan Pifer, president of Carnegie Corporation in New York, to head a special education group. President Ford continued to rely on the foundation's advice and proposals. This allowed the Carnegie Foundation to settle in, as it were, at the federal level and begin setting educational priorities from that vantage point. President Carter, as indicated, handed the organization a cabinet-level agency, the U.S. Department of Education, replacing the old Office of Education. President Reagan, apparently not recognizing the extent of foundation control or the existence of 1960s-era policy blueprints, unwittingly launched his decentralization policy, which permitted the organization's puppets at the federal level to pass off mandates emanating from Washington as mere local and state initiatives, through "decentralized" state education agencies.

President George Bush, who in 1988 billed himself as "the education President" with a bold anti-illiteracy agenda to help him win special interest votes, is today in the unenviable position of having little that is new in his America 2000 Education plan, except its blatant intrusiveness into the family — the very entity he claims to want to strengthen. Neither is the appointment of Lamar Alexander as Education Secretary likely to result in a less behavioral, more academic thrust to education. The Governors' Association, where Alexander first made his interests in education known, as Governor of Tennessee, has been important in advancing the cause of federalization of education—through a combination of policy and pressure.

Moreover, the groundwork laid some twenty-five years ago has been implemented with barely a hitch. CFAT has been, through successive Administrations, liberal and conservative, the primary mouthpiece for government policy on education. Its edicts, in the form of official reports, are nearly always carried out; its "findings" are consistently taken as gospel; its members head the most prestigious review boards, committees, and task forces on education matters.

Today, CFAT and their proxies in federal and state governments co-control educational research. They co-control three computer banks of test result data — including personal, non-academic information, opinions, and attitudes — which in 1988-89 were integrated into one large, supercomputer: the Elementary and Secondary Integrated Data System (the ESIDS).

Behaviorist extremists and their protégés in the foundations and government serve in the federally funded educational research Labs and Centers around the country, all of which specialize in behavioral psychology. As a result, curriculum and testing research now has a mandated behavioral emphasis, which was first outlined in a 1973 federal publication entitled *Handbook on Performance Objectives* (later updated in *Program Guide 44*). This is the same publication that defines "cognitive learning" as a "belief system."

As already described, the "titles," or provisions, of the ESEA law were the initial federal funding mechanisms to get behavioral programming into the schools. Title I made special provisions for disadvantaged youngsters. Title II began as school libraries, textbooks, and instructional materials, but quickly escalated to "educational technology" and so-called "basic skills improvement."

Title III provided monies for creating "innovative programs" — in the main, psychological experiments — and later added funds for "exemplary" (validated) programs; additional guidance, testing and counseling; and for "special programs" (health education, population education, global education, and some ten others).

Title IV, as indicated previously, brought in the Labs and Centers, and later libraries, "learning resources" (the supplementary materials); early childhood education; still more guidance, testing and counseling (including social workers and psychiatrists); and "innovative compensatory programs," to name a few. Title V provided grants and resources to the SEAs for data collection and management, personnel development, and spurred the formation of various official councils. Eventually other titles were added for the handicapped, migrant children, "community education," ethnic heritage programs, bilingual education, opportunities for Indian Students, emergency aid, and so on.

In no significant instance, however, were entitlement programs discontinued. The legislation continued to be infinitely expandable. What the various reorganizations did do was, first, to give the impression that financial prudence was being exercised by reducing waste or redundancy (a sham shakeup, of sorts), and to make the constantly changing funding titles and numbers confusing to the lay person. Constant reorganizations also have had the effect of making federal funds easier to dispense and/or obtain, which, of course, was the point of the exercise.

One of the questions that will surely come to mind in all of this is: Why hasn't somebody blown the whistle before now — someone at the Department of Education, a state official, a journalist, an investigative reporter, or even the President?

Probably the best answer is found in a statement from renowned journalist Hedrick Smith in *The Power Game:*

> There is a strong urge for simplicity in the American psyche...to reduce the intricacy of a hundred power plays to...up or down, winning or losing.... Television news feeds the public appetite to treat events as binary — good or bad, up or down, progress or setback, winners or losers — and to push aside more complex layers of reality.[41]

Most people both inside and outside of government, journalists and bureaucrats, focused almost exclusively on numbers; in this instance, scores. Were the scores up or down? Hardly anyone questioned the sources of these scores. Were we winning or losing the war against illiteracy and school crime? Was money being sufficiently channeled into education, or was education getting short shrift compared to other areas?

Like teachers, many bureaucrats and others working in the education establishment have not been in their positions long enough to notice, much less understand, the connection between Smith's "complex layers of reality" — the ESEA titles, the behavioral objectives and mandates, CFAT, the NAEP, the NDN, behavioral programs, change agents, and so forth. Most employees just see their own little piece of the puzzle. Even if their suspicions are aroused by some incident, most don't have the time or inclination to do the research it takes to understand the whole picture. Some, of course, do question. But, again, without the missing pieces to that jigsaw puzzle, just what does one say to a superior? Moreover, the 25-year marriage between CFAT, the behaviorist extremists, and the federal government (which includes the state counterparts of the U.S. Department of Education — the state education agencies, or SEAs) has produced a plethora of experimental initiatives which were placed under the appealing banner of "education reform." This buzz-term misled not only most parents and the public, but many sincere, hardworking bureaucrats, who were also looking for answers.

CHAPTER 18

How to "Impact" a School District

ANITA HOGE HADN'T in the least suspected the use of a Delphi Technique in her community — until she got hold of a large black notebook, called a Long-Range Planning Guide, used to implement the federal agenda in McGuffey School District. Her suspicions were aroused when she found her name on a local task force, one that reviewed curriculum. Anita knew she had never been on such a task force. She copied the list and called some fifteen names. Only three said they could remember ever being involved with such a group. Some of the others didn't even have children in school at the time.

At length it was surmised that someone had copied names of small business owners whose efforts were in any way connected with children. Anita Hoge had run a day care center for a short time.

What kind of phony task force was this? she wondered.

In further examining the *Long-Range Planning Guide*, which was obviously compiled in response to a federal directive, Anita Hoge and her colleagues thought it looked as though statistics had been manipulated to make it look as though the local school district qualified for more Title I money than it was entitled to.

Actually, there was powerful incentive to do that kind of thing. If the percentage of children in a school district who "qualified" as being, say, disadvantaged — that is, topped a certain percentage — then the entire district's *school-age population* would have to use the same federal guidelines, programs, and materials as the qualifying children.

Obviously it would be in the interests of school districts and the SEAs to pad the statistics if they could, to get more federal aid. And, as will be seen further on, it was in the interests of the federal government — for more reasons than one — to dole out this additional money. In any event, the strategy of manipulating percentages so as to qualify for massive handouts through government grants was called *"impacting."* [42]

It took 501 coordinators to set the stage for implementation of the EQA. McGuffey's federal coordinator for ESEA Title I was paid in part by the federal government and in part by the state for one year. This is one of the places where Anita Hoge found evidence of the federal funds used in creating the EQA. The point here, however, is that the Title I Coordinator in this case acted also as controller of McGuffey School District's education budget. Statistics examined by the Pennsylvania Group showed a larger percentage of "needy" children than appeared to have been the case. The Coordinator's statistics, therefore, once sent to state and federal authorities, could ensure a large influx of federal dollars into Pennsylvania school districts — in particular, into McGuffey School District.

The Group decided that if it could prove fraud, or misrepresentation of the figures they found in the Long-Range plan, it just might, well . . . pay off. That was when Anita Hoge demanded the audit of McGuffey School District in particular and the state of Pennsylvania in general.

Bob Gray of the Fraud Hotline in Washington always felt that the case should have been pursued as fraud. Now Anita was ready to try that approach. She particularly wanted the federal government to key in on the years 1978-1982 in their audit because those were the critical years when the McGuffey School District got caught up in government mandates and curriculum changes.

Such a demand was the last thing, of course, that officials in Washington expected. Damn! The lady always seemed to be one step ahead of them. How did she know to order an audit?

Predictably officials stalled. They weren't accustomed to being told by non-experts how to run their business.

With this background in mind, it is appropriate here to return to the topic of the Department of Education's regional research "Labs and Centers," as they are abbreviated in educational parlance: the places where education research and curriculum are born. Here one discovers an "impact" of a different kind.

Although "reform" initiatives are soft-sold to parents and the public using carefully constructed public relations campaigns (brochures, press releases, and other literature for the use of local school administrators), it is clear from official documents and private memos that their creators are aware of the sensitive nature of what they are doing. They know that certain words and phrases will raise alarm bells, and they carefully admonish local officials against their use. For example, a Seattle memo warns local principals and teachers in 1978 not to use the subject label "global education," calling it a "political hot potato." It tells them to substitute another euphemism, "multicultural education." (Unfortunately, neither course has much to do with history, geography or foreign language.)

Regardless of whether one approves or disapproves of the content of school subjects, however, the point is that people in high places have long been aware that their initiatives would not win popular approval if the public were privy to all the facts. Communities would discover, among other things, that in professional parlance *"the school"* is now a *"clinic,"* or *"laboratory,"* and that the term *"cognitive learning"* is a *"belief system"* (recall the *Handbook on Performance Objectives* and the Shaver document discussed earlier).[43] They also would learn that these changes in definition permit certain learning experiences to be passed off as hard subject matter when, in fact, they are attitude manipulation exercises and thought control experiments created by experts who specialize in behavioral theory (a specialized branch of psychology). They believe the average "Joe Sixpack" is not sophisticated enough to understand the potential value of their experiments to the individual and to society. They insist they are justified, therefore, in imposing their ideas from Above, as it were, using the convoluted wording of legislation as their screen and the equally convoluted legislative process as their funding mechanism.

The open-ended nature of the 1965 ESEA law, particularly Title IV, allowed the Labs and Centers to amass or re-direct enormous sums into behavioral-psychological research without making it obvious to John Q. Public.

Still other legislative initiatives, like the seven-state Cooperative Accountability Project (CAP), headed by the first Secretary of Education, Terrel Bell, (discussed briefly earlier on) targeted the states that would be used to implement the early results of this research — or "reform," as it would later be known — on a national scale. Pennsylvania, of course, was the pilot state for assessment testing. But there were many other models. California launched the computerized database under the banner of "accountability"; Michigan changed the thrust of teacher education; and goal-setting procedures were mapped out in Missouri. Wisconsin was the repository for data collected under CAP with the State Education Assessment Repository (SEAR). It evolved into the ERIC database. These, and other, states involved in the CAP were, together, the "*models* of reform."

Meanwhile, CFAT and its cohorts in government were busy cultivating a network of accommodating state and local regulatory bodies. Gradually, sympathizers in the corporate community and ambitious bureaucrats in federal and state governments were placed into state and local education agencies (SEAs and LEAs), so that as soon as the old Office of Education achieved cabinet status in 1976, they would become extensions of the federal agency — with increasingly generous budgets. CFAT created organizations like the Education Commission of the States (ECS, headquartered in Denver, administered the NAEP for twelve years) so that the federal government would have a point of contact early on in every state. They also cultivated such existing bodies as the Council of Chief State School Officers, National Association of State Boards of Education, the National Education Association, and the National Governors Association, all of which today have considerable say in what goes on in education — as long as they continue to represent the CFAT view.

So if it strikes one as odd that President Bush, and some of his predecessors, made the annual Governors' Conference, rather than the Association of School Principals or some other education-related body, the focus of discussions in 1990 on education reform, it should come as no surprise. These, and other organizations, became the "closed clubs" for education issues; that is, no one aspires to leadership (and in some cases, even membership) in these organizations unless they have the "right" philosophical credentials — approved, of course, by the Carnegie Foundation for the Advancement of Teaching, the body which seems, ultimately, to call the shots.

Cultivation and philosophical take-over of bodies like the Governors Association was accomplished gradually. Take the Council of Chief State School Officers (CCSSO), for example. Pre-1976 brochures from the CCSSO indicated a strong interest in local control and suspicion of anything that smacked of federal imposition in matters of curriculum or procedure. But by November 1984, just eight years later, the CCSSO was adopting a position paper that "challenge[s] the U.S. tradition of local control in education" and was calling for the implementation of a large-scale data collection system to promote coordination among state, national, and international assessment programs. The CCSSO suddenly was turning out brochures touting federal involvement and hyping specific curriculum content. Why the change of heart?

> The Council of Chief State School Officers and the U.S. Office of Education in 1968 jointly agreed to develop and implement a comprehensive education evaluation system in an effort to consolidate state reporting of the several federal programs as required by law. The initial meetings took place at the Belmont House in Elkridge, Maryland, and the program has become known as the "Belmont Project." Planned for eventual use in all states, the program presently [in 1973] includes 27 pilot states. Representative of these states, together with USOE [U.S. Office of Education] personnel, comprise a Task Force responsible for the general development and direction of the project. All states are tied into the project through Evaluation Coordinators appointed by their chiefs.[44]

Need more be said? If this isn't collusion, what is? If this is not conspiring to end local control and impose a top-down method of control, from the federal government using the state education agencies as proxies, what on earth is it?

A speech October 16, 1985, by Ramsey Seldon, Director of the Center for Coordination of Educational Assessment and Evaluation, provides further insight into this about face. He said that the CCSSO would be expected eventually to play a major role in implementing the new "reform" programs.

It would help ensure that school districts *complied* with federal *mandates*. The CCSSO, he said, would also help compile a system of computerized information from the data collected by the states.

This speech and other documents are significant, because one has to ask the questions "compliance with what?" and "what mandates?" The answers are quite the reverse of what is put out for public consumption.

It turns out, for example, the "mandates" in question are the strings attached to federal funds, and the federal funds are the bait used to ensure that every school district in the country is included in the "reform" effort. The ever-expandable 1965 ESEA law is the vehicle used to lure school district after school district, and eventually many private and parochial schools as well,[45] into financial dependency.

All that was ever asked in return for federal dollars was the "assurance" of some ongoing accountability. This seemed reasonable. Nobody could really object to that. So when mandates were handed down stating that goals would have to be written up a certain way and reflect certain objectives, or that children would have to be tested regularly to ensure that these objectives were being met — and if not met, then remediated — this kind of thing was deemed a relatively small price to pay for financial aid, nothing more than busywork, really.

When teachers, supervisors, and administrators started to write those first goals, however, they discovered that every one had to be written as a "behavioral change."[46] This was a little tougher, but it still didn't raise any alarms. It was viewed as bureaucratic nonsense, and people from the state could be brought in to local schools to teach teachers, department heads and principals how to write the goals the way the government wanted them.

But schools and school districts were in for a surprise. They discovered eventually that they would need a whole lot more money than they originally had asked for in order to comply with the new mandates. Of course, local school districts jumped at the chance to shift the financial burden and paperwork to the state. But once they did so, they were hooked irrevocably into Long-Range Planning (which, basically, means formulating objectives according to government specifications). What's more, their greatest new expense would be for tallying equipment — they were drowning in paperwork! It took less than five years for most districts to figure out that what they really needed was a computer. Since it was the government's fault that they were in that position, who better to ask for the money?

And that was the thing which would lock every school in America into a permanent dependence on federal dollars. Gradually, federal authorities asked that state and local computer systems be made compatible with the federal system. As with the monies for other education needs, funding was granted in blocks[47] through the SEAs for the purpose — helping the SEA staffs and budgets to grow along with their data.

Few objected. Obviously the thing had to be done.

But in complying with these directives, local schools sealed their fate. In the future, if they balked at *any* federal mandate, program, edict, or policy, they could be threatened with loss of federal funding. These funding cuts, regardless of which school programs were affected or the reasons behind the cut, always translated to loss of face in the community and angry teachers.

Schools were stuck — and they knew it. By the time locals got around to realizing that their curriculum, their books, their programs — in fact, the whole thrust of their school systems had changed in the name of "reform" — it was too late. All they could do was get serious about their public relations.

So, what's wrong with education reform? Nothing. Not a thing.

Which is precisely why the scheme worked.

As a consequence, communities no longer control their schools, and the federal government — between its educational "research" arms like the Labs and Centers; its NDN and ERIC computers; its special programs and pilot projects; its SEAs; its federal-state partnerships (like Project Best in 1981), its block and special grants, and the NAEP — *influences* far, far more of the nation's educational funding than the approximately seven percent or less of the total it directly contributes.[48] Thus the U.S. Department of Education's $50 billion-dollar-plus, tax-supported price tag is a powerful force in how the nearly $400 billion dollars is spent on education (elementary, secondary, and higher education, public and private) in the United States.

The people — in this case, parents — gave away their functions and powers and received in return "token" representation. What they did not give away, district administrators (who are now in control of most school boards) took away. The state, through the SEAs, took more, mainly because they owed their continued existence to the U.S. Department of Education. What is left of parents' rights, the courts are usurping daily. (After all, judges are not elected, but appointed, and it would come as no surprise if some have special interest loyalties on education issues.)

Moreover, behaviorist extremists in education discovered that if they really wanted to have an "impact" on education, the way to do it was to make school districts, through the states, financially dependent on the federal government.

CHAPTER 19

Running with the Ball

AFTER ANOTHER YEAR of hard work, the Pennsylvania Group had officials at the U.S. Department of Education in Washington reeling. Bureaucrats tried various tactics to defuse the group and its supporters (and to cut down the phone calls spawned by the Group's media attention; Department switchboards frequently were swamped). Officials denied, delayed, and diverted correspondence. But by March 1987, authorities realized the fire just might hit the fan unless they came up with something believable.

So, in April and May of that year Pennsylvania's SEA reluctantly responded to some of the federal Department's demands for records — budgets, expenditures lists, official goals and plans, funding applications, personnel and contractor data — which officials in Washington said they wanted in order to trace the source, or sources, of federal funding for EQA. What Department officials were hoping to get was something they could use as proof that EQA was *not* federally funded, was *not* a psychological test, and had been presented to parents before it was given to McGuffey students. Thanks in part to Pennsylvania's Senator Arlen Specter, who requested to be kept informed and then passed on copies of correspondence to Anita Hoge, she and her colleagues were able to keep abreast of the letters that went flying back and forth during that period between the federal agency's Hazel Fiers, Director of the Student and Family Education Rights and Privacy Office; the Pennsylvania Department of Education's Dr. William Logan, Acting Commissioner of Education (Bureau of Basic Education); and McGuffey School District's Superintendent, Frank Zitto.

It was Dr. Logan who tired of the battle first and passed Anita Hoge on to federal authorities, much to his later regret.

At first, the federal agency and the SEA both took the position that there "was no evidence of psychological testing in Pennsylvania's state assessment test." But by March of 1987, Fiers and her colleagues had abandoned that approach in letters to Dr. Logan and Mr. Zitto and admitted there was a "possibility" that the EQA "may be a psychiatric or psychological test...." Leroy Rooker, who replaced Fiers, wrote on May 13, 1988, a three-page letter to the Chief Counsel, stating he was worried that the test "violates one or more of the seven protected areas." He further referred to the EQA as an "attitude instrument" and "noncognitive" — all indications that the test was not what it was advertised to be.

Initially, Dr. Logan wrote that the test was "totally state funded...that no U.S. Department of Education funds were used either in the development or implementation" of the test. But by April 9, 1988, he too was equivocating, writing that "there is no way to verify" one way or the other. He wanted to know precisely "what our...burden is in providing you with reasonable proof that we did not use federal funds for this purpose. ...Until we know, we will be unable to be more responsive."

Probably to get the case off his back, he sent along the "interpretive materials" that eventually proved so incriminating — the same materials Anita Hoge and her Group had obtained through King of Prussia, Pennsylvania. Logan apparently hoped that whatever those materials contained would satisfy officials in Washington. He attached a cover note, and emphasized in boldface type:

> "those instruments [the interpretive materials] are secure and should not be shared with anyone but your staff."

It turned out that the interpretive materials were "secure," along with the tests, for a very good reason. For these materials, when coupled with the 1975 memo from the Pennsylvania Senate to the Education Committee members (alluding to the 1973 ACLU case involving Dr. Coldiron, described earlier), made it impossible for officials to deny that, first, the assessment test was mandated, not voluntary; secondly, that the mandate came from the federal government, not the state; and finally, that the test was primarily psychological, not academic.

Three strikes and the Pennsylvania Department of Education was out!

The Pennsylvania Group, of course, already had copies of the interpretive materials and the memo about the ACLU case. They knew what the "seven protected areas" of the Protection of Pupil Rights Amendment were, and had studied in particular the portion on privacy. They also found out that Pennsylvania's Chief of Testing, Dr. Coldiron, had been on Ramsey Seldon's Advisory Network for State-by-State Comparisons, and that therefore he knew far more about the federal role in education than he was telling.[49]

What the Group wanted now was a *written admission* of what they already knew. They didn't get it, of course, but a shocked and helpful federal official, Bill Riley, of Student Rights and Testing Privacy (later moved to the Protection of Pupil Rights Office) told Anita Hoge that her case was the best of its kind he had ever encountered against behavioral programs.

A month later Riley had conveniently been transferred ("promoted?") to another agency.

Clearly, the ball would stay in the complainants' court.

Part

V:
"BACK TO
THE FUTURE"

CHAPTER 20

A Hard Day's Night in Nebraska

IN 1988, A year after Senator Zorinsky's sudden death from a heart attack, Nebraska was still one of five states that had not been pulled into the assessment-testing process. However, parent groups had been alerted that there might be some attempt made to introduce a NAEP-like assessment, and they were keeping an eye out. Thus far, it appeared that all Nebraska's tests were doing what they were supposed to be doing: assessing basic skills. That year parents monitoring the legislature found a bill that had been introduced to "establish a system of student assessment." Since Nebraska already had an assessment, their ears perked up. Sure enough, a hearing was soon held, and the testimony is a case study in how a federally mandated assessment test can be made to look like a local initiative.

Michael Kurts from Stanford University and Frank Newmann, President of the Education Commission of the States (ECS),[50] went to Nebraska under the guise of "learning a little bit about Nebraska schools." Apparently, the two "found it very interesting . . . that there is a sense of . . . pride [on the part of Nebraskans] about their schools without a lot of empirical data to back that up." They claimed that when they went to other states, they found not pride, but, rather, "a sense of panic about a need to improve education . . . ." Kurts and Newmann said they were surprised to find no such panic in Nebraska and attributed it to the fact that Nebraska officials simply didn't have enough information on their educational institutions, which were comprised of many small, country schools, to know what they were talking about.

So the idea was planted: Data was needed so that Nebraska educators would know how their pupils were doing and how they compared from district to district and from state to state.

Two bills were introduced the following year, LB 337 and LB 744. The first called for a new assessment in reading, mathematics, and "critical thinking and analysis and other key competencies." The second would establish a Nebraska Education Data Center. LB 337 was eventually dropped because, as Roger Hudson, of the state education agency, indicated, LB 744 would allow the state to do what it wanted to do anyway.

An astute state senator and an aide to the Senator started asking questions. Since LB 744 called for the transfer of student data electronically to other data centers, the Senator and the aide figured there would be a connection to the new national supercomputer they had heard about. In fact the bill entailed "the exchange of data within the state and with the federal government."

The Senator's aide called the Buros Institute for Mental Measurement to obtain information on assessment versus achievement testing. A highly placed researcher who had a close working relationship with the Nebraska state education agency, and therefore access to all Nebraska's tests, returned the call and indicated there was proof that authorities intended to use the NAEP for Nebraska's assessment test all along. The test was under tight security, but the researcher urged the Senator to get a copy to look at, if possible. One portion, in particular, the researcher said, concerned what were called "societal issues." Also, it appeared that the establishment of a data center would be vital for the test to be useful.

As in other states, the consensus-builders began their work. To counteract their efforts, absolute proof was needed — proof that the NAEP was behavioral, and proof as to where collected data would go. The vote on LB 744 was just one week away, and it looked as though the proponents of testing were winning.

Proof that the proposed test was NAEP-based didn't take long to find: The fiscal note of LB 744 clearly stated the NAEP would be used, despite the side-stepping of that issue. Now, a company called Westat turned out to be under contract to none other than the Educational Testing Service (ETS), run by CFAT the reader may recall, which is joint owner and operator of the NAEP with the U.S. Department of Education.

Westat representatives denied vehemently the attitudinal testing charge. So it was suggested that somebody call NAEP headquarters and place the burden of proof on them. NAEP chief, Archie LaPointe, took the bait and indicated that, certainly, NAEP officials would be happy to prove there was no attitudinal testing. In fact, they would send down the test.

The Senator and the aide were pleased, and they expressed particular interest in certain sections of the assessment; for example, the one on citizenship.

Neither the Senator nor the aide had ever heard of Westat until the day before Westat's representative showed up in Lincoln, Nebraska. She agreed to allow the Senator and others to see a copy of the National Assessment under controlled circumstances — no writing down of questions or photocopying. Two Nebraska Department of Education employees sat in for a short time on what turned out to be an eight-hour-long marathon review with the Westat representative and the Senator's group, which included a former Nebraska-certified teacher.

The Nebraskans discovered, as countless other groups had before them, that assessment tests are held tighter than the Pentagon Papers. The Westat representative brought the tests in secured cases. She told the assembled review team that they had to agree that nothing they were about to see would be discussed with anyone else in any form or fashion, as the NAEP was "federally secured information." Therefore any discussion of the test was a breach of law. Some forms for signature were on the table, but the Westat representative got sidetracked and never actually passed them around — a technicality that proved most fortuitous for the Senator's office. The oversight led to the Westat representative's later denial that she had ever had any forms with her.

As the hours dragged on, the Westat representative had to use the restroom, and she insisted that the whole assembly troop down the hall with her. Otherwise, she said, the tests would have to be resecured in the cases and taken with her to the restroom.

The Nebraskans groaned.

But Westat was in for a surprise of its own. It seemed the representative had never actually examined the test even though she had given (disseminated and proctored) it many times.

At length, the Senator had to leave for the Senate floor, but the aide and the rest of the assembly spent the day, without even a lunch break, going over the tests. The group could hardly believe what it was seeing. Up to this point, the Westat representative did not understand what all the fuss was about. What could a test do to a kid? she asked. That was when one reviewer chanced to ask if the Westat rep had ever read the test. The representative admitted to the stunned group that, well, no, she had never really examined the questions. One of the reviewers held up a page from the reading section. "Well, then," she said, "you might like to take a look at this." And she handed over the page.

It was a passage from the reading section of the test that told how the Devil tried to deceive someone on Earth. The Devil had in his possession a large bag of uncracked nuts that he wanted to eat, but he was too lazy to shell them himself. So he looked for someone on earth to do it. He decided to hide a pearl in one of the nutmeats and put that one on top. He figured if he could find someone "stupid and naive" enough to fall for the ruse, he could get the whole sackful of nuts shelled for him. The Devil picked out "a little old lady" whom he thought might be sufficiently stupid to fall for the ruse. But the last laugh was on him. The old lady took the pearl and went her way, leaving the rest of the nuts unshelled. Later, she used the pearl to make a purchase for herself.

The test question asked students to describe the little old lady as (a) deceptive, (b) wise, (c) clever and practical, or (d) greedy. Everyone in the room tried to guess the answer, and not one, including the Westat representative, got the response which the manual called correct.

Beyond the matter of the answers, some wondered why there would be a story about the Devil in the same tax-supported environment that forbids references to God? And just what did the "correct" answer imply? That stealing under some circumstances is all right? That little old ladies are smarter than people give them credit for?

Look at the passage about the devil and the old lady again. Indeed something does seem odd about the way the question is handled, but it is difficult for most people to say just what. That is because neither the story nor the responses are aimed at reading comprehension. None of the responses would even determine what a child believes. What the question will do, however, is to indicate which values local parents are transmitting to their youngsters, and therefore, what attitudes the community holds as a whole. Combined with other attitudinal passages and responses, which are interspersed among valid reading comprehension items, this question will help analysts to do a profile of the community. Such a profile, in turn, will help behaviorists craft an approach to "planned change," discussed in earlier chapters, that will be suited to this community.

Fascinated by the implications of the story and the various "appropriate" responses, the Westat representative decided to join in examining the test.

Now, ETS officials had admonished their Westat contractor to collect any pencils, papers or other utensils that were used during this examination of tests, and to mail them pronto — Federal Express — back to headquarters that same night. The Senator's aide stayed late at the office that evening to finish up some work. Some time between 4:30 and 5 p.m., a call came in from the Nebraska Department of Education.

"Where is the Westat rep?" the caller wanted to know.

The aide didn't know, but had understood that their representative wanted to see relatives in the area.

"Well, who are they?" the callers demanded.

Again, the aide didn't know.

Well, then, the caller asked, had the tests been mailed back?

The legislative aide had no idea whether the Westat representative had made it in time or not.

The caller clearly was frustrated and left a message to have the representative call them back.

The next morning, the Westat representative called the Senator's office and got the message. Apparently, the representative had just made it to Federal Express' mailing office and hadn't arrived home until 4 a.m.

Meanwhile, the former Nebraska-certified teacher, Virgil Nabity, who had been among the legislative aide's group that examined the tests, was busy writing a letter to the Senator.

> As a former Nebraska junior and senior high school teacher certified to instruct in mathematics, physics, and the physical sciences, I find the N.A.E.P. inadequate to evaluate objectively a student's understanding of the real world or to measure his/her reasoning skills.
>
> After reviewing the sample math, science, and reading test questions, I am convinced that the design of the test is to reinforce the . . . relativistic moral position glorifying disobedience to traditional values. The framing of certain questions and the chosen "correct answers" reveals a consistent bias. . . .
>
> Not enough information was given in the description of one experiment to arrive at the "correct answer." A better answer would be . . . "I don't know." Considering the massive amount of questions on subjective opinions . . . I recommend that you reject this N.A.E.P. test for Nebraska students.

Even with the evidence about NAEP and its use, it was not enough to defeat the professional consensus-builders (probably "change agents," as described in chapter 16) who had garnered support for assessment testing in Nebraska. The great effort by those who examined the test to get the word out to all the senators as to the real nature of the test almost succeeded in defeating the bill which, under normal circumstances, would have passed almost unanimously. The vote did go in favor of the testing proponents, but by a slender margin of just three votes, 25-22, with two abstentions. The only recourse now was the Governor.

A call went out on local radio stations for people opposing the test to get busy and call in. Inside sources say lines to the Governor's office were jammed for hours with callers.

Then, at the eleventh hour, a working paper was obtained from Washington that gave a detailed description the Elementary and Secondary Integrated

Data System (ESIDS) computer. "A Plan for the Redesign of the Elementary and Secondary Data Collection Program,"[51] included allusions to the identification number that would link test information to the planned supercomputer, a number which, in turn, could be linked with other computerized information.

Unfortunately there wasn't enough time for the senators, the Governor, or anybody else to study the hundred-plus page document. Even so, Governor Orr relented and vetoed the measure, but not because of anything in the working paper.

A few weeks later, one of the consensus-builders, Roger Hudson, whom the Senator's aide had suspected of being a change agent, came up to her. He hissed: "You didn't really stop this test. Now I just have to get the money from somewhere else."

By the end of the year, none other than Archie LaPointe, head of NAEP and CFAT kingpin, was agreeing to bring back the test. The Senator and the aide decided to play hardball. They insisted this time on seeing the elusive citizenship section that they had asked to review the last time.

LaPointe suddenly waxed official and told the Senator's aide that he didn't know just when he'd be able to make it out to Nebraska after all. He was due at a press conference in Washington.

Predictably, by March 1990 Nebraska's state education agency had implemented the NAEP over the Governor's veto and was forging ahead with the trial test — using only the relatively innocuous mathematics section. Even so, the so-called demographic survey at the front had students giving chapter and verse about their parents and guardians — income level, how long lived with, education level of mother, and so on, for a whole page.

What NAEP experts hadn't counted on, however, was that many of the schools involved had an open-door policy with parents. Some parents had agreed to allow their children to take the test on a voluntary basis provided they were permitted to come in and look at it on test day. The schools put out the welcome mat, but it was reported that at one school the NAEP representatives who came to proctor the test tried to yank it up. One parent sitting in a school counselor's waiting room overheard the counselor complaining: "But we have *always* had an open policy with parents! What am I supposed to do?"

What, indeed!

Today, Nebraska parents are finding a lot more things have changed in their schools, which are moving ahead full speed with "education reform." Nebraska's Department of Education has let it be known that education there will be restructured, and that local or state board policy can be done away with.

In the January 1990 *Education: Dateline,*[52] a publication put out by the Nebraska Department of Education (that's Nebraska's SEA), Commissioner Joe Lutjeharms stated that early childhood education had become the number one priority in the state. In accordance with this, there would be:

a refusal to take the 'quick fix' approach to learning by equipping students with facts;

development of a statewide education data system, including the appointment of an Education Data Advisory Task Force;

participation in the National Assessment for Educational Progress (NAEP) field test in 8th grade mathematics.

Commissioner Lutjeharms does note in the publication that LB 744 had been vetoed by the Governor following the 1989 session — and with it, therefore, the Nebraska Data Advisory Committee and the Education Data Center which the bill would have created. But, no matter, states Lutjeharms: It was a done deed.

The goals-testing-remediation process has begun, irrespective of any veto by the Governor; for now it's voluntary . . . until the bugs are worked out. But, as in Pennsylvania, in the end it will be mandatory. Eventually, Nebraska will be asked to draw up objectives (Long-Range Plans), based on the results of the "pilot" assessment. The test will be expanded to other "competencies" once it has "proved itself" in the pilot. All will be passed off as academic testing by use of the term "achievement testing," although attitudinal data collection eventually will be soft-sold. State officials by then will know how to handle the community and where the opposition will come from.

Lutjeharms admits under whose direction and administration the test comes — the feds. He might as well, after all. Nebraska citizens don't have anything to say about it anyway.

CHAPTER 21

Paper Chases: Part Two

ABOUT THE SAME time Nebraskans were brainstorming their way around LB 744, the Regional Inspector General's office in Philadelphia moved on Anita Hoge's demand for an audit of Pennsylvania to locate the federal funding links to EQA and to the curriculum. Hugh Monaghan read the audit report[53] to Anita over the telephone. It stated that yes, federal funds had been located, but only insofar as SEA officials (the Pennsylvania Department of Education) had been paid in part by the federal government. Monaghan admitted, however, that the focus of the audit had been extremely narrow. When Anita asked about the other sources of federal funding which the Pennsylvania Group had found — the sources named on the covers of the curriculum and in teachers' manuals — he explained that no one had looked for funding links there.

Anita decided to ask Monaghan for a copy of the report, inadequate though it was, and he told her, no problem, just contact Larry Newman at Freedom of Information — which she did on August 16, 1989. Newman passed Anita's letter to Deputy Undersecretary James B. Thomas, Jr., at the federal Inspector General's office, who wrote back August 31 to tell Anita that she was being *denied access to what was, in effect, her own report.* Since it was Anita Hoge who had initiated the audit in the first place, it was inconceivable to her that she would be denied a copy of something she had heard already over the telephone.

One of the things federal bureaucrats do best is to quote obscure regulations to help their superiors out of a bind. The letter Anita got from Thomas' office was typical. First it explained that Anita was being denied access to the report because of the "deliberative process privilege" portion of Exemption b5 of the Freedom of Information Act:

> It is our policy not to disclose internal deliberative records that are being used in the Department's decision-making process.

But the masterpiece of self-serving gibberish was the rationale Thomas' staff gave for invoking this "privilege":

(1) to encourage open and frank discussions on matters of policy between subordinates and superiors.

(2) to protect against premature disclosure of proposed policies before they are officially adopted.

(3) to protect against public confusion that might result from disclosure of reasons and rationales that were not, in fact, ultimately the grounds for the Department action.

At this, the whole Pennsylvania Group doubled over in laughter. "Proposed policies" in an audit report? Open and frank discussions? Protection against public confusion? C'mon!

Anita Hoge was told that she could appeal the decision — to Ted Sanders, Undersecretary of the Department of Education. But on October 26, he upheld the decision of the Inspector General's office and again denied access:

My determination is based on Freedom of Information Act exemption (b)(7)(A),5 U.S. Code sec. 552 (b)(7)(A), as amended by Public Law no. 99-570, Sec. 1802 (1986), which authorizes federal agencies to withhold from disclosure "records or information compiled for law enforcement purposes...to the extent that production of such...records or information could reasonably be expected to interfere with enforcement proceedings."

To have put this in writing was probably a strategic mistake on Sanders' part. When the average person, unfamiliar with government gobbledegook, reads a statement like this, the immediate reaction is: What is it that the government doesn't want me to know about this legislation?

Sanders added another reason, too: that "the investigation is still pending." Never mind that it had already run for 36 months. But the final paragraph of Sanders' letter was the clincher:

> This letter constitutes exhaustion of the administrative remedies available to you under the Freedom of Information Act. You have the right to seek judicial review.

Judicial review. In other words, sue us. Spend *your* money if you expect anything from the federal government that is not in its own interests. Apparently, much of the proof Anita and her colleagues had sent to help authorities trace the funding had been diverted, including the suitcase-full Anita had taken to Washington herself. Those to whom the materials had been addressed claimed they never received them and probably didn't. (The reader who is passably familiar with the Iran-Contra scandal may remember the term "credible deniability"; if officials don't receive certain items of documentation from their staffs, the mailroom, or what-have-you, then of course they can deny ever having seen them.) These "lost" materials included the cover of the citizenship curriculum (the one with the "ESEA-Title IV-C" designation on it); pages 19-21 of *Getting Inside the EQA Inventory* under "Citizenship," where it stated NAEP objectives were being used; the references to the federally financed Intermediate Unit (specifically, the Allegheny IU), used to disseminate "supplementary materials" to schools; and one dynamite excerpt from Tyler and Wolf's *Critical Issues in Testing* pointing to Pennsylvania having been selected intentionally, back in the late Sixties, as the testing model for the nation. When it states that the Pennsylvania "state education agency has produced instruments..." it is implied that the state did this on its own initiative. But it has already been established that (a) Ralph Tyler, co-editor of the anthology from which this is quoted, is the same CFAT fellow and ETS kingpin who did most of the testing work in Pennsylvania under contract — at about the same time he was working on NAEP at the national level, and (b) the writers of the particular excerpt quoted below are ETS people who undoubtedly have worked with Tyler. Keep in mind, too, that this volume, *Critical Issues in Testing*, was published in 1974, just one year after Pennsylvania's Dr. Coldiron (who was also busy at the federal level with Ramsey Seldon's Advisory Network for State-by-State Comparisons) ran afoul of the ACLU on the matter of not giving notice of the EQA to parents. Note especially the words italicized here.

...a few states make a point of stressing...the importance of personal-social development as an outcome of the educational process....

In recognition of the importance to the student and society of noncognitive development, *Pennsylvania includes in its targets for quality education a number of attitudes and noncognitive abilities....* Consequently, *the state* [Pennsylvania] *education agency has produced instruments* to gauge how extensively schools are affecting such significant aspects...as self-concept, understanding of others responsible citizenship, health habits, creativity...*readiness for change,* and students' attitudes toward their schools. Michigan, too, has included in its testing program the measurement of three types of student attitudes: namely, attitude toward learning, attitude toward academic achievement, and attitude toward self. *Nebraska is now planning to create an assessment program which, in its first stage, will be concerned only with nonacademic objectives.*[54]

Meanwhile, letters had been written to Secretary of Education Lauro Cavazos, which wound up in the hands of Assistant Secretary Bruno Manno, who also monitors the NAEP (the Assistant Secretary of Education always monitors the NAEP, even though CFAT, in effect, controls it). Manno responded with a perfunctory letter (June 9, 1989) giving the same old saw used by his predecessors at the Department: that there was no testing of attitudes by the NAEP, that no national data bank existed, and that NAEP was in no way involved with Pennsylvania's EQA or any other state "regarding their own student assessments." A Pennsylvania Group member sent back a letter with another copy of the page on citizenship objectives from Pennsylvania's EQA, where it is stated outright that NAEP objectives are being tested. Manno responded again on July 13 to say that if Pennsylvania *seemed* to have used some NAEP objectives, it was due to the fact that officials there *may* have borrowed from the *old* NAEP, which was no longer in use because it was "inconsistent with legislation."

This response from Manno drew more bellylaughs from the Pennsylvania Group, which by this time had accumulated dozens of documents linking both state testing and curriculum with NAEP and federal funds — including a devastating document called Project 81 explaining how the EQA was nationalized in a contract between the federal government and American Telephone and Telegraph Company (A T & T), which apparently developed a computerized monitoring technology in the mid-seventies that would enable authorities to evaluate testing and learning programs. Much of the project specifically targeted Pennsylvania's Lancaster School District.

Project 81 was conceived as "the Community-Defined Expectations for School Curriculum Project." It originated as a research effort sponsored by A T & T and the Ohio Bell Telephone Company. This effort was developed and refined during 1971-72 by the Educational Systems Section of Batelle Laboratories in Columbus, Ohio, with the cooperation of Columbus Public Schools. The project model was later made available by A T & T to all Bell System Companies throughout the country. The project was designed as a method of collecting curriculum-relevant information from a sizeable cross-section of a community in order to learn what knowledge, skills, and attitudes it would be reasonable to expect from a person graduating from high school. Because the results of the first implementation of the project were incomplete, it was tested in another site: Lancaster, Pennsylvania. The choice of Lancaster was due to its size and "prior involvement with the Pennsylvania statewide Educational Quality Assessment (EQA) and Long Range Planning . . . . These broad-based efforts seemed the natural umbrella under which to place the Community-Defined Expectations for School Curriculum Project in order to provide it with an even greater degree of credibility than it otherwise might have commanded at the local level."

The "broad-based efforts" described above involved, as indicated, no one in the local community but, rather, "a group of eight men in public education in the Commonwealth of Pennsylvania who joined together under the auspices of the United States Office of Education" and two non-local colleges to find a solution to what they considered the most pressing problem of local schools: "the application of systematic planning processes for the improvement of education."

The major work of the first year was "to develop a consensus on the major categories within which the state would require [not request] districts to certify proficiency."[55]

The entire effort became known as Project '81, the "'81" denoting the year by which implementation of the effort was to be accomplished in Pennsylvania. When the group finally got around to seeking community support, they went not to local schools or town meetings, but to the Chamber of Commerce, labor unions, and state officials of the PTA.

One of the contract monitors of the Lancaster project was Dick Brickley, who later became Director of the R.I.S.E. in Pennsylvania.

Meanwhile, Emerson Elliott, head of the Center for Education Statistics (CES) apparently decided it was time to enter the fray. On July 19 he sent a letter to a Group member. Elliott claimed that Manno had shared his correspondence with him and that "as the federal administrator with direct responsibility for the NAEP" Elliott wanted to assure everyone that NAEP and the EQA were not connected, but that Pennsylvania might have used some NAEP materials since there was no way to control their usage once materials are in the public domain.

Public domain? How interesting, thought the Pennsylvania Group. How was it that NAEP testing materials were so difficult to obtain if they were in the public domain? A Group member fired off another letter demanding to see these elusive materials.

Anita Hoge jumped in as "an interested party" on the public domain issue. She wrote Manno to describe exactly how NAEP was involved in attitude collection — how, in effect, it was monitoring "a threshold level of compliance" using hypothetical questions involving reward and punishment. She explained, with copies of still other documents, how the federal government was piloting curriculum, even before the NAEP officially started testing, in 1969.

No response from Manno — another big mistake that would eventually put federal bureaucrats in a Catch-22.

On September 6 a piece appeared in *Education Week* by Peter Schmidt stating that Emerson Elliott, head of the Center for Education Statistics, was pulling three of the older data collection mechanisms. One was the Longitudinal Studies — because there were "questions" about the potential to track individuals. Of course the three old data banks were being absorbed into the ESIDS anyway, but the article nevertheless indicated that somebody's cage had been rattled. Schmidt even quoted House Education Subcommittee head, Augustus Hawkins, who admitted that, yes, there just might be a problem with what the CES was doing.

Score one point for the Pennsylvania Group.

The truth was that as early as May 10, 1988, both the U.S. Department of Education and the Pennsylvania Department of Education knew they were in trouble. Anita Hoge, in her usual mode of keeping the pressure on, chanced to call Leroy Rooker, Acting Director of Family Policy and Regulations Office (formerly Office of Student Rights) to check on the status of her complaint. Rooker told her that, as a matter of fact, the federal Department had just issued an ultimatum under his signature to the state education agency in Pennsylvania. Anita asked whether it might be possible for her to see a copy of that letter. Hoping, no doubt, that this would satisfy the indefatigable Mrs. Hoge, he agreed. In retrospect, he may have wished he had not. The letter was a scorcher — and provided just the information Anita Hoge needed to plan a winning strategy.

The admissions of the May 13, 1988, letter from Leroy Rooker, U.S. Department of Education, to Mary Rogers, Chief Counsel of the Pennsylvania Department of Education, are so overwhelming that it is appropriate to reprint it here:

Dear Ms. Rogers:

As you know, this Department is investigating a complaint by Mrs. Anita Hoge alleging that Pennsylvania's Educational Quality Assessment (EQA) was administered to her son without her prior written consent by the McGuffey School district in violation of the Protection of Pupil Rights Amendment (PPRA), Section 439 of the General Education Provisions Act, 20 U.S.C. 1232h.

By letter to you dated March 9, 1988, the Department requested certain information from Pennsylvania to support the assertions that no Federal funds from the U.S. Department of Education (ED) were used in connection with the EQA. The Commonwealth [of Pennsylvania] was requested to provide specific documentation showing whether account 181, which funded the test, contains ED funds. You were informed that the deadline for such documentation was March 31, 1988. This documentation was not received as of May 10, 1988.

. . . To avoid further delay . . . we request that you address the following issues with documentation by June 15, 1988.

First, from the EQA literature submitted to this office, it does not appear that written consent was obtained by the school before students were required to take the EQA test. This office has received EQA literature which requested that teachers give students an information booklet to take home to parents informing them that by making a written request of the school principal their children would be exempt from the test. From our examination of this literature, it is not evident that the Commonwealth [of Pennsylvania] followed the PPRA stipulations with regard to parental consent. . . .

Second, the PPRA applies to "psychological tests" that are funded in whole or in part by the U.S. Department of Education — the primary purpose of which is to reveal information concerning one or more of the seven areas enumerated in the PPRA. The regulations implementing the PPRA, 34 C.F.R. part 98, define the term "psychological test" as follows:

"Psychiatric or Psychological examination or test" means a method of obtaining information, *including a group activity* [Rooker emphasis] that is not directly related to academic instruction and is designed to illicit [sic] information about attitudes, habits, traits, opinions, beliefs or feelings.

Based on the information we have received, there remains a legitimate concern that the EQA may fall within the above definition of "psychological test." At no time have we received information from McGuffey School District or the Commonwealth which would indicate that the EQA is not a psychological test. . . . In fact, the *EQA Commentary* refers to the Educational Quality Assessment as "EQA attitude instruments." In addition to measuring students' knowledge, *Information for Parents* states that the EQA also assesses students' attitudes. *EQA Commentary* states that "noncognitive measures in EQA are those which collect information on students' attitudes, opinions or feelings . . . ."

There is also concern that the primary purpose of the EQA is to reveal private information from one or more of the seven protected areas. If you have information on the EQA which demonstrates otherwise and which shows that the EQA is not a psychological test as defined by the PPRA, please provide this Office with support for this position.

Any other information you wish to consider in connection with Mrs. Hoge's complaint also should be provided by June 15. We would prefer to have your views on these issues in resolving Mrs. Hoge's complaint. However, if they are not forthcoming, we will be obligated to draw our own conclusions based on the evidence available to us, including the allegations in Mrs. Hoge's complaint and our analysis of the EQA materials. The Department of Education will then proceed with appropriate action.

Enclosed is a similar request for information that has been sent to the McGuffey School District.

Sincerely,
Leroy Rooker
Acting Director
Family Policy and Regulations Office

Actually, Rooker's letter identified only the surface issues. It did not get into what kinds of "remedial" programs had been brought into Pennsylvania schools to "correct" the weaknesses assessed from the students' responses on the EQA test. It did not identify where such programs come from (the National Diffusion Network) or that they are funded and "validated" by federal government appointees. It did not address the question of who comes up with test questions (the Educational Testing Service), and how those questions mimic the national version of the test, NAEP, also created by the Educational Testing Service. The letter did not refer to the owners and operators of the ETS, either. If it had, the letter would also have had to reveal how much money that body and the federal government were passing back and forth, in the form of official grants going back as far as 1964.[56]

Rooker's use of the terms "academic" and "noncognitive" in the letter to Rogers leads one to believe that he, and probably others at the federal level, did know the difference. Just how many knew that the term "cognitive" had been changed by behaviorists to include the affective domain, as described in the Shaver paper,[57] is unknown.

Anita Hoge wrote still another letter to the Inspector General's office in late October — with copies, of course, to the other officials involved. In it, she informed the agency that she intended to pursue the case on the grounds that the Inspector General's office was "ignoring pertinent facts, concealing documents and harboring information to protect the Department of Education."

She also requested another audit. For although officials had at that point admitted federal funding through salary payments, they had not conducted the audit in a manner consistent with Anita Hoge's request or complaint. She wanted confirmation of federal funds through the *Intermediate Units,* with Title IV-C of the ESEA being used as the grant vehicle. This would have established in writing from the Inspector General's office the alleged illegality: the government using federal money to establish curriculum. It would have named the vehicle used to accomplish this act.

Predictably, the authorities declined. Anita Hoge received a letter in December 1989 to the effect that officials at the time of the audit saw their job as determining whether federal funds were being used in *any* phase in the development, administration, or implementation of the EQA test. Period. Apparently, by that time they knew they could not, in light of their audit, deny federal funding, but neither did they wish to go so far as to admit establishing curriculum by using test results. So they ignored — and indicated they would continue to ignore — Anita's references to the Intermediate Unit and, in turn, its connection to the "validated" programs assessed from the EQA. Officials also would continue to ignore the dates for which Anita wanted the audit: 1978-1982. Conveniently, they had earmarked their audit period for 1983-1986. This neatly circumvented the years Anita Hoge's school district became entrapped with federal funding.

The whole affair was becoming a game of chess between Anita Hoge and the federal government.

The Inspector General's office was claiming that since they already had found "conclusive evidence" of federal funds, they had "no basis" now for conducting another audit.

When will this woman quit? they wondered.

Instead of quitting, Anita Hoge decided to force the government's hand with a new move of her own. She changed tactics. It was clear that officials in Washington were under pressure from other sources and intended, therefore, to wait for Anita to file a formal suit rather than give her any more ammunition to use against them, such as a written admission of guilt.

Anita remembered recently filling out an income tax form on which she claimed her daughters as dependents. To claim exemptions for children under three years of age, parents now had to obtain a social security number for each child. Meanwhile, she understood that legislation was quietly being drafted by certain interested parties to require newborns to have a social security number.[58]

In June of 1990, Anita Hoge began focusing more attention on the questionable legality of using the social security number in conjunction with assessment testing — an approach Pennsylvania officials were using to launch the newest version of the EQA. Anita wrote to the Office of Public Inquiries at the Social Security Administration to ask whether the Pennsylvania Department of Education (PDE) could legally require a child's social security number on a test that collects personal and private information about the child or his parents, particularly if they are not informed as to how the data is to be used or where it is to be stored. Furthermore, she wanted to know whether the PDE was permitted to monitor non-academic areas from one testing date to another, using the social security number, in order to observe and/or remediate attitudinal, value and behavioral changes of the child being tested. Finally, was the federal education agency, the U.S. Department of Education, legally permitted to input personal data collected from a state test (in this case, Pennsylvania's) through the social security number into the ESIDS computer at the Center for Education Statistics in Washington, particularly if the test used to gather the data was already found to be in violation of privacy rights and federal law? Anita enclosed with her letter copies of documents outlining the ongoing federal investigations into Pennsylvania's testing procedures.

Because of the uproar earlier on, the EQA had already been pulled — due to "pending investigations," according to Pennsylvania officials. At first that seemed like good news, but in reality the Pennsylvania Division of Testing had merely renamed the test: the Pennsylvania Assessment System

(PAS). The newest addition to the test was a blank on the cover to be filled in by the student — the social security number.

At first Anita and her cohorts challenged the practice without being fully aware of all the privacy ramifications. Foiled again, officials put a moratorium on all assessment testing in Pennsylvania for a period of two years, ostensibly so that "the bugs could be worked out."

The new test, of course, was but a more sophisticated version of the EQA. The proof was in a memo dated January 3, 1989, from James Hertzog, Acting Secretary of Education in Pennsylvania, to Shirley Hughs, a legislative aide (with copies to all Intermediate Units and other state agencies). Hertzog stated:

> Testing of all other subject areas [except reading and mathematics] in the...Quality Goals of Education previously known as the Educational Quality Assessment program [EQA] will be suspended for one year while it is incorporated into the Pennsylvania Assessment [PAS]. Any testing in these areas in the 88-89 school year will be experimental tests for future programs.
>
> ...When completed the system is expected to provide information on the Quality goals of Education previously provided by EQA.

So: same goals, same psycho-behavioral educational agenda, a system still bent on making attitude-manipulation, not academics, the primary objective. Elsewhere in the memo, Hertzog admonished school systems to "proceed with caution" in administering the PAS next time.[59] People out there were watching.

By June of 1990, however, the implications for privacy with a social security number connection to the new, cross-referenceable education computer (the Elementary and Secondary Integrated[60] Data System, or ESIDS), was far more clear. Predictably, those promoting the nationalization of psychological assessment and experimentation in schools did not want Anita Hoge pursuing this line of research. The social security number was crucial to the full implementation of the ESIDS — targeted for July 1991, according to the working paper that described the computer system. The public was still in a state of relative ignorance and/or complacency about computerization of educational data. It was no time to alert them as to how the new system was going to be used, or that the social security number might be the key to linkage with other data systems.

Anita Hoge's month-by-month, year-by-year persistence was now starting to pay off. On October 10, 1989, she had met with Senator Arlen Specter's legislative assistant for two hours in the Pittsburgh office. So alarmed was the Senator's staffer about the nature of the testing and the computerization of data that she called in an aide to take notes.

Anita then forwarded to Leroy Rooker (Director of the Family Policy and Regulations Office who, the reader may remember, replaced Hazel Fiers of the Student and Family Education Rights and Privacy Office) copies of all correspondence between the Department of Education, Freedom of Information Office, other agencies, and Pennsylvania Group members, so that the conflicting responses of federal and state education officials would be a matter of record.

By December of 1989, the various federal agencies involved had gotten the message and began responding in kind — too late to save themselves — with copies of correspondences to their colleagues in the federal and state education agencies. Department officials and their bureaucratic minions started checking with each other to get their stories straight before putting anything in writing to Anita Hoge or anyone else in Pennsylvania.

Meanwhile, worried letters from state officials like Mary Ann Clausen, Counsel at the Pennsylvania Department of Education, were complaining to federal education authorities that no determination had been made as to where *they* stood on the psychological testing issue. They reasoned that federal mandates had gotten them into this mess, so was Washington going to back state officials up or not? Assistant Secretary of Education Bruno Manno's letter about old NAEP objectives being inconsistent with legislation justifiably alarmed Pennsylvania officials, who feared their own tests would also be deemed inconsistent with legislation, which they probably were. Moreover, state officials were just beginning to comprehend the magnitude of what they had opened up by passing Anita Hoge on to the federal government.

But for the time being, state education officials just wanted their documents back from the feds, along with assurances that if things got sticky the federal government would pull them out. The Deputy General Counsel at the federal level duly considered the plight of officials in Pennsylvania — and, no doubt, his own plight as well — and decided that he just might have a deal for the worry-warts in Pennsylvania. Federal authorities would negotiate with the Pennsylvania Counsel "to get a policy issue" — meaning, to get Pennsylvania off the legal hook on the EQA — if Pennsylvania officials, in turn, would get Anita Hoge off everyone's backs.

Pennsylvania SEA officials must have worked feverishly to come up with a plan to defuse Anita Hoge. But the only idea they could come up with, apparently, was an admission of guilt. Since Anita Hoge hadn't sued, it didn't take any great deductive skill to figure out that her motive wasn't money. Maybe all she wanted was a pat on the back; to be told that, yes, she was right, and a promise that officials would get their act together and make sure it didn't happen again.

So a carefully worded letter was drafted, something that might appeal to her ego and recognize her achievement, but which would include nothing so specific that she could nail them with it in the courtroom or in the press.

On April 18, 1990, nearly four years after Anita Hoge had filed the complaint against Pennsylvania's Department of Education, U.S. Senator Arlen Specter's local office in Pittsburgh called to say her complaint had been resolved. She had won. The staffer who telephoned on the Senator's behalf oozed enthusiasm. She held a letter in her hand, she said, a copy of which would be forwarded to Anita.

Anita was skeptical. She had heard this sort of thing from officialdom before. She pressed for specifics. In the course of the conversation, the staffer indicated that the Education Department and the Justice Department had ruled favorably on Anita's case: saying that yes, the EQA was a psychological test (which Anita already knew from Leroy Rooker's May 13, 1988, letter to Mary Rogers); that yes, federal funds had been involved (which had been verified already in the Pennsylvania audit and other documents); and yes, that some of the seven areas "protected" under the

Protection of Pupil Rights Amendment had been violated. Now the impression was given that here it all was, nice and neat and set out in a letter that would henceforth make it unnecessary for Mrs. Hoge and her research network to drag out all those damning documents.

If the letter the staffer was talking about really did contain those three admissions — that EQA was a psychological test, that federal funding was involved, and that areas protected under PPRA had been violated — then all those other letters forwarded earlier on by Arlen Specter's office would prove conclusively that officials at the highest levels of government had been lying for three years when they denied the charges earlier. The only thing that would be missing was a flat-out admission that the federal government was conspiring to establish curriculum.

No matter, thought Anita. She had the 1982 paper out of NDN — the one stating that only programs which were funded by the federal government could be validated by the Joint Dissemination Review Panel and, from there, be placed into the NDN — proof enough the federal government was "establishing curriculum."

She had them! It was too good to be true. Surely even bureaucrats wouldn't be so stupid as to think she hadn't saved copies of previous correspondence!

They weren't.

Nearly a month later Anita got the long-awaited letter.

The letter admitted wrong-doing and mentioned the EQA as well as to repeat the wording of Anita's original complaint. But there were no specifics. Not a single one of the so-called "violations" were named. All there was of a substantive nature were allusions to policies being made that would "preclude any future violations." Like what? Anita wanted to know. Which violations were they going to avoid in the future?

Anita Hoge called Senator Specter's office to tell them what she thought of the letter and the so-called admissions of guilt. "Believe me, you've won," insisted a desperate staffer. "You should be very pleased!" she gushed.

Hellfire and damnation, thought Anita Hoge. *They think they've ended it.* Why was Specter's office suddenly cutting her off?

She was just mad enough to reexamine all previous correspondences, wondering what, if anything, she could do. She assumed, rightly, that there must be some reason why Washington and Pennsylvania officials were going through this charade.

Then Anita remembered a fellow named Mark Shiffrin, General Counsel at the Education Department in Washington. He had told her that if she ever found that authorities "weren't complying in Pennsylvania," to let him know. Letters between the federal and state Departments of Education that had been forwarded to Anita by Senator Specter and others frequently mentioned Mark Shiffrin, either in the "copies to" list at the bottom, or by implying that the substance of the letter had been "run by" Shiffrin's office. Leroy Rooker, it turned out, had been keeping Shiffrin in the loop, and so, Anita reasoned, she might be able to use that fact to find out what was really going on.

Anita found out more than she bargained for. She discovered that once the case was closed, it couldn't be reopened unless she had children in public school. She also found out about the "deal" hatched between General Counsel and Pennsylvania, to get the latter officials off the hook on EQA and Anita Hoge off everyone's backs.

Hmm, she thought. *They must want to close the case rather badly all of a sudden. Had the social security number ploy gotten under somebody's skin after all?*

It was time to pull out all the stops. Time to take their "king." All Anita Hoge's instincts told her that authorities in Washington and Pennsylvania wanted her out of the picture once and for all. If she was going to do anything, now was the time.

First Anita contacted the renowned attorney William Ball, who some years before had won an unusual case. In a daring move, Ball had succeeded in proving that atheism was a religion — albeit a non-theistic religion (one not based on a belief in a single god). But because certain brands of atheism were nevertheless a "worldview" and had written-down lists of doctrine, Ball said they were subject to the same strictures about separation of church and state as any other religion — i.e., the government could not promote atheism, either directly or indirectly, any more than it could promote Presbyterianism or Catholicism or Judaism.

It had been a gutsy maneuver, and Anita Hoge needed somebody gutsy.

Anita forwarded to Ball all her copies of correspondence between state and federal agencies and herself as well as several of the key documents pertaining to her case. She talked at length with Ball's aide explaining what she had done and what the case was about. It turned out that Bill Ball had a very full slate of clients which precluded his taking on such a weighty case at this juncture, but he was intrigued nevertheless, and for future reference agreed to hold her documentation.

Anita shut herself in her room and pored over the regulations concerning resolution of complaints. She knew average citizens were not supposed to have to hire legal counsel in order for state and/or federal authorities to hear and rule on complaints. That's why legislation such as the Protection of Pupil Rights Amendment is written in the first place, to give average citizens recourse without taking on the whole system.

She read through the legislation again, and again, and still again.

Then she found it: Section 98.9a and b, "Investigation of Findings"; a clause which stated that authorities cannot ignore the letters of complainants, and also stating that the *"office must provide to the complainant written notice of its findings and the basis for those findings."*

That was it! Officials had to specify the **basis for their findings!** They couldn't just mumble something about avoiding "future violations" and not say what the violations were or explain the basis upon which their experts had concluded violations had occurred in the past, or might occur in the future.

What's more, Anita had copies of some ten letters she had written over the course of four years to federal officials — letters which still remained unanswered — such as the one she had written to Bruno Manno, Assistant Secretary of Education.

About that time the long-awaited letter from the Social Security Administration's Privacy Office regarding the use of the social security number as an identifier arrived in Anita's mailbox. Sure enough, the use of a child's social security number was covered by the provisions of the 1974 Privacy Act. Stated Privacy Officer Stephen Siff: ". . . the Privacy Act of 1974 (P.L. 93-579) does impact on Pennsylvania's collection and use of the SSN [social security number] as a personal identifier. Section 7 of this law provides requirements concerning the uses of the SSN . . . with which all government agencies must comply."

Attached was a copy of the legislation, with the all-important Section 7. Section 7a made it "unlawful for any Federal, State or local government agency to deny to an individual any right, benefit or privilege provided by law because of such individual's refusal to disclose his social security account number." But Section 7b was the clincher:

> Any Federal, State, or local government agency which requests an individual to disclose his social security account number shall inform that individual whether that disclosure is mandatory or voluntary, by what statutory or other authority such number is solicited, and what uses will be made of it.

In other words, explanations like "demographic research" would hardly suffice for an assessment test like the EQA. Finally, Siff's letter suggested that Anita contact the U.S. Department of Justice which, he stated, had proved "most helpful in providing guidance on issues concerning . . . section 7 of the Privacy Act."

Anita Hoge had a wide grin on her face when she drafted what she thought was her final letter to the legal Counsels at the Pennsylvania and Washington, D.C., Education Departments. She had been patronized, now it was time to turn the tables.

First, she commiserated with her antagonists by explaining that she understood how anxious they were to close her case. Tsk! Tsk! Such an awkward situation. But according to Section 98.9b of the Protection of Pupil Rights

Amendment, they couldn't quite close it yet, not until they provided the *basis for their findings* — for the "violations" alluded to in their previous letter.

And while they were at it, there was the little matter of ten outstanding responses to letters she had written to their various offices.

Anita signed the letter and typed in at the bottom:

> *cc: William Bentley Ball, Esq., Attorney at Law: Ball, Skelly, Murren, & Connell; Mark Shiffrin, Deputy General Counsel, U.S. Dept. of Education; Peter Wathen-Dunn, Office of the General Counsel, U.S. Dept. of Education; and Ernest N. Helling, Assistant Chief Counsel,Pennsylvania Dept. of Education.*

Anita had passed her most important test: She had learned to think like a bureaucrat. She thoroughly understood her opponents in Washington and Pennsylvania. She knew no one would bother to check whether she had actually retained Ball or not. She knew officials at this point wouldn't know, or want to know, just how much documentation had been placed in Ball's able hands. She knew no one would believe that it was she, and not the lawyer, who had found the obscure Section 98.9b.

And soon someone at the U.S. Justice Department would know, if he didn't already, that Anita Hoge held in her hands the key to the issue of linkage with the social security number: Section 7 of Public Law 93-579, the Privacy Act of 1974. Using the social security number to link attitudinal-value data through the new ESIDS computer wasn't going to fly.

"Checkmate!" Anita Hoge said to herself as she sealed the last envelope. This time, she decided, she had really won.

CHAPTER 22

Resurrecting the Educational Blueprint

IN THE SPACE of just the last year or so, it has become a relatively simple matter to find officials publicly hyping psycho-behavioral teaching strategies, if one is keeping an eye out. As recently as June 16, 1990, a letter to the Editor on the *Washington Post's* editorial page by a University of Maryland professor of Education and Psychology, Donald K. Pumroy (who is also the Director of the university's Psychology Program) wrote:

> ...the same approach that is used in special education, helping people with weight control and the cessation of smoking...is referred to as the science of behavior, behavior analysis, or behavior modification.
>
> It is the teacher's job to change the behavior of his or her pupils. The theory and technique are based on research that goes back several decades, and we know they work because of this research. While many individuals do not understand or appreciate the behavioral position, there are serious efforts underway to help teachers learn and use this approach in their classes. The general public will hear more of the science of behavior in the future.

The good professor, of course, does not bring up the fact that using behavior modification to help people change their eating habits or stop smoking is in a different ethical category from changing pupils' behavior in a classroom setting. In the former case, individuals have made a conscious decision to seek help in changing undesirable behavior. In the latter, the child is in a captive environment and has no choice. As to whether the child's parents have been given the opportunity to make the choice for the child — well, that was at the heart of the Anita Hoge case.

The above editorial was a response to an earlier *Washington Post* article on teacher training, one that described "resistance to change" in teacher training (June 3, 1990). The professor, like others in his field in government and at CFAT, is becoming more public in promoting psychological teaching strategies. Instead of denying what they are doing, proponents and promoters of psycho-behavioral education are giving it the soft sell.

But that is only because, now, it is a *fait accompli*. As the professor points out, the research has been going on for decades. For decades, experiments have been conducted using people's children as unsuspecting guinea pigs.

The so-called father of progressive education, John Dewey (1859-1952), was the first to come out publicly for the "socialization of the child" as the appropriate main thrust of all formal education. To Dewey, subject matter was entirely secondary. He is portrayed in most college teacher preparation programs as the Father of modern education, or at least its most eminent guru. Other educational philosophers, like Piaget, voiced similar theses, but they did not say it in quite the bold way Dewey did.

The year 1967 was a pivotal year. Two voluminous documents were written establishing large-scale blueprints for the kinds of changes Dewey had promoted. One, a multi-state project in 1967-68 called "Designing Education for the Future," headquartered in Denver, Colorado, supports the charge of collusion between the federal and the then-independent state education agencies. The other, nicknamed B-STEP, completely revamped teacher education.

The "Designs" papers comprise five lengthy documents — the most revealing being papers Number 3 and Number 5.[61] These outline a procedure for changing educational objectives on a national scale — from the top down. Local initiatives, according to these documents, would continue to be of interest only if they served the interests of the U.S. Office of Education in Washington.

For example, states page 280, Paper 3: "Education is . . . a means to achieve important economic and social goals, usually of a national character." Nothing about education being a means to financial independence on the part of the individual, or a means to knowledge of history or culture.

The paper goes on to espouse "advanced measurement techniques" for attitudes and values, and to stress the importance of *social scientists* as consultants on the project. Even at that date, just two years after the ESEA law created those five little titles, the call was out for a "state assessment" that was "closely coordinated with the national program." The result would be the NAEP and its clones in the states.

Paper Number 5 makes it clear that the so-called "service function" of state education agencies, or SEAs, is just a façade. On page 184, this "Designs" paper emphasizes, by using italic print, that *"a state education department's basic responsibility is not necessarily to provide a service or perform a function . . . , but to ensure its provision in the most effective way."*

What is meant by "its provision"? The SEA's new role as "policy enforcer."

Here is nothing less than the key to changing education. The state education agency, formerly independent of the federal government, would henceforth exist to enforce the directives of those in control at the top. The SEA would ensure compliance of local education agencies — thus individual schools — with federal directives. The first federal directive, the cardinal principle, was that a *"state education department must be an agent of change"* and *"change must be institutionalized."*

A scheme had been hatched, beginning with the five titles of the ESEA law, and now here it is, explained step by step. "Designs" paper 3 indicates that henceforth, the SEA would pass itself off as a service agency, "helping" local agencies and school districts to get the things they needed to do their job of educating local youngsters. Only CFAT and federal sources knew that what locals would need would not long be confined to items of their own choosing, but would include primarily money — and lots of it — to carry out federal directives. Page 170 of "Designs" paper 3 confirms the point, then links it right to the Carnegie Foundation for the Advancement of Teaching:

> A major strategy in getting change is the use of dollars. It is no accident that the recent Secretary of Health, Education and Welfare was, prior to his government service, a [Carnegie] foundation president. An emergent function of a state education department is to act more like a combined management and consultant firm and philanthropic foundation,...to offer money to bring about correction and change....

"Designs" paper Number 5 details how local school districts would be reorganized, how SEAs would "lose their identity as well as their authority" and "form a partnership with the federal government."

No wonder Anita Hoge and other parents didn't get satisfaction from the state agencies! They had thought, when they went to the SEA, they were going straight to the top, to the people with clout. That was what they were supposed to think. But the SEA existed only to serve the federal government; to be the whipping boy when the federal agency didn't want to deal with a complaint or problem; and to act as dispenser and withholder of federal funds. With the SEAs "running interference," the federal agency could remove itself from any political fallout over its role in local education.

The "Designs" papers even go so far as to warn SEAs to "use happy, persuasive words" like "service" and "assistance" rather than words that pertain to its regulatory function, like "mandates," "compliance," and "controls."

The most important term of the three, of course, is "compliance." Only by ensuring compliance with federal directives could so-called "reform initiatives" — like the EQA in Pennsylvania — be made to look like state initiatives. As state initiatives, complainants could be kept running around in circles for years at state education headquarters like Harrisburg — and be kept away from officials in Washington.

In case the state agencies ever took a notion to balk at the heavy-handedness of the federal government, plans were set early on for the federal bureaucracy to run right over them. Page 181 of another "Designs" paper notes significantly:

> State education departments . . . will have to consider two things: (1) the necessity to cooperate with federal officials . . . in order to ensure that data systems are compatible . . . ; and (2) [that] unless state education departments establish sophisticated information systems, they will soon find that Washington has to go directly to local institutions in order to secure data, thus bypassing the states.

Clearly local educational institutions were never to have a chance, from the moment the ESEA law was enacted. There is no question from the foregoing that education was to become a federal prerogative, existing legislation notwithstanding, or that the establishment of an integrated data system was the long-range goal. SEAs and LEAs were to be kept in line and cooperative with promises of ever-larger budgets and staffs, and when that didn't work, there was always force, through the use of mandates.

In a final caveat the "Designs" paper states:

> Planning and exhortation are important, but it helps to hold out a carrot to accomplish given ends.

That carrot, of course, was federal dollars.

CHAPTER 23

The Carrot and the Stick

AS INDICATED, MANY additional "titles" were quickly added to the original ESEA law, encouraging school districts to become trapped in such a way that they would have no choice but to commence psycho-behavioral testing and hand over their data.

It may be useful here to summarize again the flow of federal dollars as they go from the federal to the state, and finally down to the local level:

When local school districts request federal aid, the dollars come from the state education agency, or SEA. The state is block granted federal money each year on the basis of expected demand. The first local school district to request financial aid from the federal government starts the ball rolling in the whole state.

Before the federal government will give a single dollar to the state for education purposes, the state must formulate a set of broad educational *goals* and narrow these down to specific objectives, called *Long-Range plans*. The U.S. Department of Education sends the state directions, called "guidelines," detailing how goals and objectives are to be written and how measurement devices are to be constructed. The locals, or LEAs, discover their goals and objectives must be written in behavioral terms. Through the state agency, or SEA, the federal government then demands that there be some accountability device to ensure that the goals and objectives are being met. That accountability device is assessment testing. Later, results of these assessments will have to be presented in a form that is compatible with federal computer systems. Organizations like the Council of Chief State School Officers (CCSSO) and the Education Commission of the States (ECS) will "help" the state education agencies get their act together.

Pupil *weaknesses* are identified from the "pilot" tests,[62] and student population groups are *targeted* for change. From there, testing and remediation becomes a continuous "recycling" and refining process: that is, resources are requested and obtained in order to meet the new directives; change *programs are implemented,* with the help of change agents and state facilitators; *results are evaluated.*

This, in a nutshell, is "planned (or managed) change."

If, somewhere in the eight-step process described above, a local education agency or individual school district complains, the state can threaten to withhold funds, a threat which local institutions by this time can ill afford. If the state as a whole objects — that is, the SEA objects — the federal government can do the same to it, in the form of budget cuts and staff reductions.

What tests measure — and what schools are evaluated on — are known technically as "indicators." There are three types: input indicators, performance indicators, and societal indicators. The latter are all those survey questions about the students' families — income, occupation, educational level, how many magazines in the home, and so on. But the important one for purposes here are the *performance indicators.* These are the "educational outcomes," which according to federal guidelines (like the *Handbook on Performance Objectives*) are to be "measurable and observable behavioral" changes. That is why "cognitive learning" had to be redefined as the child's belief system.

Moreover, the federal government runs, in effect, state and local education policy, while maintaining the opposite fiction, and federal education policy itself is run by behavioral institutes and psycho-behavioral engineers, the most influential of which is the Carnegie Foundation for the Advancement of Teaching. CFAT, through its Educational Testing Service, co-owns and operates the major testing mechanisms at both the federal and state levels (sometimes under subcontracts so as not to be obvious). It jointly owns and runs the data banks, NAEP, and even grants money to the U.S. Department of Education.

Today the loop is nearly complete: testing, validation, textbooks and materials, curriculum, data banks. Curricular programs in most cases are licensed, thanks to the publishing deal with LINC out of Columbus, Ohio.[63]

Officials at the state or federal level can say to prospective curriculum developers: Yes, you can have a contract, providing you write your materials according to government (i.e., ETS') guidelines. Curriculum developers require, in effect, top-level approval to market their wares; curriculum and tests are linked. The only thing left is consolidation: only 31 states are completely hooked in to the loop (i.e., every school district in a state). The Anita Hoge case is the story of how federal funding became the carrot and the stick — and the key to the Pandora's Box of psychological probes and mislabeled goods in education.

The primary scapegoats in the scheme, of course, are classroom teachers. On teachers has fallen the brunt of "accountability." They have to justify the entire education system in the eyes of parents and the community, and at the same time satisfy the mandates of an education bureaucracy-run-amok. They are trained in techniques that don't work: teaching methods that turn even bright children into discipline problems and functional illiterates. Their supervisors in the administration practice an arrogance passed off as public relations, which, of course, evokes the wrath of the community. These supervisors — the local administrators and superintendents — frequently know little about managing children, but a whole lot about toadying to state and federal agencies. Frustrated and demoralized, good teachers leave; average-to-poor ones stick it out — with ne'er a clue as to how they've been had.

That's fine with the U.S. Department of Education. Teachers who are just sticking it out aren't likely to cause trouble. A teacher strike now and then is a small price to pay for power — in fact, it's helpful to the Department if teachers are worrying about their salaries instead of poking their noses into where student and teacher data goes and how federal education policy is made.

Part

VI:
INTO
COMPUTERIZED
SLAVERY?

CHAPTER 24

Evolution of Data-trafficking and the Supercomputer

MANY OFFICIALS, PARTICULARLY local ones, continue to maintain the fiction that state and national assessment tests are anonymous; that no individual student can be targeted through a test. Initially, this was true. What analysts were most interested in at the beginning was not individual students, but *group* trends in both academics and attitudes. They wanted to know how various regional, economic, and other specialized clusters of individuals compared in basic subject areas, and while they were at it, compare their attitudes, too. If behaviorists could figure out why certain groups were disposed toward specific attitudes and viewpoints, there might be a way those attitudes could be manipulated, or changed.

As time went on, the computerized numbers on tests and answer sheets, disseminated in chronological batches, made it theoretically possible, at least, to key in on small class sets of fifteen or fewer tests or to tell which teacher gave what batch of tests.

By 1983, the use of social security numbers began rising dramatically in elementary and secondary schools. Younger and younger children were being asked to record their parents' social security numbers on forms. College students, of course, had long been putting their social security numbers on forms, including surveys and standardized tests, which virtually no one challenged because it was more or less assumed that that was the only way to manage enormous amount of paperwork. But the missing children phenomenon coupled with more complex accounting procedures everywhere encouraged legislators to lower the mandatory age for obtaining a social security number, and its use became increasingly convenient.

It was the late Sam J. Ervin, Jr. (D-N.C.) — the old Watergate Committee chairman — and former Attorney General Elliot Richardson who were among the first to key in on potential abuse of the social security number.

The *Washington Post* carried a long story June 19,1974, detailing their concerns. Ervin released the results of a four-year study on "Federal Data Banks and Constitutional Rights." Referring to the 53-page summary of the 4,000-page report, he charged that federal agencies "understate, if not hide, their data banks." The *Post* article discussed the interlinking that was possible even then, and quoted Rep. John E. Moss (D-Calif.) as charging that the system would soon allow government to assemble "dossiers on any individual or institution."

The article also cited a significant report by the American Civil Liberties Union, "Records, Computers, and the Rights of Citizens." In fact, the ACLU referred to the privacy issue at the time as "the son of Watergate." It was even theorized that those overzealous culprits in the Nixon Administration who broke into Daniel Ellsberg's psychiatrist's office could have saved themselves the trouble by going to the MIB computer system — a then-popular source for insurance companies — to uncover such tantalizing tidbits as somebody's alcoholism, sexual deviations, or criminal record.

Ervin's interest in this subject spurred a group of knowledgeable Maryland citizens, Parents Who Care, to go to him in 1973 about what they were seeing in education. The NDN already was disseminating its behavioral-attitudinal contents by that time, and the group had plenty of Show and Tell. Ervin was outraged by many of the learning programs. He called it "the biggest scandal in the history of the United States." But he was even more interested in some of the questions that were being asked of schoolchildren on surveys and tests.

Ervin continued his personal meetings with the group and collected hundreds of documents. As a result, he co-sponsored Amendment 1289 (to Senate Bill 1539) which, he said, "would prevent schools from making guinea pigs out of children and delving into their personal attitudes and privileged information about their families, as has been done in schools throughout the United States."

The bill went nowhere. Ervin was furious and insisted that "a person held in a compulsory environment has a right to be left alone." But just about the time Ervin was prepared to pursue the issue more aggressively, he was named to head the Watergate Committee. After that, his health declined. While he was on the Watergate case, however, an odd thing happened. Ervin's legislative assistant, Anne Sullivan, started to complain that some of the education documentation he had been collecting was "disappearing" from his office. The missing documents were never found, and Sam Ervin died without ever having had a chance to pursue the privacy issue as it related to education.

Using a social security number to link sensitive and private information in non-secure national data banks brings up obvious legal and ethical questions. That the computers housing the data have the capability to align microrecords on individuals monitored by the federal government brings up visions of Big Brother.

In 1988, a parent from the Hopewell School District in Pennsylvania was told her daughter had done poorly on the mathematics portion of an assessment test and would, therefore, have to be "remediated."[64] The parent previously had been led to believe, however, that the test was anonymous, so how, then, could authorities know that her daughter had done poorly? It seems the children were asked one day to obtain their parents' social security numbers, which had then been placed on so-called basic skills tests. Parents in Hopewell never questioned a request for such information; they accepted that their children had forms to fill out.

The Tax Reform Act of 1976 permits state and local governments to use the social security number in administering their tax, drivers license, motor vehicle registration, and welfare payment programs, but, as Anita Hoge discovered, no *legal basis* exists for using it to collect other data, much less to monitor the private domain of individuals.

In May 1988, two General Accounting Office (GAO) reports came out — *Computer Security: Status of Compliance with the Security Act of 1987* and *Information Systems: Agencies Overlook Security Controls During Development*. They reiterated what the Office of Technology Assessment had stated in its embargoed release of two years before — that computer data was not secure. The first report points to the Department of Education's sensitive computer systems (which includes the CES), and the federal agencies' for a total of 53,443 sensitive computer systems, not counting the CIA (which is exempt from the Act). *The Information Systems* report shows that appropriate security measures still were not being incorporated into the development phase of many automated information systems. The report was mentioned in the popular press, but otherwise didn't get any special attention.

These two reports were not the first to receive short shrift. Back in 1983 — at the same time Anita Hoge and her husband were moving to McGuffey School District so that their children might have a healthy, rural, school environment — the government was swamped with complaints from other sources about behavioral education. The Comptroller General was assigned the task of ascertaining whether the federal government was, or wasn't, funding such programs. The GAO published *Questions Persist About Federal Support for Development of Curriculum Materials* and *Behavior Modification Techniques Used in Local Schools.* The research was thorough and admitted quite frankly that, yes, the federal government was funding behavior modification programs and yes, the federal government was involved in funding and promoting curriculum. (Oddly, no mention was made in the report of the legal prohibition against the federal government "establishing curriculum.")

The year 1978 was, in fact, a bumper year for official protests about behavioral goals, tests, and curricular programs. That was the year Senator Orrin Hatch (R-Utah) protected students from psychological tampering with the Protection of Pupil Rights Amendment, which was passed by the Senate and used by Anita Hoge as the basis for her original complaint. It took some strong words to pass such an amendment, and Senator Hatch had them:

> ...The techniques used to change young children's attitudes and values are an invasion of privacy in the first degree, especially in some of the innovative testing questions soliciting young children to pinpoint their father's or mother's faults, or in another ESEA-sponsored program which actually had the students of an elementary school class collectively put their parents on trial — following which the mother and father were always found guilty.... Again, what I am concerned with, as are my colleagues who have co-spon-

sored the parental consent amendment, is not the monitoring of basic education, but of the behavior-probing tests, games, and surveys currently being
conducted....[65]

But that was that. Again, no follow-up. No headlines. Certainly no hype.
Presumably the GAO would not have been assigned to research and write
the report if nobody had questioned the propriety of such activity. What
happened?

When it comes to technical subjects, reporters don't always understand the
significance of what they are reporting, particularly if they don't happen to
write frequently on the same topic. In 1978, the terms like "behavior
modification" sounded technical and didn't draw a lot of attention from
people outside the field. The revolution in the computer industry is another
technical nightmare that results in stories which newspaper editors have to
simplify for lay readers. The fact is, stories on technical developments may
not make it to the popular press at all. It is more likely that a technical story
will go to a specialty publication where, presumably, there is a better
audience for such material. That is what happened to the story of the
education supercomputer: The Elementary and Secondary Integrated Data
System (ESIDS).

Stories involving computers and computer traffic tend to be reported by
technical experts, rather than average reporters. They occur just far enough
apart so that mainstream reporters and average readers (if they read the
articles at all) don't connect them.

Take, for example, a story that appeared in the *Washington Post* science
and editorial section (and was picked up, perhaps, by a dozen other newspapers across the United States), "Networking for the Future," on July 15,
1990. The author of the piece, Senator Al Gore (D-Tenn.), who chairs the
Senate Subcommittee on Science, Technology, and Space, described a
proposal for a "national superhighway for computer information" — a
revolutionary technology in the works that would enable "a school child
[to] plug into the Library of Congress every afternoon and explore the
universe" or "a doctor in Carthage, Tennessee, [to] consult with experts at
the Mayo Clinic in Minnesota on a patient's CAT scan in the middle of an

emergency." Gore went on to describe in relatively uncomplicated terms how already "dozens of separate computer networks link more than 500 universities, laboratories and hospitals throughout the nation." Now, he and other members of Congress and the scientific community are advocating passage of an "information superhighway bill" so that more than one million computers can be linked in some 1,300 locations among the 50 states. That is why he wrote the piece for the newspaper.

Most of the technology to do this already exists; it involves switches, software, and digital libraries that use existing fiber-optic cables to carry the billions of "bits" of information per second required to their destinations. The concept already is old-hat to researchers in the field. "[O]ptical fibers," states Gore, "are the first transmission lines whose capacity can be expanded without laying additional lines." The goal, which sounds worthy enough, is to do, essentially, what was done with the railroad — exploit the existing technology to link people and information. Gore thrusts the reader into an idyllic scenario of the future, when "teams of scientists and engineers could work together in a 'co-laboratory' if their supercomputers were linked."

Congress passed the Supercomputer Network Study Act, which Gore introduced in 1985 — on the thirtieth anniversary of the signing of the Interstate Highway Act. It provided research and development money to the computer field. Today, four Senate committees have endorsed moving forward with the new network, which is billed as "a springboard for [America's] technological leadership" — a good bet since the United States already has "the largest telecommunications system in the world."

Now most people who read Al Gore's piece in the *Post* probably didn't read the more technical versions of the Supercomputer Network that appeared in professional magazines on computer networking, artificial intelligence, and robotics. Similarly, average people don't read specialty publications like health care trade publications or *Education Daily,* in which they might find applications of this same technology.

Certainly the mainstream audience didn't link the work toward an education statistics computer to objectives other than simple recordkeeping. Consequently, there was never an investigative report of what was going on at places like the Center for Education Statistics. Besides, computer security is not considered a "sexy" issue. To understand what went wrong with American education — specifically, how psychological research was misdirected into a scheme to collect personal information and use that information to mold public opinion and create dossiers, all at the expense of real learning — it is helpful to return to 1981, to the old National Institute of Education, where Willard Wirtz and Archie LaPointe coauthored their working paper, "Measuring the Quality of Education." This document can well be considered the philosophical basis for establishing a national, cross-referenceable supercomputer.

There was nothing secret about the project. Every phase over the years — from research on the prototype computer, WICAT,[66] in Utah, to the planning-programming-budgeting system (PPBS) that was piloted in California, to the culmination of years of work toward a federal data Center — was reported in publications like *Education Week*, read primarily by educators and technocrats, of course, with watered-down versions appearing from time to time in mass-audience newspapers like the *Washington Post* and *New York Times*. It was all there, but too few people recognized the connection between the stories.

The Wirtz and LaPointe document makes absolutely clear the connections between the Carnegie Foundation for the Advancement of Teaching, the Educational Testing Service, and the National Assessment (NAEP), along with the work toward a centralized computer bank and the funding arrangements to make it all happen. The paper explains how NAEP could be used by the states to create "their own" assessment tests. It describes the existence and purpose of earlier educational data banks — the Common Core of Data, including the Public School and LEA Universe Files, and the Longitudinal Studies — which most people outside the field knew nothing about. "Measuring the Quality of Education" explains where their data came from and what the data contained. It tells how these data banks would be absorbed into a new system. In a footnote on the Longitudinal Studies, page 6, is a blatant admission about collection of *parent* attitudes:

...achievement data are not the primary focus of the studies, which also collect data on educational attainment, student characteristics and attitudes, parent attitudes, and school programs.

Moreover, "Measuring the Quality of Education" makes no bones at all about the attitudinal nature of much of the data already collected — or of data that would be collected in the future. Indeed, it is clear from the paper that the authors know they are getting into some very touchy areas:

> Getting into the students' personal characteristics and situations invariably prompts warnings that the NAEP purpose is not to analyze human development, and injunctions against confusing the measurement of educational results (outcomes) and the analysis of cause (inputs). But it is being recognized increasingly that the measuring of achievement is incomplete without an accompanying identification of whatever educational circumstances may affect these results.

The Wirtz and LaPointe paper shows that its writers are aware of possible political fallout over attitudinal data collection — not to mention local control and funding issues — which they addressed elsewhere. Wirtz and LaPointe appear so sure of themselves that they gloss over the warning signs of trouble; they already have formulated their rationale for "getting into students' personal characteristics." Moreover, the authors maintain that this and other potential sore points, like local control, can be overcome with enough money and the right public relations policy.

They were right.

Data collection proponents like Wirtz and LaPointe and their colleagues at the National Center for Education Statistics (now, CES; the word "national" was removed from the agency title in 1985) had long insisted that data from earlier computer banks, like the Common Core of Data and the Longitudinal Studies, was "inadequate to provide policymakers and practitioners with the information they need to address ... key questions about education." Almost annually, they decried the lack of a central source, or "clearinghouse," and the difficulties of comparability, integration, and monitoring education systems.

In 1985 another enlightening paper surfaced, this one out of the Office of Educational Research and Improvement (OERI)[67] called "Alternatives for a National Data System of Elementary and Secondary Education."[68] It was the proposal for a national, linkable data collection system in elementary and secondary education — a "national educational information system" of the type alluded to in the earlier Wirtz and LaPointe paper.

The proposal's authors set out a model and two basic alternatives for setting up the system, suggest which agencies should be involved, what the system ought to accomplish, who would have access to it, and how it should be paid for. They do not give the computer system a name at this time, but they do break ground for the most important parameters of the system, which got underway a year later.

Right away, in Chapter 1, the "Alternatives" authors establish a rationale for the system: universal dissatisfaction with the quality of elementary and secondary education; a dissatisfaction so pervasive as to force major changes and new decisions; the need for massive reforms.

Then the coup — the thing that behaviorist extremists and turf-conscious bureaucrats worked toward for more than 15 years: a decent burial for the concept of local control (thus the emphasis).

No longer do these decisions fall within the exclusive purview of local school boards and local school administrators.

Fortunately for supercomputer proponents, the recent *A Nation at Risk* and *The Nation's Report Card* publications lent an urgency to their pleas. The public was suddenly aware just how poorly American students were doing thanks to excellent journalistic reporting on the two booklets. The do-something-even-if-it's-wrong mentality took over, and it became relatively easy to sell the idea that testing and centralized computerization were the way to "reform" education.

The bold, new system is to be built, states the "Alternatives" paper, around the format of a microrecord, which is defined as "a datum on an individual person or an individual entity." No longer is the Department of Education to concern itself with mere group comparisons and trend analyses; henceforth, it will zero in on "individual persons and individual entities." Further on down page 60, under Privacy and Security, the authors comment that some "elements, records, and files [will] contain information about individuals" and that "personal identifiers" will be necessary. Although the need for confidentially and security measures is mentioned in the same sentence, the following page states that since privacy and security have not come up as a problem in earlier reports on the National Center for Education Statistics, there is no reason to expect it to be a problem in the future. Throughout the rest of the paper there is every indication that access to the new data system is to be made easy, that the information is to be infinitely linkable with other computer systems, and that there will be virtually no limits on who has access to what. The authors envision "a network of channels linking potential users to each other and to the data base" with the same ease as they might set up a telephone conference at a business meeting.

CHAPTER 25

Of Men and Microchips

THE MICRORECORD IS different from the older, more commonly used aggregate record. The latter is a summary of many records, so that one is left with an overview and generalities, rather than specifics. In the old Common Core of Data, for example, there was not room to give chapter and verse on each year of a student's school life, or each teacher and school course or activity. All that changes with the microrecord, however, which is more like a tracking or accounting system than a summary.

If one entered into a data base the records for each employee in a company, or a high school catalogue containing information on each course taught, or a transcript for every pupil in a particular school, each of these categories would be considered a "basic" file, or microrecord.

The new data base proposal for education includes a long list of categories and even subcategories. There are *pupil files* containing personal information about "the child's family background and home environment," including community and family characteristics, as well as special needs, difficulties, activities, pursuits, and experiences. Results of attitudinal surveys and tests like the NAEP will also be included so that other affective information, like opinions, can be extracted. These will be linked to *personnel files* on teachers, which include information about salary, position, responsibilities, credentials, employment history, and participation in educational activities of the district. All these will be linked, in turn, to *school files*, which is an in-depth look at characteristics of the immediate community (or neighborhood) served by the individual school, and to *district files,* which describe the characteristics of the larger community, such as how much money it has and the various sources through which that money comes. All this information, and more, is to be made interlinkable, not only with each other, but with statistical records in computers at the Census Bureau, the National Center for Health Statistics, and so on.

"Only microrecords for personnel, pupils, and activities can produce the kinds of analyses and reports necessary to inform and evaluate . . . new policy initiatives," states the "Alternatives" paper.

What can be accomplished with a data base like this? Just by processing individual pupil records to the level of the school, the district, the state, and nationally, analysts can see test averages, course taking patterns, and home environmental characteristics — not just for a group or community of students, but for *individual* students. Students can be tracked from kindergarten through college and on into the job force. Teacher characteristics can be linked, too — via course taking — to pupil performance. This means the teacher has to teach the objectives, the tests must be scored for these particular objectives, and tests must reflect these objectives. Thus there is a three-way control mechanism in place that affects teachers every bit as much as students.

The "Alternatives" paper proposes two basic ways for the federal government to get this information from every school district and every individual school, including private ones, in the nation. Option A is an integrated survey approach to gathering information on state and local education agencies, individual schools, teachers, students, and households. The method would involve interviews by highly trained personnel sent out to America's cities and towns from the federal level. They would conduct their interviews in person, by telephone, and by mail using questionnaires and "other instruments." Under Alternative A, data is supplied directly to a Federal Data Center from the survey site and doesn't make a pit stop at state or local headquarters. The federal government does all the work, and the state does not have to alter its current data collection methods (although it will be urged to do so anyway and will give in in the end).

Under Alternative B, states are to use their own management information systems, revamping them if necessary, so they will link up and be compatible with the federal Center system. The revamped state systems will go into place in successive stages. Under this option, the states get a first look at their own data, and they get money from the federal government to update their systems.

There are various levels of participation in between the two options, but none in which a state or school can "just say no."

Page 87 of the"Alternatives" paper posits that once "all 50 states adopt a common management information system, state and federal needs . . . could be accommodated through the state systems and the need for federally-operated data acquisition projects would be eliminated." What isn't stated in the proposition is that it is in the political interests of the federal government to mandate large-scale data collection so that it looks like a state initiative — and as soon as possible.

According to the proposal, however, the new data base will be federally maintained and operated. Sooner or later all schools and school districts will have to comply. Should a state fail to force them, the federal government will take on the job. Thus if a state's officials want any say about anything, they had better jump on the bandwagon and not wait to be coaxed. (Private schools, one surmises, will lose accreditation, not to mention any federal funds, if they opt out.)

Unsurprisingly, the Council of Chief State School Officers (CCSSO) is called to "establish a consortium of all states and develop an agenda for identifying specific information . . . and data elements required for the system." The federal Center, however, will be responsible for staffing the consortium and establishing working groups. The Powers That Be don't want any heretics among the troops.

To get the states' cooperation on a nationalized computer system, its designers knew they were going to need help. Fortunately, that consideration had already been addressed with a contract between the CES and the CCSSO, to get the states moving on computerizing their records.

Recall the chief state school officers and their Position Paper at their 1984 annual meeting in Wilmington, Delaware.[69] It established that two of the most important functions of the organization were going to be, first, providing technical assistance to the state education agencies (the SEAs) for developing new data systems, and second, "promot[ing] coordination among international, national, and state assessment programs." The CCSSO accomplished this feat by presenting the baffled SEAs with a long and technical must-do list. States had to substantially increase the comparability of their data, standardize terms and definitions, and then break down information into four categories (for input into a data base) — resources, teaching strategies, student characteristics, and policy. They had to report a "core set of indicators" annually and align programs with one another, while the CCSSO decided how to refine the data so as to "promote coordination among international, national, and state assessment programs." The ultimate aim of all this, stated page 9 of the 1984 Position Paper, was to establish criteria which, over an approximately five-year period, would result in states testing a *common set* of grades, skills, and attitudes.

The key, as always, was NAEP, along with one other thing: *legislative changes* in the various states to "assist" (read "ensure") their timely response.

Costs for the new system, of course, were expected to be astronomical and therefore shared by federal, state, and local education agencies (which by that time would be pretty much one and the same anyway), with the higher distribution of costs usually falling to the federal government. But tax dollars are tax dollars any way you look at it, so in the end the bill is footed by the taxpayer. Near the end of the "Alternatives" paper, the authors point out that "most, if not all, of the data collection formats for elements required in the early phases of implementation . . . already exist within current Center data programs (e.g. NAEP . . .)." This serves as a reminder that NAEP is not about mere academic testing but, rather, is a first step toward a permanent, interlinkable dossier and data bank on the nation's citizens — and a way of imposing a national curriculum.

Very little appeared in the press in 1985 about the proposed data collection scheme. Neither political faction, liberal or conservative, had much to say. Only one lone voice over at the "conservative" Heritage Foundation raised an eyebrow at the expensive — and expansive — proposal. Even the usually vocal National Education Association on the liberal side, which had for years taken a position against testing, was strangely silent.

Then, in 1986, *Education Week* reported on the new generation of educational computers, with the headline "'Radical' Overhaul Offered for E. D. [Education Dept.] Data Collection." The story reported "a proposal [that] would allow researchers and policymakers for the first time to examine all nationally collected data on a state-by-state and even classroom-by-classroom basis" with "an unprecedented level of federal, state, and local cooperation."

By the time that story appeared, however, another landmark paper had come out, this one by the Center for Education Statistics: "A Plan for the Redesign of the Elementary and Secondary Data Collection Program."

It sounded like a follow-up to the 1985 "Alternatives" paper — as though the government had already started work on the system. What was new was that the data system now had a name: The Elementary and Secondary Integrated Data System, or ESIDS.

Like the 1985 proposal, the CES paper described a cross-referenceable computer system that combines millions of previously existing records with still more coming in from the states through testing programs like the Educational Quality Assessment, and its successor, the Pennsylvania Assessment System. The key, again, is the "microrecord" that permits linkages on individual students, teachers, and learning programs (or "strands"). Under the new system, teachers, students, and courses could be "monitored."

With the 1981 Wirtz and LaPointe paper, Office of Educational Research and Improvement's 1985 "Alternatives" paper, and this last, 1986 CES paper side by side, the first seems to be a trailblazer for the actual proposal, to see just how much flak there is going to be. The 1985 paper is just what it appears to be: a proposal; whereas the 1986 "Plan" sounds like a *fait accompli.*

Meanwhile, the *Washington Post* reported on May 11, 1986, that while the federal government could not require a state to computerize its records, it could craft its regulations in such a way as to make it prohibitively expensive or impossible for states to meet federal requirements unless they did so. This small, but significant, mention should have signaled trouble. But investigative journalists were still asleep.

Even as far back as 1969, Walcott Beatty wrote in *Improving Educational Assessment and an Inventory of Measures of Affective Behavior,* that federal funding for schools would hinge on data collection at the local level and that the use of NAEP objectives in obtaining this data was important. Like Wirtz and LaPointe twelve years later, Beatty emphasized that the arrangement must avoid the appearance of establishing a national test or curriculum.[70] Wirtz and LaPointe show how terribly sensitive this issue continued to be when they wrote on page 13 of "Measuring the Quality of Education" that "[s]pecial precautions were taken against [NAEP's] appearing a step, taken under Federal Government auspices, toward 'standardizing' American education." Page 20 expands the point:

> Arrangements can be made for the inclusion in a state assessment instrument of enough National Assessment [NAEP] items to make possible a comparison of state with national results. State officers can . . . use all or part of a NAEP instrument for their own assessment purposes . . . .

> Other possibilities of reciprocal arrangements might involve building into the National Assessment sample some of the students assessed as part of a state program. These prospects go beyond cooperation with the states to include comparable opportunities involving local school systems.

> ...It remains important, both politically and administratively, that the Assessment's principal clients are not the Federal government but, rather, whatever is meant by "the public"....

What was not understood for a time was why a National Assessment is still needed if states can be cajoled into having their own assessment and turning over their data to a central source in Washington. Since it was obvious that the federal agency wanted to make testing look like a state initiative, while the federal agency kept a low profile, it didn't seem to make sense to keep the NAEP going.

But since the NAEP was around *before* the state tests (and there were still states and districts within states that had not been bullied into starting "their own" assessment), federal authorities may have been just plain reluctant to give it up. In fact, the NAEP took on an additional role: that of overseer. If a state's results showed marked differences from NAEP results of the same population group, then perhaps school districts there were not complying fully with federal/state education mandates. Maybe they were not remediating ("recycling") students as often as they should, or something else. Moreover, if, for political reasons, the data had to come through the states for the whole scheme to work, there had to be some mechanism that was independent of the states to oversee what they did.

Today, the NAEP assumes more importance than ever — to the tune of a whopping $18.4 million. As George H. Johnson of the Educational Testing Service indicated as far back as 1974:

> ...NAEP staff can serve as a catalytic influence to promote interpretive activities.... A number of activities are contemplated, such as sponsoring work groups, reaction panels, or study groups made up of educational specialists and lay people...working with curriculum projects and publishers of instructional materials....[71]

This foreshadows a 1984 prediction of the Chief State School Officers:

> Ideally, one can imagine a perfect world in the future when one program of student testing and . . . data collection would provide everyone from the classroom teacher to the international analyst with the information they need to do their work.

It was former Education Secretary William J. Bennett (former "drug czar" in the Bush Administration) who, according to several newspaper accounts, moved to expand the NAEP so as "to include more students in more subjects and provide state-by-state and reliable private school data for the first time." A 22-member panel appointed by Bennett and headed by former Tennessee Governor Lamar Alexander (now himself Education Secretary) recommended a sixfold increase for NAEP in 1987. It was reported in the *Washington Post* that ETS conducts the test and that "[u]nder the new program, the number of students tested would increase from 70,000 in each subject to nearly 700,000." The panel also called for expanding the NAEP to more subject areas. Chester Finn, then Bennett's Deputy Undersecretary, continues to be one of NAEP's staunchest supporters. In 1989 he came out publicly in favor of a national curriculum, something he indicated he didn't believe in just three years before.

Despite appearances, it is doubtful that Secretary Bennett ever examined the contents of either the NAEP or the NDN computer personally, although someone in his position never admits such a thing. The fact is, most cabinet-level secretaries are kept too busy to get into specifics and depend on staff to do it. That is why staff has become so important in recent years. Lofty, appointed positions, like Secretary, increasingly tend to be political and to serve as mouthpieces for Administration policy and as public relations point-men and -women.

Staffers, therefore, frequently view themselves as the ones who actually do the work, and in many cases it is true — too much so, perhaps. The career people are there, of course, from Administration to Administration, Republican or Democrat, Liberal or Conservative or Moderate, doing their thing. They construct the language of bills and legislation. They know the rationales behind the words. They have their own axes to grind — which are sometimes at odds with the political appointees they serve. Consequently, the quip about giving "the appearance of doing something," even if one has no intention of doing anything, has become a standard joke among governments, democratic and otherwise.

Occasionally, of course, it all backfires — as in the case of Watergate, Irangate, and numerous other scandals. A staffer blows the whistle. Politically appointed underlings sometimes deliberately mislead their superiors in an attempt "to serve two masters." Or an administrative aide might decide to do some personal investigating. As a result, some go out on a controversial limb, as did Education Undersecretary Gary Bauer, when he publicly lambasted social science textbook publishers, and U.S. Department of Education Region VI Representative, Thomas G. Tancredo, at the time he published his legal staffer's (Gregg L. Cunningham) scathing indictment of so-called global education programs, itemizing exactly what was in them.

But such whistle-blowing is the exception in government rather than the rule. One can easily jeopardize a career — and maybe even one's life — by too much prying or outspokenness in the wrong place at the wrong time.

Cunningham had to find new employment, despite the fact that the Education Secretary was supposedly in his camp. Others have had death threats and other forms of harassment. It's risky business.

Nowadays, NAEP officials like Archie LaPointe are toadying to think-tanks and policy groups in Washington with claims that the Governing Board of NAEP is becoming more representative (politically?) and that ETS has gotten out of a lot of the testing — apparently to defuse charges of monopoly in testing programs. Along the same lines, carefully worded releases have come out in the press to the effect that the government is seeking *bids* to conduct an "expanded" NAEP. The implication is that ETS will have some competition.

But proctoring, scoring, and analyzing a test is not the same thing as creating it. News accounts do not say the NAEP is going to be revamped or thrown out. The term "expanded NAEP" merely means larger and more often. What competitors sometimes bid on is the proctoring, scoring and statistical analysis, like Westat, for example, in Nebraska and other states.[72] The fact is, ETS is contracting out in many states. Of course, the organization helped create the tests in many instances, and in so doing they ensured that state assessments would complement and/or borrow heavily from the national test. Efforts to move the NAEP into private and parochial schools are progressing, too. Even die-hard Christian Fundamentalist schools are succumbing to carefully worded ploys about how testing and technology, together, will allow school administrators to know how well their teachers and students are doing. Dr. Norbert Matts, who runs Dr. Jerry Falwell's private Christian schools, was busily examining sample NAEP tests in 1989, with a view to possibly including them in Lynchburg, Virginia's, Christian academies.

Different pitch. Same results. As soon as a private or parochial school is locked in, behaviorist extremists and their helpmates at the federal level will descend like vultures, with a shopping list in hand.

In any event, the system is in place. The test will continue to reflect the behavioral objectives ETS created. It matters not a whit who owns NAEP now, whether ETS continues its involvement with the test, or whether some other organization gets ETS' contracts. Curricular programs are already linked to NAEP and learning programs are linked with textbook publishers and disseminated through the NDN. Many companies can run a computer and analyze results.

Behaviorist extremists know this. They know they hold all the "aces" and are in a position to do as they please, including determine whatever "quality" is supposed to mean as they go along. Page 16 of "Measuring the Quality of Education" conveys a decided smugness:

> Those in charge of the Assessment are in a position to guide their policies entirely by the determination of whatever "quality" means. They face no competition and are subject to no political pressures. Innovation and experimentation are part of the Assessment's authentic tradition. It can provide...courage in the implementation of the new national purpose to impose educational standards.
>
> Its [the NAEP's] administrators have pioneered and innovated and experimented. They are in a position to provide critically important service functions to state and local educational testing and assessment agencies...
>
> [A]n educational standards policy depends for its effectiveness on the perfection of "value judgment" elements in measuring educational achievement; and this can be best attempted by an independent agency working from a nationwide base.

The "independent agency" alluded to in the last line is CFAT/ETS.

CHAPTER 26

Target Practice

TODAY, TEST RESULTS — including family information and something called "family problem" data — go into state and, ultimately, into national data banks at the Center for Education Statistics. Until 1988, that might have meant any one of several older computers: most likely the Common Core of Data, the Universe Files, or the Longitudinal Studies. But with the new supercomputer, the ESIDS, files can be merged and cross-referenced with any number of other federal record-keeping devices, not to mention state records: motor vehicle registration records, county marriage and divorce records, housing (Register of Deeds) records, IRS records, criminal records, the State Data Exchange Network, credit records, and on and on. Even insurance records (including medical) and pharmaceutical records increasingly are being computerized and linked to other computerized information. Ever more linkages are made annually among different types of data.[73]

Many commercial firms provide time-sharing arrangements where the customer pays by usage. No questions are asked. Profit and non-profit multinational organizations use various private circuits for their internal communications worldwide. Take any bank issuing VISA or Mastercard: A large bank might use as many as three satellites to provide their headquarters with instantaneous access to operations on four continents. Or a large airline: How is it a person can change an airline ticket in Bangkok, even if he bought it in Billings?

Smaller companies can, in turn, plug into larger corporations' terminals for a modest fee. In many countries, like Britain, an average person at home can order up on the television screen hundreds of different data bases, simply by using the telephone. The charges are added to the phone bill.

Moreover, the merging of computer and communications technologies is facilitating direct transfers of sensitive personal data, without the subject's prior knowledge and consent. How will American citizens be protected against the exploitive use of computerized data in foreign countries if they are not even protected in this country?

Interestingly, NAEP tests have given professionals other than behavioral scientists, educational theorists, and company managers[74] something new to play with. A highly placed source in the NAEP organization, for example, said that data is being sold to just about any domestic or international group billing itself as a research organization. The Pennsylvania Group discovered that in one U.S. locality, authorities wanted to expand a local airport, but expected to encounter resistance. So they had a marketing research firm buy into attitudinal assessment data to get an idea how to craft an approach to win support of area residents for the planned expansion.

Here is additional evidence that attitudes assessed from school children are reflecting to greater or lesser degrees the views of their parents. It is not particularly comforting to consider that the same approach used to market an airport might also be used to "market" a political candidate for public office.

On January 20, 1991, the *Washington Post's* business section ran two articles, "Peering Into Private Lives" and "Keeping Tabs on Card Holders." Both articles confirmed what many have already suspected: that non-secure data banks are linking information on demographic, and other, groups of individuals (in these articles, for marketing research purposes) and that the newest wave of technology may soon make it possible to build dossiers that include information on lifestyles, personal habits, and just about anything else. As you read the following excerpt, keep in mind what is already possible using the attitude collection data from school assessment tests and surveys, particularly the latest models that include the social security number, which of course serves as an identifier:[75]

Until recently,...profiles [on individuals] have been available only to a few big retailers, banks and other credit services willing to pay handsomely for the right to take advantage of them.

But that could change dramatically this spring if Lotus Development Corp. follows through on plans to bring out a controversial product that has the potential to put lifestyle, demographic and income estimates of about 80 million American households into the hands of almost anyone who wants it.

A joint effort with the credit agency Equifax Inc., the product is a compact disc that would hold the names, addresses, approximate income levels and personal buying habits of people nationwide. It would mark the first time that the mammoth databases of credit bureaus and marketing powerhouses would be married with the personal computer — a combination that is fueling questions about individuals' rights to privacy because it vastly expands how and by whom such data can be used.

Lotus says it has been barraged by some 30,000 callers and letter-writers who believe the product is a clear invasion of their privacy and don't want their names included in its data bases....

What has privacy advocates concerned is that the Lotus product appears to be moving the nation a bit closer to a day when all the information on one person could be gathered in one place and then easily retrieved, sold or manipulated by virtually anyone.

Today there is no simple way to retrieve all the information stored about a single individual simply by punching that person's name into a computer. While data about a person's credit-worthiness, criminal record or driving history can be easily obtained electronically, information about an individual's lifestyle and other personal buying habits is retrieved only as part of a group of people with like characteristics.

The new compact disc..."opens a window of vulnerability," said Evan Hendricks, the Washington publisher of *Privacy Times*, a newsletter on privacy issues. *"Once they have established this precedent, there is nothing to stop the next guy from selling anything he wants [for use on personal computers], from your Christmas purchases to your genetic history."*

With the Lotus disc, a small business would essentially build a profile of the type of customers most likely to respond to its sales pitch...The computer would digest all the desired traits and then spew out a tailor-made list of residents in a certain neighborhood, including their addresses.

Information for the disc was gleaned from 40 different sources, including the U.S. Census, Internal Revenue Service, Postal Service, and surveys taken at 8,500 shopping centers and retailers nationwide. As one of the country's largest credit bureaus, Equifax has also drawn on its own records, which contain specific information about a person's marital status, sex, age range, and likely income level.

In essence, the company creates "a profile of an individual based on their credit files," said Robert Hilles, an Equifax vice president. The most sensitive information...is blended with that of nearby households to build a general profile for each neighborhood....

...Lotus vows to sell "Marketplace: Households," as the product is known, only to businesses *and nonprofit groups,* although it admits policing that process will be a difficult task.

The portions italicized here for emphasis warrant a second look. In the seventh paragraph, the *Privacy Times* publisher mentions setting a precedent. He may not know it, but one may already have been set — if the NAEP has, in fact, been selling data to research groups for some time.

The ninth paragraph mentions the 40 different sources from which information was garnered for the new product. Notice that the IRS is one of them — and IRS records utilize the social security number as an identifier.

Notice also that the article did not say that it was *impossible* to retrieve information about a single individual today, by "punching a name into a computer." It said there "is no *simple* way" to accomplish it. The point is that one may not need a name at all, but only a number to identify an individual.

And just who are the "nonprofit groups" to which the final paragraph in the excerpt alludes? Is it assumed here that nonprofit groups are automatically benign? This writer could find no one who was willing to assure that education-related nonprofit groups inside and outside of government would not be considered as legitimate markets for the Lotus data.

"Peering Into Private Lives" provides additional insight as to how Americans are categorized by computer:

Particularly useful for marketers are the handful of huge databases that profile nearly all Americans. In the computers of TRW Inc., which operates both a credit bureau and a marketing information service, . . . any one of 150 million Americans can be characterized in up to 600 different categories. Some categories describe easily obtainable data . . . . Other traits are more personal. Based on previous mail-order purchases you've made, TRW may classify you as a health and fitness fanatic, a fishing enthusiast or a literary scholar.

Another database is alluded to further on, National Demographics & Lifestyles, a Denver company, which has detailed the characteristics of some 30 million people from buyers' returned product registration forms.

Why wouldn't surveys and questionnaires returned by schoolchildren not also be entered into a data bank and cross-referenced? Personal and attitudinal information (which, again, tends to reflect the parents' views), gathered over many years of the child's school life, may soon determine, if it hasn't already, whether an otherwise qualified student is accepted or rejected by the college of his/her choice, whether a student is turned down for employment, whether a person is later passed over for a promotion, or a dozen other things that can occur many years after the child is grown up and the survey, test, or form in question is forgotten.

The second January 20 article in the *Post*, "Keeping Tabs on Card Holders," explains how data is used to predict which groups of accounts are likely to become delinquent. To do this, the computer assimilates data on personal buying habits, characteristics, and traits to see which combination tends to contribute to eventual delinquent payment and which do not. The horror stories from people who have come out on the losing end of a computer system — one that somehow confuses two identical, or similar, names — underscore the validity of concerns about privacy and potential abuses of personal data:[76]

...there is a good chance that the computer not only took note of your [Visa or Mastercard] payment, it gave it some thought. Like whether you paid the bill on time and maybe even what merchants you dealt with.

The reason it did all this was simple: The bank that issued you your credit card is a lot more interested in you than it used to be. . . .

...Though civil libertarians and others concerned with privacy issues worry about the potential for disseminating data to people who might abuse it, the banks regard these efforts as a key tool to remaining profitable in an intensely competitive environment.

Personal information is frequently collected for any number of purposes —
and by organizations that would amaze many people. Take, for example,
the results of an exercise research study conducted by the Institute for
Aerobics Research (Cooper Clinic) in Dallas from 1970 to 1985. The
physical fitness of 10,224 men and 3,120 women was measured over this
time period, and the results appeared first in *The Journal of the American
Medical Association.* Participants were given questionnaires to fill out over
the period in question in order to obtain the statistics, but some of the
participants didn't respond and had to be tracked down. Here's how it was
done:

> Most of the subjects were white college graduates employed in professional,
> executive or white-collar positions....Those who didn't respond to follow-up
> questionnaires were bird-dogged via the Social Security Administration's
> files, the Department of Motor Vehicles in the subject's state of residence, a
> nationwide credit bureau network and the more recent National Death Index.

International organizations repeatedly have documented the use of NAEP
data. The purpose, according to CFAT and Department of Education
officials, is to promote international coordination and comparisons of data.
The major organizations involved in this effort are the International Education Achievement Organization (IEA) in Sweden; the Organization of
Economic Cooperation and Development (OECD) and UNESCO, both
based in Paris; the Committee on Coordinating Educational Information and
Research (CEIR), which is part of the CCSSO in the United States; and the
U.S. Department of Education's Office of Educational Research and Improvement (OERI).*

Two of the most revealing papers about such transborder data flow are
"NAEP and International Comparisons" by Richard M. Wolf (Columbia
University) and UNESCO's "Development of Educational Technology in
Central and Eastern Europe."[77] They are worth the read for the similarity

---

*   For background on the OERI and OECD, see endnote 67.

of terms and to understand the direction this international "cooperation" in education is taking.

A more immediate question, however, is whether national security is being violated. Whose laws will all these various countries be abiding by when it comes to "privacy" considerations and Fourth Amendment rights — ours or theirs? How will these countries use our data, and how will we use theirs? Will the United States work to make foreign systems compatible with ours — to "facilitate" transfer of data — in the same way the U.S. Department of Education got the CCSSO to facilitate transfer of state data banks to the federal Center?

Given the personal and attitudinal nature of data-trafficking that is going on in this country,[78] the possibility of an international database containing such information — a kind of Interpol on average citizens — is not amusing. What would, say, Iran[79] or Iraq do with information like this? Cuba? The Soviet Union?[80]

Any way you look at it, the non-secure, cross-referenceability of large numbers of federal and state computer banks portends a massive government dossier-building capability. With the addition of attitudinal and psychological data, any political, religious, social, racial, or geographical group can be targeted for change — for psychological manipulation — under the present system, just as it stands. Once the requirement for a social security number is lowered to newborns — an event that appears imminent — behaviorists will be able to single out ("target") individuals of any age for psychological exploitation.

Part
VII:
HOW TEACHER EDUCATION WAS REVAMPED

CHAPTER 27:

Where the Bucks Are: The Big Push in Behavioral Science

THE MEN AND women who conceived the re-design of American education are, as indicated, primarily psychologists who specialize in the behavioral sciences. But there is a unique breed in this field who are heavily into what is known as the "futurist movement." They are not the only ones into futurism. Many businessmen and even politicians are into it, too; for example, Senator Claiborne Pell (D-R.I.), Chairman of the Education Subcommittee, has attempted time and again to pass legislation promoting the views of "the Human Potential Movement" — a quasi-religious futurist cult.[81] He even has a full-time staff member researching psychic phenomena. The World Affairs Council also is heavily involved in the futurist movement, especially in education.

Not every behavioral psychologist is a futurist, any more than, say, every science fiction writer is a futurist. To further complicate matters, not everyone who latches on to the futurist label is into its more extreme aspects. Space program enthusiasts, for example, have a club with the futurist label. But most members are more interested in building colonies in space than any kind of social engineering. So making generalizations about who is and who is not into futurist cultism is touchy business, although some fields do tend to attract the fanatics.

The Carnegie Foundation for the Advancement of Teaching, as well as two other Carnegie organizations that help fund one another — Carnegie Corporation (banking and finance) and Carnegie Endowment for International Peace (international politics) — has long supported futurist extremist causes. Unfortunately, all three organizations are so well-heeled financially and highly placed politically (since as far back as 1911) that they are entrusted by nearly every administration, Republican and Democrat, with performing all sorts of vital functions, from negotiating foreign treaties with the Soviet Union to setting policy in education.

Futurism is by no means a U.S. phenomenon. Great Britain and Australia, for example, have their futurist proponents in very high places, including education. On January 23, 1990, Lady Caroline Cox from Great Britain's House of Lords addressed a packed room at the Russell Senate Office Building in Washington, D.C., concerning the behaviorist education trends in her country, and in 1988, the popular show *60 Minutes* aired a segment from England on psychologically manipulative education. Parents who were interviewed let the education establishment have it with both barrels.

It should be emphasized that behaviorist fanatics are *not* necessarily Communists, nor do they see themselves as such. They do, however, appropriate some elements of Marxist philosophy. Behaviorist extremists are not out to destroy the United States, nor are they against freedom. Their concept of freedom, however, is different from the norm. Freedom to them means to be liberated from hunger, worry, job loss, and the like. In other words, futurists are not Jeffersonian democrats. The "rugged individualist" vision of freedom is not theirs. In the extreme futurist view, the individual is not the all-in-all that is portrayed in Western novels. Futurists believe the interests of the individual can best be served by the collective. Therefore the collective good is considered more important than the individual good. With that, any similarity to a Marxist ideal ends.

In 1948 Dwight D. Eisenhower, in an "Open Letter to America's Students" that appeared in Reader's Digest, remarked: "If your generation fails to understand that the individual is still the center of the universe and is still the sole reason for all man-made institutions, then the complexity of life will become chaos."

Futurists would take great exception to that statement. In fact, they would turn it around. They would say that if our generation fails to understand that man*kind* (in the collective sense) is the center of the universe and the reason for all man-made institutions, then the individual will not be able to cope at all, and life will become chaos.

That is why futurist fanatics — those individuals we are talking about here — believe that a representative democracy such as is practiced in the United States, or even a participatory democracy, is not a viable model for the future. Rather, they argue that the checks-and-balances concept of multi-governing bodies is confusing, wasteful of time, and inefficient. They dislike the terms "capitalism" and "competition," too, as these seem to lead to grasping ambition — a success-at-any-price mentality. Futurist extremists equate this negative human characteristic with the rich getting richer and the poor falling through the cracks. According to them, nobody should have to pull themselves up by their own bootstraps in a free society.

To help eradicate the trend toward what they see as blind ambition, planned change is steered very deliberately *away* from the concept of excellence and *toward* "functional literacy" (or "minimum competency").

About the best definition around of "literacy" comes from Michael Brunner, a top-notch expert on phonics and reading instruction, formerly with the National Institute of Education at the U.S. Department of Education. He currently heads up a team to brainstorm workable, phonics-based literacy programs for juvenile offenders.

Brunner describes *literacy* as "the ability of individuals to read and write what they can talk about, hear, and understand." The word *functional* connotes "usefulness." Thus "functional *il*literacy" means the *in*ability to put this knowledge, however skimpy, to use. It means a person may be able to read the traffic signs on a freeway (and possibly pass a driving test), but not be able to do anything more advanced, such as follow a written set of directions or write a coherent paragraph about the importance of safe driving. "Functional illiteracy" in the nontechnical sense is usually taken to mean the inability to read at all; but technically, it means that while a person may be literate in the sense that he or she can recognize enough words to get by, this word recognition *per se* will be of little practical use, and all school subjects eventually will be affected.

Thus "minimum competency" is the *least* amount of knowledge a person can get by with and still be said to have passed a course. This minimum can be set anywhere officials choose. If they select "functional literacy" as the standard for passing a course, a student may go from one grade to the next without having gained anything from the various courses outside of a vague idea concerning what they were about.

The following example shows how a minimum competency standard in reading (particularly using the look-say method) can be as bad as out and out illiteracy, and it shows, by implication, what happens to a youngster's self-esteem as a result. Look at these random sentences taken from two typical textbooks:

> Thomas Jefferson was the first president to be inaugurated in Washington.

> As the *Spirit of St. Louis* touched down on the turf, the crowds surged toward it.

Using the look-say approach, which, remember, is based on sight memory and context clues, a minimally competent student might read these lines as:

> *Thomas Jefferson was the first president to be assassinated in Washington.*

> *As the* Spirit of St. Louis *rolled along the surf, the cowards surged toward it.*

The student will, of course, do poorly on his test — even though he did, in fact, read his assignment. Worse, however, is that because of the nature of his errors, the rest of the paragraphs in both selections will make no sense to him. Why was Thomas Jefferson assassinated? he will wonder fleetingly. The rest of the selection seems to indicate the man lived on a good while! And did the Spirit of St. Louis have water-landing gear? Why did cowards go up to it instead of away from it? And so on.

Passed on from grade to grade, this student eventually will throw up his hands in exasperation because nothing in any of his classes makes sense.

With this in mind, look at a quotation from the all-important Wirtz and LaPointe paper. It seems to be suggesting, in effect, that educational standards be set at the very *minimum level* possible, or functional literacy:

A different kind of assessment would help correct the tilt in the educational standards concept toward functional literacy and away from excellence.

Repugnant though this statement may be, it does not, however, translate to mean that futurists are against all free enterprise and privatization. Indeed, futurist extremists believe that socialism and capitalism can be combined, and they have coined a term for it: *free-market socialism*. This is the soft-sell term for "democratic socialism," the model, apparently, for future governments. Under free-market, or "democratic," socialism, the best of both worlds join hands for the common good: government-guaranteed incomes, jobs, medical care, housing and food coexist with certain well-regulated, quasi-privatized industries and businesses that do not lend themselves to government ownership and control. Proponents also are helping to move nations toward a worldwide currency, which they hope will replace old national currencies like pesos, marks, francs, and dollars. Such a move, of course, would also make both money and people easier for government to keep track of.

Futurists tend to be against nationalism. They believe national boundaries should be eliminated. National boundaries, they claim, have been the cause of wars throughout time (a good example, they will claim, is Iraq under Saddam Hussein), and the way to permanent peace is to get rid of sovereign nations. Toward that end, *it is in the interests of the futurist movement to create a generation of cultural illiterates.*

Futurists believe the world needs people who will not be eager to focus on those constant reminders of nationalistic pride: the common store of heroes and villains, stories and poems, and other culturally based ideas and attitudes (including the Constitution and the Bill of Rights)[82] which make for emotional ties to homeland and nationality.

In fact, two organizations which today have a tremendously large say in matters of curriculum and textbooks (along with the government's Labs and Centers) — the Association for Supervision and Curriculum Development and the National Council for Social Studies[83] — joined in a cooperative venture shortly after the second World War to study how to change elementary and secondary attitudes toward nationalism. The result of their study was a large book, *Education for International Understanding in American Schools*. Excerpts from that publication provide overwhelming evidence of an intent to re-direct attitudes on a national scale. Take special note of those portions boldfaced here for emphasis.

From pages 44-45:

> The nation-state system has been in existence for about three centuries.... The nation-state has not been able up to the present time to abolish wars.... enduring peace cannot be achieved so long as the nation-state system continues as at present constituted. It is a system of international anarchy — a species of jungle warfare. Enduring peace cannot be achieved until the nation-states surrender to a world organization the exercise of jurisdiction over those problems with which they have found themselves unable to deal....
>
> Nationalism is the product of the modern period and of the nation-state system. It is a feeling of loyalty to one's nation-state. Loyalty to one's family, to one's local community, to one's own group seems to develop naturally when the contacts are agreeable to a person. An extension of that loyalty to a larger area, such as a nation, has been attained by the adoption of patriotic songs, setting aside national holidays, teaching the greatness of the nation's heritage, use of uniform language, and establishment of schools where youth are taught patriotism and their duties to their native land.
>
> Unfortunately man did not attain peace through the nation-state system.... A spirit of narrow nationalism was stirred up in the people by impressing them with an idea of their own superiority.... People were taught to look down on other nations as inferior.... So long as these narrow nationalistic ideas continue to be held by many people in nations today, there is a threat to world peace.

From page 82 (note this view toward home and free press):

> Teachers can maximize the effectiveness of their instruction and minimize the adverse counter effects of such out-of-school influences as home and press and motion picture....

From page 33:

> Education for international understanding involves the use of education *as a force for conditioning the will of the people.*

The futurist cult believes nations should substitute a world government, or world authority, and cull the best and the brightest from all nations to sit, as it were, on the Board of Directors. They believe this will inevitably be the case anyway, and they might as well help it along so that humanity doesn't wind up with thugs like Panamanian dictator Manuel Noriega at the helm of world affairs. Even in light of what is happening today in Eastern Europe — the crumbling of totalitarian communism, thanks in part to the strength of nationalism, which Josef Stalin tried, and failed, to eradicate — those who head the education establishment remain convinced of the deleterious effects of nationalism and continue to equate patriotism with Nazism.

That is why futurists are among the biggest proponents of the United Nations and the organizations connected with it. Not that there is anything wrong innately with the concept of a United Nations. But unlike Woodrow Wilson, who conceived the League of Nations, forerunner to the present U.N, futurists see a global government with more clout than discussion prerogatives. They deny the potential for abuse in this scheme — as long as the "right" people are steered toward leadership positions. And that is the key to understanding what futurist extremists want: *to steer the "right" individuals toward positions of leadership.* Now one begins to see the unique importance assigned to education. The only way the "right" people can be steered toward power positions is to begin seeking them out among children, like a talent scout looking for a potential Olympic champion.

Intelligence alone, obviously, cannot be the deciding factor. Neither can creative genius, or good health, affability, or a number of other characteristics, all of which may help, but cannot be the basis of selection for leadership.

The basis of selection must be, in a word, *attitude.* Or perhaps one might prefer the term "philosophy," or "world view." In any case, if a person's philosophy is not "right," he or she cannot be a leader.

Who will decide whether a person's philosophy is "appropriate"? Not an electorate. Not those ignorant, swarming masses of humanity who can be taken in by anything. No, the selection process is better controlled by a dedicated cadre of experts whose quiet, ongoing Pavlovian[84] mission is to cull the best individuals from among the world's populations and place them, programmed and loyal, into various leadership roles. Meanwhile, the masses (humanity, in the abstract) must be made amenable to their inevitable subservience to the collective, preferably within the space of one or two generations. That way the planet survives; mankind survives.

In our weaker moments — perhaps while listening to that excruciating Presidential campaign of 1988 — many of us non-futurists might be tempted toward this idealistic scenario, even to think it logical. But upon reflection it may occur to the thoughtful person that the future "leaders" in this scheme will not — cannot — actually be leaders. The "leaders" behaviorists envision will be tools, or puppets, of whatever group selects them and steers them to success. *To that end, the "leaders" of tomorrow will have to be the best "followers" who have ever existed!* They can never be "their own man" or "their own woman."

When one examines the futurist scheme in detail — and it is set out quite clearly in many popular books as well as in technical papers, among the latter being the B-STEP paper, which completely revamped teacher education[85] — the scheme promises mankind everything it has ever wanted. A job. Reasonable comfort. Human rights. Even freedom — from hunger and loss. Everything, that is, except the one thing mankind can no longer "afford" if there is to be a safe planet: independent thought. People will have to learn how to express their "individual differences," declare futurist experts, in a way that is "appropriate."

If the futurist cult gets its way, their hand-picked "selection team," culled from the so-called best and brightest, will be running the show in the year 2020. That's CFAT. The Aspen Institute. The School of Ageless Wisdom. Whoever.

It's not a new theme. It's an old science fiction theme — another version of Utopia. Every extremist group that ever was thinks it will be the one that "rules the world." Futurists are dreamers, working to create not only the perfect world but perfect people to inhabit it; playing King of the Mountain, all over again.

The difference this time is that the behaviorist faction of the futurist movement — the real fanatics — have the money, the influence, and an incredible technology in place to pull it off. They believe they've hit on a strategy to launch what they call "a planned society." The idea involves tapping the tremendous material resources of free nations to finance research and development of a science already demonstrated to have unlimited potential, behavioral psychology, then use that science, first, to unmake, then re-make, the world — starting with education.

For years, scientists have been on the cutting edge of breakthroughs in mind control psychology. What was done during World War II to prisoners of war was only a small beginning, and, ironically, it has been "peace-loving" futurists, of all people, who have gone on to exploit the idea. Advertisers, of course, increasingly have been making use of mind-control techniques developed by psychologists. So have rock musicians, religious fanatics, and others.

Subliminal messages. Self-hypnosis. Assertiveness training. Fourth-Force Psychology. Regression therapy. Programming and de-programming — of people, not computers. Just take a look at the self-help section of any bookstore. Yes, some of it is pop psychology. A lot of it is pure rubbish. But a lot of it isn't, too. Much, in fact, is based on real breakthroughs in behavioral research. People who couldn't get a job in the field 25 years ago are advising their sons and daughters to major in behavioral science today. Thought-manipulation. It's big business. And that includes the business of political persuasion.

The futurists are élitists first and socialists second. As in the book *Training for Change Agents*, they believe the results of their efforts will be so positive once their ideas are fully implemented that public approval is virtually assured. Therefore they are justified, they think, in not telling people the full story about the "science of planned change" until it has been accomplished: the *fait accompli*.

Adolph Hitler is sometimes referred to by the media as "extreme right-wing," but never as a "conservative." Behaviorists may call themselves "socialists," but not "left-wingers." Futurists say they believe in human rights and peace on earth. But they also claim to believe in a top-down method of promulgating their social and political ideas. Their actions imply that the ends justify the means. If a few individuals get hurt because of their experimentation, apparently it doesn't matter. The masses are viewed as too idiotic to be trusted in the decision-making process. Futurists therefore believe in a controlling world elite which "provide[s] bread and circuses" to the masses and which is empowered to remove children from their homes if they are judged as "lacking the sensory input [at home] to build normal intelligence." They view the teacher as "a learning clinician" or "facilitator" who, among other things, acts as "biomedical therapist...dispensing memory [and intelligence]-improvement chemicals" to their young charges.[86]

This is not the Flower Children of the 1960s who wanted to go back to nature and living in communes. This is extreme, pure fascism, totalitarian — and very high-tech. It's the futurists' "new world order."

CHAPTER 28

People-shaping Through Programming

THE FUTURIST CULT wants to create, through behavioral programming, people who will be able to cope with what they envision to be the challenges of the next century. A comment which, perhaps, best sums up the futurist vision of education is this dynamite quote by Harvard's Dr. Chester M. Pierce:

> Every child in America who enters school with an allegiance toward our elected officials, toward our founding fathers, toward our institutions, toward the preservation of this form of government . . . all of this proves the children are sick, because the truly well individual is one who has rejected all of those things and is what I would call the true international child of the future.

The Behavioral Teacher Education Project (or B-STEP) is a thousand-plus page landmark document published in 1967 (compliments of the U.S. Office of Education).[87] It not only revamped teacher training in this country (and others), but it sets out in plain language the world view, the intent, and the strategy of the futurist cult. A sister text, often referred to as the "bible of educational theory," is the *Taxonomy of Educational Objectives,*[88] edited by behaviorist kingpin Benjamin S. Bloom, who also received a federal grant for his effort. Both texts are very reminiscent of popular authors Aldous Huxley and Alvin Toffler, with an eye, apparently, to speeding their predictions along. There are other equally revealing works, especially in the high-tech vein, but it will be enough to cover B-STEP and Bloom's book here.

The world vision of B-STEP and *Taxonomy* rely heavily on what B-STEP calls "impersonal manipulation" — a future world in which *"people will be so saturated with ideas and information [that] few will be able to maintain control over their opinions;"* a world in which pleasure-seeking, drug-induced escapism, and indiscriminate "chemical experimentation" on minors and adults is normal; a world where *"each individual receives at birth a multi-purpose identification number"* so that *"all will be in constant contact with their employers or other controllers, and thus exposed to direct and subliminal influence."*

These, supposedly, are "givens." They will occur, say futurists, whether anyone does anything about it or not.

Remember this is not an excerpt from a science-fiction novel. This is a document written under contract to the U.S. Office of Education for the purpose of outlining proposals to revamp teacher education. Keep in mind also that there was a shortage of teachers at this time, and a program of student loans had been set up under the National Defense Act to attract young people to the profession.

Exactly why behaviorists obtained the grant to do this particular work can only be surmised, but it no doubt had a lot to do with the influence of CFAT and the behavioral colleges, which already were strong at that time. The "givens" are but the introduction to the B-STEP document. It goes on to provide the rationale — the why — behind techniques and changes that are going to be recommended further on. The three major goals of B-STEP, cited next, are:

> 1. Development of a new kind of elementary school teacher who . . . engages in teaching as clinical practice . . . and functions as a responsible agent of social change.
>
> 2. Systematic use of research and clinical experience in decision-making processes at all levels.
>
> 3. A new laboratory and clinical base, from the behavioral sciences, on which to found undergraduate and in-service teacher education programs, and recycle evaluations of teaching tools and performance.

The language could not be plainer. The behavioral sciences will not merely be incidental to the revamping of teacher education; they will be the primary vehicle. The introduction to B-STEP goes on to say that the world the authors are preparing future teachers for is one in which "the Protestant Ethic will atrophy as more and more enjoy guaranteed sustenance" and a world in which "a small elite will carry society's burdens...." In the end, "[p]articipatory democracy in the American idea will largely disappear" and no government anywhere will be able to protect its citizens without risking all-out nuclear holocaust. The authors add to this dismal vision an ever-expanding global population with ever-shrinking resources; thus a necessity to redistribute the world's wealth to provide equitable resources to the world's starving masses.

Despite futurists' calls for "human dignity," often published in the popular literature and in some school textbooks, treatises like James M. Becker's *Education for a Global Society*, paint quite a different picture: "...mankind is by far the most destructive of all species that inhabit the earth."[89]

Perhaps. But mankind has also been the most constructive of all the species that inhabit the earth, and that isn't mentioned. Most of the educational films and texts put out by futurist-behaviorist groups echo the philosophy of Becker, whose primary rationale for everything from education to international politics is "safeguarding the human species." Taken together over time, children absorb the idea that mankind desperately needs to be controlled and regimented in order to keep from harming self, others, and the planet. Precisely the attitude that futurists would call "appropriate."

In B-STEP the authors make clear that their aim is to create, through education, an elite that does the controlling and the regimenting (that "plans" society), while the masses are fed the equivalent of educational pap:

> curriculum content [is] focused on value-building, process competency...interpersonal relationships, and pleasure cultivation...and other attitudes and skills compatible with a non-work world.

If mankind is to survive, maintains Benjamin Bloom in *Taxonomy - Handbook I*, people will have to be taught *"'proper' attitudes before others are developed."* To accomplish this task, educational data banks must be set up to *"classify . . . the ways individuals are to act, think, or feel as the result of participating in some unit of instruction."*

Thus the purpose of attitudinal testing, and the purpose of a "new world order."

Testing, of course, will show where students are at each stage in the quest for "appropriate" attitudes. The goal of instructional programs, particularly those that "remediate" attitudes, will be "the integration of these beliefs, ideas, and attitudes into a total philosophy or world view."[90]

Thus, "human dignity" in the cultist view appears to mean freedom from torture, starvation and other forms of physical abuse, but not freedom from regimentation.

The most significant point in B-STEP, for practical purposes, is that the teacher's role is to change so as to assume the function of *therapist*. States the B-STEP introduction:

> The program [B-STEP] is designed to focus the skills and knowledge of behavioral scientists on education problems, translating research into viable programs for pre-service and inservice teachers. The traditional concept of research as theory is not discarded, but the emphasis is shifted to a form of practical action-research in classrooms and laboratory.

It would be impossible to state any more clearly the fact that the authors intend to perform psychological research in the "laboratory" of the classroom. Again, this is not science-fiction. This blueprint for teacher education has been used in nearly every major college and university in the country.

Unfortunately, to the undiscerning college sophomore or junior of nineteen or twenty, this stuff sounds good. Most prospective teachers are at an age when they are beginning to leave the nest to go their own way. They're idealistic, rebellious, and vulnerable. Raised on a never-ending diet of entertainment that depicts young people as either misunderstood or tweaking the noses of their elders, these young people are only too ready to hear that life as an adult will be different, and that as teachers the emphasis henceforth will be on soothing their young charges' feelings rather than encouraging them to attain knowledge.

The educational changes these young people are advised in B-STEP to make as teachers are, if anything, more shocking than the introductory pages explaining the "world of the future."

Page 246 calls for the use of personality control drugs.

Page 250 calls for "clinical experience with youth in varied settings" and "extensive and intensive laboratory experiences which develop . . . group attitudes...." (Was busing originally part of a "varied settings" experiment?)

Page 251 calls for the "use of medical tools to produce children of desired learning potentialities" (Desired by whom? Higher or lower potentialities?)

The whole of page 253 is devoted to an intended manipulation of the media!

Comparing B-STEP's 1967 predictions for the world with what has transpired in the interim, one is tempted to say that the authors were pretty much on target. But while they may have been correct about the communications revolution and information saturation, they did not foresee such innovations as the video-cassette recorder (VCR), which actually provides the individual with the capability to screen out what he doesn't want to hear (or want his children to hear). In a sense, the individual has more control over his information, not less. Parents have more control over what is presented as acceptable at home (i.e., the values their youngsters learn), not less — if parents will only take advantage of it.

B-STEP forecasts the negative effect of computers on the individual, too — machines taking over the work of people and moving the United States toward a "service economy." But they didn't foresee, apparently, the advent of affordable home computers, which even now are giving men and women the opportunity to work at home, to spend in some cases more time with their families, and to communicate their ideas on word processors, disseminating and even publishing their own work.

Moreover, people have more control over their own destiny, not less.

But that is not the message schoolchildren are getting. Instead they are absorbing what may in the long run be a self-fulfilling prophecy — that their lives are essentially out of their own hands.

Another futurist who has figured highly in revamping teacher education is John Goodlad. He, too, has received a number of government grants for his work, as well as foundation money. His best-known works are *A Place Called School* and *Education Curriculum and Inquiry*. Goodlad, at this writing a professor at the University of Washington and Director of the Center for Educational Renewal, focused his government-supported research primarily on three areas: on how well positioned schools and colleges of education are to make substantial changes in the training of teachers; on development of cooperative ties between colleges and universities so that such change can occur; and on the status of teacher training, including the perceptions and beliefs faculty members hold about their work and their students. This may explain why at least half of the National Teachers' Exam is attitudinal and why (for at least 20 years) neither test-takers nor their parents have been permitted to see that test or the results. Rather test-takers receive only a notification of having passed or failed. To fail this test means to be denied a teaching certificate regardless of an otherwise acceptable, even outstanding, grade point average.

Teacher training took another leap in the behavioral direction when the National Education Association (NEA) launched its National Training Laboratory. Its primary purpose was to re-educate teachers who were already in the field. At the time it was launched, many teachers had not been exposed to the revamped college programs.

What did the NEA want to re-educate teachers for? States their pamphlet: "to change teachers' inflexible patterns of thinking." The National Training Lab is a multi-day encounter program featuring strong psychological techniques to change attitudes. Just how strong can be surmised in the application form, which carries at the bottom the following disclaimer:

> Any person undergoing treatment for emotional difficulties or in psychotherapy is expected to discuss the advisability of program attendance with the person directing his/her treatment and to secure written approval for attendance. No person concerned about entering a stress situation should participate in NTL programs.... [A] small percentage of participants have experienced stress reactions in varying degrees. There is no means of predicting such reactions or screening out or otherwise identifying those predisposed to such reactions....

At least prospective teacher-applicants are being warned. One has to give the NEA that. But what of the students whose teachers take the course? Participating teachers also are learning "innovative teaching strategies" in the NTL program. These incorporate some of the same behavior-manipulating features — like the encounter group "games."

The thrust of what the NTL is re-training teachers to do is explained on page 47 of the NTL manual, under "Issues in Training" (note the futurist overtones):

> Although they [children] appear to behave appropriately and seem normal by most cultural standards, they may actually be in need of mental health care in order to help them change, adapt, and conform to the planned society in which there will be no conflict of attitudes or beliefs.

When the teachers who take this course get back into the classroom, their students will have no application form to warn them or their parents about what kinds of strategies will be used. The NEA disclaimer admits "there is no means of predicting . . . screening out or otherwise identifying those predisposed to [stress] reactions. . . ." If that is so, what are teachers doing playing with these kinds of techniques in their classrooms? But most teachers never take the high-stress NTL course. They don't understand what has happened to their profession any more than parents understand what has happened to their schools or their children. Unless teachers, first of all, have been in the profession long enough to have seen the change of thrust, and, secondly, have somehow become knowledgeable enough to find and read for themselves texts like B-STEP, there is no way in the world they could know they are being set up as therapists, or "clinicians," transmitting the attitudes and values of futurist cultists.

But that, nevertheless, is the logic behind the recent push toward "recertification" of teachers — recently made popular in well-publicized, new CFAT proposals. The public, of course, is enthusiastic about the idea — because they think it means forcing teachers to meet tougher, academic standards. Teachers generally take a dim view — because they see recertification as insulting to their profession and disparaging of their hard-earned credentials.

Both are wrong: the public and the teachers. Recertification is not about toeing the line or academic standards. It is not about credentials in the sense of individuals being "licensed" to perform a job. Recertification is re-education — to formally legitimize changing the role and function of "teacher" to one of "therapist." The long-range goal is to change the fundamental value system in America.

Yes, it sounds crazy. But as people around the world have discovered through recent events in the Middle East, and, long before, this is the nature of fanaticism — a lopsided kind of logic that can be, with enough financing and the right "packaging," both appealing and fatal.

Sometimes it takes a lot of legwork to find the pieces of a puzzle — and how American education could have sunk to such a deplorable state is surely one of the most complex puzzles of all time. Occasionally, however, there is one little gem that makes it all worthwhile, that one piece that makes all the other pieces fall into place.

One such is a 1948 paper entitled "International Conciliation", by the Carnegie Endowment for International Peace. The paper introduces the World Health Organization (WHO). The Preface is written by its then-president, Alger Hiss, the same man who was later tried and convicted of being a spy. Hiss' Preface points out that the term "health" is to have a whole new meaning: "a state of complete physical, mental, and social well-being, and not merely the absence of disease or infirmity." In particular, Hiss states, it means "mental health, housing, nutrition, economic or working conditions, and administrative and social techniques affecting public health."

Hiss goes on to introduce "an eminent psychologist," Dr. Brock Chisolm of Canada, who writes the short introductory article for the paper in question. And that is when the "little gem" turned up. Following up, it seems that Dr. Brock gave many lectures on psychiatry, its importance, its direction and its mission. One careful read of what he has to say, especially in the context of education, explains volumes about how American curriculum, tests, and surveys came to have their present psycho-behavioral emphasis. No additional commentary is necessary to the following speech by Brock Chisolm, published in *Psychiatry* in 1946.

> It would appear that at least three requirements are basic to any hope of permanent world peace. First — security, elimination of the occasion for valid

fear of aggression. This is attainable...by legislation backed by immediately available combined force prepared to suppress ruthlessly any appeal to force by any peoples of the world. . . . it will be necessary that all disputes be submitted to arbitration by a world court of highest integrity.

Second — opportunity to live reasonably comfortably for all the people in the world on economic levels which do not vary too widely either geographically or by groups within a population. This is a simple matter of redistribution of material....

It follows inevitably that the third requirement...is that there be enough people in the world, in all countries, who...are sufficiently free of neurotic symptoms which make wars inevitable.

All psychiatrists know where these burdens come from. The burden of inferiority, guilt, and fear we have all carried lies at the heart of this failure to mature successfully. . . . [W]e must ask ourselves why the human race is so loaded down with these incubi and what can be done about it.

...It would appear that this quality of maturity, of growing up successfully is what is lacking in the human race generally....

This fact puts the problem squarely up to psychiatry. The necessity to fight wars, whether as an aggressor or as a defender . . . is as much a pathological psychiatric symptom as is a phobia or the antisocial behavior of a criminal...

What basic psychological distortion can be found in every civilization of which we know anything? It must be a force which discourages the ability to see and acknowledge patent facts, which prevents the rational use of intelligence, which teaches and encourages the ability to dissociate and to believe contrary to and in spite of clear evidence, which produces inferiority, guilt, and fear . . . . Is there any force so potent and so pervasive that it can do all these things in all civilizations? There is — just one. The only lowest common denominator of all civilizations and the only psychological force capable of producing these perversions is morality, the concept of right and wrong....

In the old Hebrew story God warns the first man and woman to have nothing to do with good and evil. It is interesting to note that as long ago as that, "good" is recognized as just as great a menace as "evil."....

[This] artificially imposed inferiority, guilt and fear, commonly known as sin,...produces so much of the social maladjustment and unhappiness in the world.

...[S]urely it would be more advantageous to the world for psychiatrists to go into the preventive field where the big job needs to be done. The training of children is making a thousand neurotics for every one that psychiatrists can hope to help with psychotherapy. To produce a generation of mature citizens is the biggest and most necessary job any country could undertake, and the reward in saving of misery and suffering would be colossal.

The reinterpretation and eventually eradication of the concept of right and wrong which has been the basis of child training, the substitution of intelligent and rational thinking for faith...these are the belated objectives of practically all effective psychotherapy.... Would it not be sensible to stop imposing our local prejudices and faiths on children and give them all sides of every question...?

...Freedom from morality means freedom to observe, to think and behave sensibly...free from the outmoded types of loyalties and the magic fears of our ancestors.

If the race is to be freed of its crippling burden of good and evil it must be psychiatrists who take the original responsibility.

The battle, if it is to be undertaken, will be long and difficult. . . . With luck we have perhaps fifteen or even twenty years before the outbreak of the next world war...twenty years in which to change the dearest certainties of the human race, twenty years in which to root out and destroy the oldest and most flourishing parasitical growth....[91]

The futurist-behaviorists rose to the challenge, and a "new world order" was set in motion.

CHAPTER 29

The Politics of Popular Consent

IF FUTURISTS AND their behaviorist cohorts had been totally candid in their approach from the beginning, they would have said something to the effect of: "Look, Parents, here is what we believe and we'd like to try it out. We will show you the real goals of our program and ask for volunteers. We will set up experimental facilities using endowments from certain foundations that believe in what we are trying to do. If you would like to enroll your child(ren), here is where you can go to do it; here are the forms you can fill out."

It is true that the child still would not have much choice in the matter, but then children rarely do anyway. Parents typically have been deemed responsible for their children (until recently), so this approach would at least have been ethically acceptable to society.

But cults and fanatics are rarely that "up front," and the futurist extremists are no exception. Instead, they decided to operate on the edge of the law. They engineered their inclusion on important boards and task forces, influenced legislation, and channeled billions of tax-free dollars into the de-programming and re-programming of the child using an educational setting.

That such tampering with human lives may already have diminished the incentive of many couples to raise children according to their own standards — which is the only way, really, people *can* raise children — is probably beyond doubt. Arguably, the declining birth rate among the prosperous nations reflects to some extent the fact that parenthood, in the eyes of the professional and semi-professional classes, has become a no-win situation. It isn't terribly surprising that many couples opt out.

The American public has been amazingly patient through thirty years of educational decline. It gave up phonics in reading instruction, which thus far had produced a predominantly literate population. It relinquished proven techniques for teaching mathematics, nearly all instruction in geography, penmanship, essay writing, English grammar, and chronological history. The American people acquiesced on the issues of school dances for pre-teeners, lax dress codes, explicit sex education as a separate course (separate, that is, from biology and physiology), and something called "social studies." In essence, the public gave up the three R's and got back the three "I"s: ignorance, illiteracy, and illegitimacy.

Parents of the fifties and sixties wanted a "kinder and gentler nation," too. They were living in the shadow of the horrors of World War II, and they were in no mood for a repeat performance. So they were, in some ways, vulnerable to the arguments of futurists, which came at them, first, through articles and books on child-rearing, and later through educational institutions.

Today we can look back and see that the American public (and some of the other free nations) have put up with one fiasco after another in the name of psycho-behavioral education passed off as "reform":

"Open" classrooms are labeled differently now. They have been such a disaster that many teachers have hung rugs on the walls to keep the noise level down until engineers can come back and restructure the rooms.

Time-Out Boxes are such a vicious form of psychological "education" (youngsters are placed in boxes for anywhere from one class period to a full day while classmates throw in trash and grass) that some children have had to be taken to child psychologists to undo the damage.

Since death education and suicide-prevention courses were introduced, the teen suicide rate has tripled. "Suicide is a declaration of freedom," reads one lesson. In some cultures, suicide is not a sin, points out another lesson, but rather it is a way of handling an unsolvable problem.[92]

On December 26, 1990, the *Washington Post* reported the results of a new study on this subject headed by David Shaffer, Director of Child and Adolescent Psychology at Columbia University's College of Physicians and Surgeons in New York. The study investigated the impact of suicide prevention programs on the attitudes of ninth and tenth graders who said they had tried to commit suicide. The researchers found that the teenagers who went through the prevention program continued to believe that suicide was a possible solution to their problems and that they were even less likely to ask for professional help than they were before they took the course. Another psychologist not connected with the study was quoted as saying that these results were "not surprising and add support to theories that teenagers have a romantic vision of suicide." The study concluded that "[t]here is a clear need to evaluate such programs to determine their efficacy and safety."

This account is typical of many psychological programs and leads one to wonder whether studies like this aren't more appropriate *before* experimental programs are unleashed on thousands of unsuspecting schoolchildren rather than waiting until damage is done. Not only would this help restore parents' confidence in their schools, it would help teachers who are the ones who bear the brunt of complaints when something goes wrong.

Similarly, illegitimacy and venereal disease rates have gone nowhere but up since explicit sex education became hyped as a course of study in its own right. On June 24, 1990, the *Washington Post* ran a front-page story, "Failures Seen in Education on 'Safe Sex'." The subtitle was "AIDS Experts Worry As Warnings Are Ignored."

No surprises here. This result is precisely what the studies on the subject of explicit sex education foretold.[93] What is surprising is the recommendation. You guessed it: More explicit sex education at still younger ages.

Behaviorists, of course, claim that other factors caused these disappointing statistics, not their programs. But even if one gives them the benefit of the doubt on that, the question still arises: Is there any evidence that their programs helped?

T-groups, encounter sessions, operant (Skinnerian) conditioning, altered states of consciousness, and change agents: It's time to take a look at the track record. And while we're about it, perhaps it is time to ask whether the Carnegie Foundation for the Advancement of Teaching belongs in the education business.

CHAPTER 30

CFAT Does the Bureaucratic Shuffle

THERE ARE A few good books around on the history and evolution of the three Carnegie organizations. Although one such book was commissioned by the Carnegie Foundation for the Advancement of Teaching (CFAT) itself and, therefore, was bound to contain nothing particularly damaging to or critical of the organization, *Private Power for the Public Good* by Ellen Condliffe Lagemann[94] is very good and worth the read. Perhaps because it was commissioned and approved for publication by CFAT, it is all the more revealing because the author surely would have had no previous bias against the organization. Otherwise, she wouldn't have been selected to write the book.

The title reveals how CFAT views itself: a powerful organization that exists only to perform functions that are in the public interest. But even the author concedes in the *Preface* that as she was researching the book, doubts began to surface in her own mind concerning the "dilemmas associated with the traditional philanthropic claim that 'private power' can be 'for the public good.'" Comments Lagemann:[95]

> ..."the public good" is a theoretical concept that becomes elusive when one begins to consider the actual variety of group interests that have existed and still exist in the United States;...any form of purposive social action, including foundation philanthropy, must represent the interests of some groups better than others and must advance some social priorities at the expense of others;....

It was twenty-five men, says Lagemann, who gathered in old Andrew Carnegie's mansion in New York City in 1905 to set up CFAT. Most of the twenty-five were college presidents — of Harvard, Yale, Columbia, Stanford, Cornell, Princeton, and others. They could not have known it then, but this would in a sense help to ensure the philosophical support of the major universities, as well as their financial support in future years. They elected Henry Smith Pritchett to serve as the Foundation's head, and beginning with him, it can be seen that little by little the Foundation moved in a philosophical direction that might have made old Andrew Carnegie turn over in his grave.

Through its various studies, for years restricted to the university level, CFAT defined the standards of professional education that still prevail. It started with Abraham Flexner's famous study of medical education, sponsored by CFAT. It was discovered from that study that the United States was behind Europe in many aspects of its medical training. This study was received so well that it was repeated in other university disciplines. In the process, formal training and certification became a basis of social status in America.

> ...In the same way, the Foundation promoted the use of standardized testing...the Foundation delineated purposes and administrative procedures for different levels and types of academic institutions and thereby helped to foster systematization of American education.

> The Educational Testing Service of Princeton, New Jersey grew out of the Foundation's activities...commissions and task forces, today, are frequently organized by CFAT, and its proposals are generally implemented by government.

Little by little CFAT got away from being a university pension fund — and from the principles and vision of Andrew Carnegie. By the time Alan Pifer, president of CFAT and the Carnegie Corporation in New York (and the one who asked Lagemann to write the book), was appointed by President Richard M. Nixon[96] to head a special education group, CFAT had long since extended its efforts and influence to elementary and secondary education. By 1968, too, there was a real problem with Congressional oversight of tax-exempt foundations in this country — that is, Congress' monitoring was minimal at best.

Pifer sought to set educational priorities and to win Presidential blessing for a strong policy center for higher education "close to the summit of Federal Government." This would provide a channel for a tight, interlocking directorate of large foundations, corporations, law firms, and quasi-government organizations, such as the National Governors' Association, the Council of

Chief State School Officers, and other institutions. Behind the lofty claims of disinterested public service, there began to emerge a politically motivated foundation machine that brooked no interference in its affairs.

In an attempt, apparently, to stifle mounting criticism in the 1960s, Pifer suggested in the Carnegie Corporation's annual report that foundations set up an independent commission to recommend forms of public accountability. This commission, of course, would serve as a lightning rod to deflect criticism so that it could be managed by the foundations themselves, much as the state education agencies became lightning rods for complaints about educational policy so as to keep irate parents away from Washington. This move also helped to ensure that no outside body was free of ties to the big foundations and, therefore, made it difficult to oversee CFAT's activities in an objective manner. From such a haughty citadel, foundation publicists then could brand as "anti-intellectual" or "crackpot" any honest attempt to delve into their operations.

By 1978, the year the GAO report on behavioral modification programs came out — unnoted and unsung in the press — current CFAT president Ernest Boyer was sitting as the U.S. Commissioner of Education. CFAT indeed had come a long way; in fact, to the very top of the educational hierarchy. No one ever stopped to ask whether such a position constituted a conflict of interest — and Boyer certainly wasn't about to work against his own interests by pursuing the results of the GAO investigation. In fact, he was busy calling for a "new curriculum, one that gives us a clear vision of the unity of our world, in both a social and physical sense."[97]

Protests against Carnegie influence in education, particularly its love affair with behavioral laboratories, is of long standing (along with concern about behavior modification). In 1968, parents were aghast at textbooks financed by the Carnegie Corporation under "Project Read" — a project to provide programmed textbooks for schools in "culturally deprived areas." An estimated five million of the nation's children used material produced by the Behavioral Research Laboratory in Palo Alto, California.

The texts in several passages of the reading series could well be taken as incitement to arson and guerilla warfare, such as took place in Watts and

Washington, D.C., in the sixties. A picture on one page shows a lit torch next to a porch; the innocent caption is "a torch, a porch."

But further on, there is a picture of a smiling man holding the torch aloft. That caption reads: "This man has a t_rch in his hand" and the student is supposed to supply the missing letter, "o." The next picture shows the burning torch touching the porch, with the appropriate caption, and the children are gradually led in stages to the point where the porch is burned. The final picture in the series shows a man moving the hands of a clock to twenty-five minutes past one, while the shack is being devoured by flames.

A subliminal message? You can't prove it is, or isn't. That's the beauty of behavioral education. One can do all kinds of manipulative things with it, and when faced with protests, just shrug shoulders and say the message had been "misinterpreted" by "crackpots." Other pictures include a flag compared to a rag — well, it rhymes, after all — and a picture of worshippers kneeling in prayer beside a picture of a horse being taught to kneel in the same way — well, kids are just learning common terms, aren't they? Then there's a picture of a boy stealing a girl's purse; and one of another boy throwing pointed darts at a companion whom he is using for target practice!

Ellen Morphonios, a Florida prosecutor and then-chief of its Criminal Court Division went on record saying, "It's a slap in the face and an insult to every member of the [Black] community, saying that the only way to communicate with minority children is to show a robber or violence. It's like subliminal advertising."

The fact is, the first behavioral programs under the ESEA law were all aimed at the disadvantaged, under Title I. There is now a considerable body of evidence to support the hypothesis that minorities were the first guinea pigs for psychological change programs — which were then improved, refined, and extended to the whole school-aged population. Apparently, it was okay to let minority children fall through the cracks, to see what would happen if they were manipulated this way or that. Perhaps behaviorists expected less fuss to be raised by their parents?

Without any adverse political fallout either from Carnegie involvement with curriculum or from the GAO report, *Questions Persist About Federal Support for Development of Curriculum Materials and Behavior Modification Techniques Used in Local Schools*,[98] the old Education Office went on to compile a 584-page compendium of almost solely psycho-behavioral learning programs called *Pacesetters in Innovation* (PACE). Even the U.S. Department of Education staff who later reviewed the programs were aghast. Coded "project accession numbers" for the PACE programs reveal "Psychotherapy," "Behavior Modification," "Psychoeducational Clinics," "Change In Parent-Student Relationships," "Total Environment Control," "Sensitivity Training," and "Attitudinal Measurement Devices." In due course, the lot was dumped into what would become known as the National Diffusion Network. The PACE programs reached more than seven million children at a cost to the taxpayer of more than $250 million. A decade later, the NDN would become part of the now-regionally accessible network, filled with PACE and other mind-bending programs carrying the government's Good Housekeeping seal of approval ("validation") that America's classrooms use today. When a highly respected psychologist and educational researcher, Shirley Correll, reviewed a printout of the PACE programs in 1983, she wrote the Department, saying: "Total Government Control of the . . . schools, for the purpose of molding society to the will of a small elite, [is] not responsible to the general populace . . . and steps must be taken . . . ."

None were.

CHAPTER 31

Some Observations on the Almost Perfect Crime

SERGEI PETROV, THE Soviet refusenik/photographer who after eight years finally succeeded in emigrating to the United States, has observed that "this [democratic] system here is an extremely fragile system . . . . If more than 30 percent of Americans stopped paying their income tax, there is no way the IRS could prosecute them [all]. If only 30 percent of the drivers started to break the rules, it would be a complete mess."

Petrov was praising the American tendency toward smoothing out the conflicts. But he was also pointing to another aspect: that our form of government depends on a general acceptance of certain concepts and principles, a certain consensus, if you will, that Americans don't often think about. If Americans did not agree IN CONCEPT to the legitimacy of an income tax, there wouldn't be one. If Americans didn't accept IN PRINCI-PLE a common driving code, life in the drivers' seat would be altogether different, as it is in some other countries. If Americans, en masse, were to view the state schools as more a menace than a boon to the welfare and health of their children, there would be no way to prosecute all the parents who kept their kids out, or all the Americans who refused to pay, say, their property taxes. That is one reason why so many public school proponents are anxious to see the bulk of school monies come from the state or federal government, so that the dependence on smaller tax scales, like property taxes, will shift instead to those taxes that Americans are less likely, in the end, to refuse paying.

Despite the efforts of social engineers and behaviorist extremists, the American populace remains quite independent-minded when sufficiently aroused. Although few would go to the trouble Anita Hoge and her husband did when faced with the bureaucratic runaround, once the trail has been blazed and people are aware they've been lied to or taken advantage of,

Americans tend to respond loudly and without reservation. Once trust is lost in any institution or individual — remember Watergate and the Vietnam War? — it is a long while before it is quite regained.

Professionals in the education business know that pollsters have vastly underestimated the general discontent with American education. Mainly, the surveys ask the wrong questions. Querying parents as to whether they feel their child's school is doing a good job, for example, begs the question. Those "C+" and occasional "B-" ratings don't sound too bad. What many parents say they want to add is the phrase "considering all things, my son's or daughter's school is doing this or that kind of a job."

"All things considered" can cover a lot of territory: general atmosphere or environment; dress codes and their effect on student performance and behavior; substance of curricula; policy toward disruptive students and juvenile delinquents; relationships between teacher and pupil and between teachers, administrators, and parents; ease of input from parents — just to name a few. Any one of these factors, dramatically altered, can — and does — greatly affect what and how much students learn. A poll that asks parents simply to rate their schools, or even the teachers, simply does not cover the subject.

Parents know, of course, deep down that school environment, dress codes and other policies don't really come from the local school and are not, therefore, the fault necessarily of the local school, and they tend, therefore, to give the local school the benefit of the doubt. They know such questions as those above transcend the boundaries of any one school, even though the questions are put to parents as if they were local issues. All public schools — if, indeed, they can be called "public"; in reality they are "state schools" — are inexorably tied to one another by federal policy. When private schools become involved with federal funding in any way, their policy is necessarily affected, too. That is why the "voucher" alternative is a poor idea — it would provide a credit (that's a form of money) for dissatisfied parents to place their public school youngsters into a private school. Inevitably, one result will be that parents of problem students — chronic misbehavers, truants, straight-F pupils, and juvenile delinquent-types —

will be prime candidates for the voucher system. This means that private schools may not be able to retain their current policies regarding the acceptance or rejection of new students. Parents, therefore, who have been paying thousands of dollars to keep their children out of the public school (the "state school") environment will be hurt because private school authorities will no longer be able to make policy decisions about who can stay and who must go. They will abide by the state codes. Polls, of course, do not reflect what Americans think about public, or "state" schools. But when the education establishment looks at the growing numbers of home schoolers and the increasing demand for more private schools (one reason for the huge increase in cost is that there's simply not enough of them), they can envision a backlash that would alter their plans dramatically. That is why organizations like the National Education Association are so sensitive on the issue of private schools. That is why increasing lipservice is given to "basics," even while the emphasis is on "fluff." Pupils are more attracted to fluff than to academics, and that fact will help state school advocates stay one step ahead of vacillating parents.

Of course, there are exceptions. The Fairfax School system in Fairfax, Virginia, for example, can do things, like expel chronic disrupters, that wouldn't be tolerated elsewhere. That is because many members of Congress have over the years gravitated to that Washington, D.C., suburb and can afford to throw their weight around. It used to be that Congressmen and -women sent their children to area private schools. Some still do. But the cost is high and they, like others, resent having to support two school systems. They take what, for them, is the easy way out. (Interestingly, the publicized cost per pupil of both tax-supported and private schools, except boarding and certain small parochial schools, seems to be about the same: between about $5,000 and $6,000 a year.[99])

There are public school districts here and there, of course, that enjoy short-lived love affairs with their communities, eschewing the guiding hand of federal and state education agencies. A Joe Clark-type[100] principal here, an independent-minded superintendent there. But it never lasts long. No matter how successful, no matter how loyally supported by the community or canonized in the press, these individuals eventually are discredited, their hands tied. Some of these mavericks never know why the tide turned against them, except that they dared to sidestep "standard" establishment operating procedures.

Private schools, meanwhile, are scrutinized for any sort of technical infraction with a view to closing them down or rendering them unable to compete. Private foundations, such as CFAT, with close ties to government, continually woo corporations, professional organization leaders, and philanthropists, enticing them to give large sums to the state schools instead of to private ones. Adopt-a-school programs, computer labs, track-and-field facilities, and learning centers are among the arsenal of ploys used to get wealthy organizations and individuals to pump up the state schools. Substantive learning, however, stays the same. The money provides, at most, a temporary boost. More important school problems, like inadequate curricula; disruptive and delinquent students; lack of discipline and authority; poor parent-school relations; and, of course, behavior modification experiments are not seriously addressed.

What remains to be seen is whether events overtake the education bureaucracy before behaviorist extremists do. Even ignoring the issues of data banks and testing devices, the marriage between CFAT, behaviorist-futurist extremists, and the federal government cannot be called a roaring success for American education. Whether one is talking about the past 25 years — or just the past two — the results hardly read like an advertisement for more of the same. That the education establishment is no longer denying behavioral programming, but, rather, is soft-selling it, does not bode well for America's future. The extremist faction of the education establishment seems indeed to have pulled off the almost perfect crime. How long before the public says "enough"? Most Americans reading the newspapers over their morning cup of coffee don't link behavioral programming and recycling to reports like the following:

> MCI Corporation screened applicants for customer service jobs, then had to teach the new employees how to express themselves and do simple calculations.

A study by the American Management Association found that 42 percent of those tested for basic skills in the professional services were deficient.

Some 135 American businesses are working to define the basic characteristics of 1,000 real-world jobs and 5,000 tasks. Based on this information, at least one large school district, in Fort Worth, will soon consider necessary changes to its curriculum.[101]

Erica Kenney points out that government does not act; it *reacts*. That is one reason why most government agencies hire a news clipping service: to take notice of unpleasant statistics and other negative news about them. Agency heads then react. They may defend their position, form a committee to study the problem, initiate legislation—whatever is the least trouble and the most likely to mollify Americans who read or watched the negative report. The following serves as a typical example of government reaction:

As if there were not enough commissions plus one cabinet-level agency that have sufficiently screwed up education, still another was convened in 1989 — a Commission on Achieving Necessary Skills (SCANS). Reportedly, this noble organization would bring together business, labor, education, and *state officials* to formulate "national competency guidelines." (Does this begin to sound familiar?) These guidelines would be used throughout the country to help develop (ahem!) new curricula and training programs for schools.

The real eye-opener, however, was the intended mentors for the guidelines: Marc Tucker, past executive director of the Carnegie Forum on Education and the Economy, at this writing president of the National Center on Education and the Economy; the Project Director for the Project on Information Technology and Education, sponsored by (surprise!) the Carnegie Corporation; the past Assistant Director of the Northwest Regional Laboratory (one of the Education Department's official Labs); and one advisory committee member from the Carnegie Foundation's Educational Testing Service.

Here we have a country whose greatest educational achievement of the past two decades has been to turn out functional and cultural illiterates. We have change agents posing as teachers, teachers posing as therapists, and therapists posing as curriculum specialists. We find education foundations using their largesse to modify behavior, achievement tests barely touching on academics, and teacher-training institutions specializing in mind-control games.

What else could possibly go wrong?

Well, the commission could "discover" that the problem with education is "too much emphasis on lower-order thinking skills."

So just what is it that knowledgeable parents and activists want government to do about education?

For openers, they want to see an honest and thorough Congressional investigation of tax-supported education and tax-exempt foundations. "Instead of spending time 'freezing' and 'unfreezing' people's values," Anita says, "the Administration should be 'freezing' the National Assessment and its counterparts in the states" until an investigation has resulted in the purging of psychologically manipulative learning programs.

Other angry parents and activists are calling on the Administration, Congress, or the states (if it is their prerogative) to:

- dismantle the Change Agent/Facilitator program;

- locate and pull psycho-behavioral curricula from the NDN and ERIC computer banks;

- review legislation relative to the social security number and enact measures to protect individual privacy as it relates to federal and state data banks;

- revoke CFAT's charter;

- shut down the Department of Education's Labs and Centers;

- review antitrust laws as they apply to educational testing and curriculum;

- revamp the House and Senate Subcommittees on Education so that these bodies will not function as a rubber-stamp for the education establishment;

- provide taxpayers with clear options that permit them to support either public or private education, *without* forcing them to support both;

- provide monetary (or tax) incentives, and remove disincentives, for the business community to create/operate *new* private schools;

- pass clearly worded legislation to ensure parents access to any private- or public-school curriculum, test, teaching aid, or supplementary material;

- strengthen and broaden existing legislation allowing parents to review their children's records and test results (including computerized);

- implement the Zorinsky legislation as it was written, including his proposal to investigate the colleges of education with emphasis on how teachers are trained in psychological techniques and reading methodology;

- initiate a public referendum on education to find out whether the American people want a nationalized, "accredited" system of education or to reinstate state and local control; and finally,

- initiate a public referendum to establish whether the American people want education to have an academic or a psycho-behavioral base and focus.

But if President Bush is correct — and there is every indication that 1991's myriad changes will continue throughout the world — and a "New World Order" is coming . . . in whose image will that Order be structured? Will it be a heterogeneous Order, tolerant of individual differences and desires, seeking to establish a consensus through education and discussion, as the United States is — or, at least, once aspired to be — or will it be an intolerant bureaucracy whose only goal is a homogeneous, "politically correct" citizenship? From what we have learned of tne EQA and NAEP, the vision of their writers is evidently the latter.

The solution? In the short term, of course, we must defeat those who would use our school systems to "guide" or mold our children into lives constrained by the imagination of only a single world view. After all, diversity is healthy; homogeneity is boring. One way to do that is to work to strengthen proposals or initiatives that have to do with choice, and independence, and diversity in education, and fight those that increase governmental control and stifle innovation. We must also do the same things at the local and state levels, because values imposed from Harrisburg, Austin, Sacramento, Tallahassee, or Lansing are no more tolerable than those from Washington, D.C. At the same time we must encourage alternatives in schools and educational systems — from innovative public school programs to vouchers or tuition tax credit options which include private schools, and even to home schools — whether any of them are schools to which we would send our own children or not. Every new freedom for others is an opportunity for greater freedom and tolerance for our own beliefs.

Tolerance, however, need not — *should* not — extend to permitting others to impose their beliefs upon our children.

In the final analysis, the only way we can assure that those whose beliefs differ from our own cannot intrude into our lives . . . is to guarantee that *no* special interest — from *whichever* end of the political, social, or religious spectrum — can impose their beliefs on the rest of us. We must deny the Federal Government the right to dictate *any* such doctrine . . . or to make us or our children fearful of speaking what we believe because a file deep in a computer somewhere still records how we answered test questions when we were eight. That the Founding Fathers believed they had enacted such safeguards has not stopped social reforming bureaucrats from trying, as we have seen.

Therefore, we must redouble our commitment to always be aware of what our government is doing for (or *to*) us, and our conviction that government must *not* have the right to impose any but the most minimal standards of behavior upon any of us. Remember, if we give the government the right to impose our beliefs upon others, we have also given it the right to perhaps impose the beliefs of others upon *ourselves*.

We must be careful what we ask for . . . we might get it.

Epilogue
(. . . And the State Board's Christmas Surprise)

On March 24, 1990, an eight-year-old Michigan boy saw an affective film entitled "Nobody Useless" as part of a self-esteem exercise in his second-grade class. One purpose, supposedly, was to encourage compassion for the physically handicapped. But among the "lessons" in the film was a blow-by-blow description of how to hang oneself, specifically, how to apply a rope to the carotid artery and cut off the air supply.

Young Stephen Nalepa had an IQ of 130, was well-liked and played soccer. His teachers described him as a "visual learner." Encyclopedia Britannica, which distributed the film, and the Osmond family, who made it, both said nothing like what happened to Stephen had ever occurred before. But, then, the film had never been used as part of a "feelings exploration" in a class full of little children before.

The Nalepas didn't follow education reform issues. They knew nothing about threshold-level "strands" or affective curriculum, nothing about the use of supplementary materials, nothing about the testing process, noncognitive learning, or the role of behavioral Labs and institutes.

The Nalepas had to learn on the job.

The boy in the film was rescued from his suicide attempt at the last moment. In real life, Stephen Nalepa was found dead in his bedroom, his feet a couple of inches off the ground. After their initial shock and grief, his parents began pursuing legal action.

December 1991

Despite a motorcycle accident that nearly took his life in 1988, the Hoges' son, Garrett, Jr., recovered and was accepted by a top college, Bucknell, due to his exceptional mathematical ability. He kept between a 3.9 and 4.0 grade point average and received a university grant for research in organic chemistry. In 1990, he was accepted into the University of Pittsburgh's Honors College where he continues his studies. Physically, Garrett, Jr., is a combination of his parents — six feet tall like his father, with Anita's dark brown hair and facial features. Like his mother, Garrett, Jr., also tends to be soft-spoken and has tremendous "presence" and speaking ability, which he is just now learning to exploit. Whenever he talks, people listen.

Dr. Robert Coldiron (Chief of the Department of Testing and Evaluation in Pennsylvania) and Dr. Bill Logan (Commissioner of Basic Education in Pennsylvania, the fellow who originally passed Anita to the federal level) both decided to call it quits just about the time Anita Hoge's requested audit report came out in Pennsylvania. Both men resigned.

Erica Kenney, the late Senator Zorinsky's legislative assistant, left the Senate in 1988. Today she has her own consulting business, specializing in energy and environmental issues as well as education.

Anita Hoge's letter to the U.S. Department of Education, with copies to various legal parties, including General Counsel at the Pennsylvania and U.S. Departments of Education, did get somebody's attention, but not in the way Anita had hoped.

Instead of issuing a "release of the findings," in accordance with Section 98.9a and b, the Education Departments cut her off.[102] In following up, Anita was told that the Pennsylvania Department of Education (PDE) had entered "voluntarily" into "extensive negotiations" with the federal level Department for the purpose of resolving her complaint and closing her case.

So, Anita thought, *they agreed to do what they wanted to do in the first place: Pennsylvania got off the hook on the EQA business, and I am out of everyone's hair. Someone must have found a way to do it.*

Anita still hadn't found out exactly *which* conditions of the Protection of Pupil Rights Amendment (PPRA) had been met in her complaint, that is, which "future violations" Pennsylvania supposedly would try to avoid.

Then, in December 1990, Anita Hoge received another letter from Leroy Rooker (Student and Family Education Rights and Privacy Office), dated November 29, 1990, in response to Anita's repeated demands to see the "basis of the findings" that closed the cases she had supposedly "won."

"Clearly . . . your complaint satisfied all of the conditions under the [PPRA] regulations for commencement of an investigation, and in fact, an investigation was conducted," Rooker wrote. He reiterated that the Commonwealth of Pennsylvania had "failed to substantiate" its earlier positions that (1) EQA was not a psychological test, that (2) "protected areas" of PPRA had not been violated, and that (3) federal funds had not been used in development, implementation, or administration of the test (or, by extension, in curriculum developed from the test results).

But the fact that Anita Hoge had been right did not entitle her, apparently, to a statement regarding the "basis of the findings." Rooker explained that the very next section of the PPRA legislation, 98.10, on "enforcement," made it clear that in the event the state agreed to "comply voluntarily" with the law, then General Counsel was under no obligation to disclose "the basis of its findings" as per the usual procedure when a decision is rendered. Since the matter was "resolved voluntarily through a negotiated agreement" and "a policy [had] been issued" on the matter, nothing further needed to be done.

Thus, whatever agreement had transpired between the state of Pennsylvania and the federal government when they entered into "extensive negotiations" in late 1989, Anita Hoge was not going to be told about it.

Anita received letters from other officials, too — one of them stating that it was "not clear the EQA was covered under PPRA" legislation. So, on

January 2, 1992, Anita wrote again to Leroy Rooker, asking, among other things, how such a thing was possible. She also pointed out his error on Section 98.10 of the PPRA, "Enforcement of the findings." The clause was intended to be a *separate* step, to be taken only *after* written notice of findings had been issued, she wrote. How does one *enforce* findings if no one knows what they are?

Of course that was the whole point. Pennsylvania officials undoubtedly knew what the findings were. It was Anita Hoge who did not.

Meanwhile, Mark Shiffrin, the helpful General Counsel for the U.S. Department of Education, whom Anita was counting on to lower the boom, had "left education" to become an attorney for the Commodity Futures Trading Commission. Someone named John Christy had taken his place at the Department.

Anita Hoge was determined to find out what kind of deal had been cut, and why she wasn't entitled to any information about it. In looking over all the letters she had received from various officials, including the all-important copies of letters Senator Arlen Specter had forwarded to her between the U.S. Department of Education and Pennsylvania officials, she realized that one letter in particular, a June 12, 1987, letter from Dr. Richard L. Kohr, Measurement and Evaluation Supervisor, Division of Testing and Evaluation at the Pennsylvania Department of Education, had been all she ever needed to prove her case; she just hadn't realized it at the time.

Kohr had responded on behalf of Pennsylvania Governor Robert Casey to a letter from a Mrs. Virginia Fischer, who apparently had complained about the TELLS test, which was also under fire for attitudinal testing and bringing in behavior modification programs. In the first paragraph Kohr stated that the TELLS was composed of "reading and mathematics test items, not attitudinal items." In the second paragraph, he allowed that although EQA included "some attitudinal type items, the vast majority of the test deals with the measurement of knowledge and skills in reading, mathematics, writing skills, ...analytical thinking and health" which he went on to describe as "cognitive areas." All of this, of course, constituted the same *pro forma* responses that later were shown to be grossly misleading. EQA was over half attitudinal, for example, and the definition of "cognitive" was "belief system," not academic knowledge. But it was the next statement, the final sentence, in Kohr's letter that would have "done in" the PDE:

> "Behavior modification is not advocated by our program, rather it is a specialized clinical technique used principally by psychologists to achieve a therapeutic goal with their patients."

That statement proved Pennsylvania's state agency staff knew the definition of behavior modification, knew it was a medical technique, which, used by anyone other than a licensed practitioner or in circumstances other than those for which parental consent had been obtained, constituted a violation of law. So when Anita Hoge opened the EQA-based Resource packet, "Interest in School and Learning," taken from the manual *Getting Inside the EQA Inventory,* and saw a footnote on page 3, in which credit was given to Dr. Kohr for the behavior modification attitude scale he developed for scoring the EQA, she knew the response he had given Mrs. Fischer in his letter, about not advocating behavior modification techniques, was a bald-faced lie. Dr. Kohr's attitude scale was one of those where the student selects responses like "Strongly Agree, Mostly Agree, Mostly Disagree, Strongly Disagree," and such-and-such "makes me Very Happy, A Little Happy, A Little Unhappy, or Very Unhappy." Dr. Kohr weighted (scored) these various options using both norm referencing and criterion referencing. The criterion-referenced items, of course, were the ones measured against preferred answers and wound up in the national data bank.

Anita Hoge had in her possession the R.I.S.E. computer printouts of curriculum, which specifically linked "EQA test areas" with federally "validated" curricula (on the printouts and on the curriculum covers themselves). These were clearly labeled "behavior modification" and even "therapy." Moreover, there was no way any official could say that EQA was not covered under PPRA regulations.

Well, there was *one* way, actually: To conveniently "lose" Anita's documentation.

More than one letter over the past four years, even as late as October 11, 1990, alleged that Anita had not supplied evidence — even though she always had made it a point to include any relevant documentation and sent the whole package by *certified mail* every time she made a demand or allegation.

Anita knew that unsubstantiated allegations were a sure way to lose credibility, and much of the costs she incurred over the four years were for photocopies and certified mailings to accommodate skeptical officials. So when faced with comments about unsubstantiated allegations, or lack of documentation, she would write back, detailing the contents of the packet she had previously sent with her certified letters. Either she would get no response at all to these follow-ups, or no comments specifically relating to the materials she sent. Only twice in the correspondence she received over the four years was there ever any mention concerning the contents of her documentation — comments indicating whether the materials substantiated her allegations or failed to substantiate them.

In May of 1991, just two months before this book was first released, Anita Hoge telephoned Larry Newman at the Freedom of Information office in Washington, D.C. Newman was the man who in the summer of 1989 had forwarded Anita's August 16 letter, about getting a copy of the Pennsylvania audit, to James B. Thomas, Jr., Deputy Undersecretary at the federal-level Inspector General's office.[103]

Just maybe, she thought, Newman would turn over everything in her file if she demanded it. Since she intended to seek legal recourse anyway, it would be good to have the folder now — and there she would possibly located the elusive "basis for the findings."

Larry Newman remembered Anita Hoge from her 1989 letter. *That's odd,* Anita thought. Their brief contact could hardly have been memorable to someone in his position. Or could it?

Newman left her to consider the idea as he trudged off to locate her folder. Anita was just beginning to wonder if she had been forgotten, when suddenly Newman picked up on the line and stunned her with: "Mrs. Hoge, I don't know how to tell you this, but your file's not here."

"What do you mean, 'not here'," she spat. "I know good and well there's a file on my case there because General Counsel told me so and..."

Newman interrupted, "I didn't mean that your *folder* isn't here; I mean that there's nothing in it. It's empty."

Three more attempts were later made to secure the contents of the file, in which there were reportedly hundreds of pages. In one attempt by another party, it was implied that the contents were being photocopied. Nothing was received by anyone for months. Finally, multiple copies of a few of Anita's own letters were forwarded at her own expense and with names of individuals mentioned blackened out, as is customary with *classified* documents. But the whereabouts of the intact file, including opinions by legal counsel, the Pennsylvania audit, negotiations, and findings, remains a mystery to this day.

The Pennsylvania Assessment System (PAS), which appeared to be the EQA under a new name, was again placed "on hold" and, even then, limited to the subjects of reading and mathematics. At least two individuals who were reluctantly permitted to read through the 1989 test wrote to Dr. William R. Kirk, Assistant Superintendent of the East Penn School District, to say that the first few pages alone appeared to be a repeat of the EQA, and in Section 7, questions 139-158 were judged as attempts to elicit personal information in the form of opinions.

In any event, the literature accompanying both PAS and TELLS stated that the tests were based on Pennsylvania's Quality Goals of Education, which, as detailed in previous chapters, are primarily behavioral and "fail[ed] to conform to legislative intent," according to the Pennsylvania General Assembly. Although the PAS test was suspended for one year in 1989, when complainants alerted school boards throughout the state that testing-programming practices might be in violation of federal laws, the PDE incorporated the Quality Goals into still another version of the PAS, called

Pennsylvania School System of Assessment (PSSA). Renaming tests, apparently, had become a favorite pastime. Test questions, the literature stated, were developed to assess "higher order thinking skills and application of knowledge." (No mention of basic subjects.) An official circular to the schools, the December 1988 issue of the Pennsylvania Education Bulletin, stated that, when completed, the new test was expected to provide information "on the same Ten Quality Goals previously assessed by EQA."

Since Anita Hoge no longer had children in public school, she probably was deemed no longer a threat — at least for the moment. So in September 1991, Pennsylvania's Armstrong School District in Ford City, Pennsylvania, tried another gambit to reinstate the EQA — this time in just the fourth and sixth grades. To conform with the requirement to inform parents ahead of time, what officials did was to include it in a list along with several other types of tests the children would get at various grade levels. So unless a parent read closely, he wouldn't even see "Educational Quality Assessment" among the entries — which included everything from the California Achievement test, to the Stanford Diagnostic, to hearing and vision screenings.

But an Armstrong District school board member, Lee Ruffner, did read closely the letter of "Informed Consent" that was also sent home to parents. Oddly, the letter had no place for parents to sign. It didn't even have a date on it. There was no designation as to whom the letter was to be returned.

The letter, it turned out, wasn't sent for signature, In point of fact, it had nothing to do with "consent," despite the title. It was instead a notice *informing* parents what the school district was going to do whether parents liked it or not:

> "... During the coming school year, the following tests may be administered to your child as part of the elementary school testing program:"

Three columns followed: Grade Level, Kind of Test, and Purpose. To the district's credit, beside "Educational Quality Assessment," under PURPOSE, was the statement "determines attitudes and knowledge possessed by student."

Lee Ruffner confronted the district, and the EQA was withdrawn two weeks later, before any children were tested.

So for the school year 1991-92, it appeared that Pennsylvania would cool its heels. Not only did the state place a "hold" on the PAS (or PSSA) and withdraw the EQA, it was the *only* state to pull out of the NAEP, ostensibly because the test was taking too many of the state's resources. At least that was one story going around the press offices.

But a piece that appeared in the *Philadelphia Inquirer* on June 23, 1991, "The Dropout State," quoted Pennsylvania Education Secretary Donald M. Carroll, Jr., as saying, by way of explanation, that "the state was reform[ing] state curriculum standards and develop[ing] new ways to evaluated performance of students and ...schools, and...it would take too much time and effort to participate [in NAEP]."

Carroll's statement should have been a warning to those following testing and curriculum issues. Instead, his comment was taken as a lame excuse for opting out of NAEP, to avoid admitting the state was in trouble over its testing procedures, especially the charges that the EQA was the early prototype for the national test, was utilizing federal funds, and was largely psychological.

Less than three months later, in a bold, preemptive strike against the opponents of psycho-behavioral testing and curriculum — a move that surprised even veteran legislation-watchers in Washington, D.C. — Pennsylvania's State Board of Education announced its intention to "adopt revised assessment and curriculum regulations for public *and nonpublic* schools." The announcement was highly irregular for several reasons, not the least of which was an attempt to regulate the curriculum of private schools.

Now, whenever this kind of announcement is made, it is because officials know that public hearings must, by law, be held so that professionals (in this case, individuals representing the Intermediate Units, universities, and education organizations and associations) as well as laypersons can examine the proposal and offer comments. This means that there must be a draft of the proposal available for people to look at. Once feedback on this draft has been obtained, in the form of oral and written testimony, those who drafted the proposal go back and produce a second draft which addresses the concerns and comments. Sometimes several drafts must be written before the final product is acceptable to the various interested parties. Other times, concerns are minor and a final draft is whipped out right away.

It is important to note that a proposal for "changes to regulations" is *not* voted on directly by the public. Such proposals are adopted by decisionmakers; in this case, by the same *unelected* representatives who drafted the proposal in the first place, the State Board of Education.

There is one avenue of recourse, however, if one is lucky enough to find out about it. In Pennsylvania, the state's General Assembly gives authority to an oversight committee to provide an independent review after the public hearings are over. This committee, the Independent Regulatory Review Commission (IRRC), gets 30 days to review the proposal. If it decides that the proposal is **contrary to the public interest,** it will see that the General Assembly brings pressure to bear upon the State Board to reconsider the proposal. Even so, the State Board drafts the proposal, calls the hearings and in the end passes or rejects the proposal. It doesn't *have* to pay attention to the findings of the Commission or the pressure of the General Assembly.

So why have hearings? Why bother with all this "Mickey Mouse"?

Because it is the law; the public has the right to the information, to ask questions and provide input. And if there is too much opposition, elected representatives may use their influence to oppose the measure.

In this particular instance, the initial announcement came out September 12, 1991. For some reason, area newspapers were virtually silent about the proposal and the first round of hearings. So when a second draft came out November 11, with the most important portions missing — a list of expected "student outcomes" and the section on "planned course requirements" — no one balked until it was almost too late. It was a classic case of trying to put one over on the public.

Here's what happened:

The second round of hearings was set for the Thanksgiving and Christmas holidays — a time when most people would be preparing their turkeys instead of preparing for a fight with the State Board. The proposed "revisions" applied to what are known as Chapters 3, 5, and 6 of Pennsylvania's Curriculum and Assessment Regulations. Chapter 3 is the testing (assessment). Chapter 5 refers to student goals and outcomes, and Chapter 6 refers to vocational and technical training. Of the three, Chapter 5 is the most important.

The regulations in question are based upon expected educational results, known as "student outcomes." This term has become increasingly popular among behaviorists nationwide because it implies a focus on educational goals instead of educational deficiencies, or weaknesses. In other words, instead of conveying a public perception of zeroing in on student "weaknesses" assessed from testing, which carries a distinctly negative connotation, educators are presenting themselves as goal-oriented, which comes off as more positive. To paraphrase Pennsylvania's State Board, the *new* focus is on what students *can* do, not on what they *fail* to demonstrate.

Again, wording is everything.

Thus for every one of those Quality Goals of Education (which meanwhile were expanded from the original 10 to 12), there exists a corresponding "student outcome." Indeed, the proposed revisions to the assessment and curriculum regulations hinge on the wording of the "outcomes." And that was the important piece the Board left out of its second draft. There were no student outcomes to look at.

People had to sign up two weeks in advance to testify at the hearings, so only those who found out about them in time showed up. Those who did asked to see the student outcomes. They were told that the outcomes were still being rewritten and that it wasn't necessary for people to see them. So a few stalwart souls brought out the previous year's outcomes to show how crucial they were to the regulations. Many outcomes were completely unmeasurable, such as:

> [All students] accept personal responsibility for effective relationships in family, workplace and community.

> All students demonstrate caregiving skills and evaluate, in all settings, appropriate child care practices necessary to nurture children based on child development theory.

How will the school evaluate, or test, whether ninth graders accept personal responsibility for effective relationships in the family? Who decided that "appropriate" child care should be based on existing child development theory, which is of questionable merit at best?

The newest two additions to Pennsylvania's Quality Goals center primarily on an entry labeled the "Common Core of Goals," which, if one doesn't read too carefully, are taken to be "basics." The term *core curriculum* has been around so long that it is automatically thought of in terms of the three R's, with some history and geography thrown in. But Pennsylvania's 1991 Core Goals are: Self-worth, Higher Order Thought, Learning Independently and Collaboratively (*learning what?*), Adaptability to Change, and Ethical Judgment. The rest of the goals are the same as before: Appreciating and Understanding Others; Career Education and Work; Wellness and Fitness; Environment and Ecology; Citizenship; and Personal, Family and Community Living. The only goals that approximate "basics" are Communications, Mathematics, and Science and Technology. Even so, when broken down into their sub-goal components — that is, what each child will actually learn at such-and-such a grade level — they come out like the following for mathematics:

> K-6th grade: [All students] use estimation to predict outcomes of problems and to check the reasonableness of a solution.

Most parents would be tickled, if by sixth grade, their children could read the word "estimate."

Moreover, Pennsylvania's goals are filled with how students will "demonstrate life skills, coping skills. and critical evaluation"; how they will "examine attitudes," "make appropriate decisions," and "bring about change." The goals and the outcomes are the EQA, all sliced up. This means, of course, that revisions to the regulations will not result in a change of *thrust* in either the testing or the curriculum. The thrust of education in Pennsylvania will remain behavioral, and the so-called "revisions" to the regulations can only further entrench that thrust.

In the Introduction to the draft, the State Board wrote that their "starting point" for the revisions on assessment and curriculum was the question: "What must Pennsylvania's students know and be able to do in order to succeed in the twenty-first century?" (Does this, too, begin to sound familiar? Like the B-STEP[104] paper, perhaps?)

"We concluded that the agenda for the 1990's and the next century must be higher order learning for all. . . . What matters is what students know and can demonstrate, not how many credits they accumulate," boasts the Introduction, which explains the rationale for adopting the revised regulations.

Not only would the PSSA replace EQA and TELLS under the revised regulations, stated the Board literature, but the new test would focus on how well *curricular programs* are doing, *not* how well individual students are doing.

If this was intended to lull parents into believing their children's attitudes would not be tracked, the ploy failed. The obvious objective of assessment testing all along was *to find out if behavior modification programs worked:*

How well do the programs change attitudes?

At what point will students adopt the state-desired (behaviorist-desired) attitudes?

Since Pennsylvania citizens made such a fuss about the state focusing on student attitudes, the Board simply changed the wording to say that, well, they were really evaluating the *programs,* not the kids.

A few paragraphs later readers discovered a proposal for a third "local" test which would track students, using "portfolios." This local test was not defined any further. No details were given about it except that the test would evaluate *individual* students, be standardized, and be contained in "portfolios," a term already in use in Michigan, Kentucky, and elsewhere, to mean "electronic monitoring." That's what it means in Pennsylvania, too — the revised Pennsylvania regulations stated that "it will be the responsibility of the Department [of Education] to recommend the criteria for judging the portfolios," and that portfolios would be continually analyzed and monitored. How does one continually monitor and analyze anything today against a set of criteria? By computerized tracking, of course.

Besides the timing of the hearings; a lack of student outcomes to examine; a thinly disguised scheme to institute a system of continuously monitored electronic portfolios; and a slate of goals that focused, once again, almost exclusively on psycho-behavioral, attitudinal objectives, there were two other oddities about the second draft of revised regulations.

In place of the "planned course requirements," the word **"reserved"** was repeated 58 times in boldfaced type. Every course requirement, apparently, was privileged information. Whenever anyone questioned the Board on this point, Board members simply refused to answer, saying, in effect, that they were there to take comments, not to answer questions.

Taking all these anomalies into consideration, a top lawyer with the Rutherford Institute,[105] William A. Bonner, summed up the matter in a stunning testimony delivered in Philadelphia, Pennsylvania, December 12, 1991:

> . . . education has now ventured into new and complex territory which goes beyond transmitting intellectually challenging curricula into reforming and remolding the attitudes and personalities of our youth . . . .

> While the public has assumed it retains its historic input into education on a local school district level, in fact education has been progressively federalized, with the bold new America 2000[106] as the ultimate expression of the consolidation of power over education directed from Washington. The revised Chapters 3, 5, and 6 respond to Washington's demand that the states effect strict compliance with federal regulation, in exchange for federal dollars. Freedom, diversity, and local control are being increasingly sacrificed in that exchange.

> Undergirding this federalization of education, and necessary to its implementation, has been a massive invasion of the family and the rights of

individual students through curricula utilizing psychological programming and experimentation, as well as a broad spectrum of behavior modification techniques. Data periodically gathered through invasive testing within the affective domain has then, through the illegal demand for students' social security numbers and other identifiers, been compiled on computer systems storing vast amounts of intimate and private information on our children and youth, in violation of their constitutional rights.

The time is long overdue for those in public education to honestly reveal to the public that "assessment" testing is going far beyond reading, writing, arithmetic and history into invasive exploration of the whole student. . . .

. . . While labels like TELLS and EQA will be obsolete, students will really face increasingly effective tracking of their psychological development, their values, their attitudes and political predilections couched in terms of mental health as a justification. . . .

The traditional interests and rights of parents have been trampled upon, as educators have proceeded on the proposition that professionals know better than parents how to raise children. The impact of these educators, some of whom hold behavioral science credentials instead of education credentials, has created further distance between public education and the public it is intended to serve. The results create a further attack upon the already weakened family units in our society. Both the assessment tests and the related curriculum increasingly reinforce the message that conformity to government-established values and attitudes is the key to future success in life. . . .

The increasing efforts to effect "security" of the assessment tests has hidden from the public the true breadth and depth of "higher order learning skills" testing. The State Board's lack of clarity regarding the implications of this testing deceives the public. The government initially sets the criteria determining which attitudes and values young citizens should possess. The public does not understand that the government is establishing criteria to assess attitudes, values and opinions, nor do they understand that a "planned course" will be introduced to "remediate" attitudes, values and opinions not meeting government standards.

Moreover, Pennsylvania, once again, appeared to be trying to establish a model for other states to follow. In ushering in their "revised" regulations using behavioral outcomes and goals as well as unspecified curricula, it would be a short step to legalizing *federal* involvement in curriculum, because the state would be giving, indirectly, its permission for the feds to step in. How? By using federal monies in their testing programs and federal monies in parts of their curriculum. By extension, therefore, the federal government would be controlling curriculum. Not that it hasn't been doing so in the past few years already, but so far it hasn't been legal to do it! This fact has given parents clout they otherwise wouldn't have to force their schools to be responsive to their concerns. Even if all other things were above-board, that in a nutshell is the danger of nationalized curriculum and testing. Too many layers of bureaucracy eventually will push parents out of the system because the directives and mandates of the bureaucracy become more important to local officials than the concerns and desires of parents. This is one reason why the grievance procedure typically doesn't work for parents but, rather, works in favor of behaviorists who have "bought in" to the bureaucracy.

So while most Pennsylvania citizens decorated their Christmas trees, the State Board was on the offensive to take away the last vestiges of parents' rights.

Anita Hoge and her family were also decorating their tree when Anita got wind of the State Board's "Christmas surprise" and the Holiday Hearings. Don't these guys quit for a moment? she wondered.

Anita was tired. Both sides of the family were due in shortly, and she would be planning dinner for 18 people. Anita hadn't even finished her grocery shopping. Her son, Garrett, Jr., would be home soon from college. Anita was behind on everything. The last thing she needed was another fight with education officials.

The question was, could she stop the State Board even if she testified? There was so much that was wrong, it was difficult to know where to even start in preparing a testimony. But, again, if something wasn't done, the Board would say it had the blessing of Pennsylvania citizens and the revised regulations would go into effect in March 1992. And EQA-based testing would continue as before.

Why had the State Board forged ahead with revisions at this particular time and in so blatant a manner? Did the Board really expect to succeed in passing the revisions and that nobody would put up a fight? Or was the whole exercise a diversion? Were policymakers in Pennsylvania, and perhaps at the federal level, too, really after something else?

Meanwhile, another measure — this one, an amendment to Pennsylvania's Public School Code of 1949 (P.L. 30, No. 14) — had already passed and would take effect beginning in school year 1992-93. At first glance, it looked good. A section was added to the 1949 law which *appeared* to provide for educational choice; in fact, that's the way the section was titled. The first hint that the measure might not be what it seemed was in the first paragraph:

> The General Assembly finds that many disadvantaged school-age residents of this Commonwealth enjoy comparatively fewer educational opportunities than their counterparts of greater economic means. . . and their parents . . would benefit from the lifting of limitations and restrictions on their ability to select the educational setting best suited to their needs. In order to assist in equalizing educational opportunities . . . the Commonwealth hereby adopts a program to enhance educational choice in the Commonwealth.

The words "disadvantaged" and "equalizing," while they set the stage (i.e., provide the rationale) for the addition of the amendment, are misleading and diversionary. Later it is clear that "disadvantaged" can mean almost anything, not simply low-income, as implied. Secondly, the "choices" are limited to alternate public/non-profit schools; they did not include private or parochial schools. Third and more important, perhaps, is that a new layer of bureaucracy was established to administer this program, the Office of Educational Opportunity, placed within the Pennsylvania Department of Education. This Office, in turn, was to be advised by an *appointed* (again, not elected) board of 12 members who supposedly would represent different political perspectives.

This new Office would decide who was eligible for a $900 (or 90% of tuition) grant to pay to the parents of each child attending an alternate school. The dollar figure would increase annually by a factor equal to the percentage increase in the State appropriation for "equalized subsidy" for education. That is, the school receiving the new student would get an additional subsidy to cover the increased head count. Parents would have to make formal application to the Office to move their children to this alternative school.

So far, not too bad — except for the fact that tax dollars would, in effect, be expended twice for the benefit of the same student, and that those overseeing the whole business were not accountable directly to the public. But six pages later was the "zinger":

> The State Board of Education, with concurrence of the Office, shall by regulation prescribe such further procedures as are needed for the determination of the availability of public school attendance slots . . . and for the establishment or operation of the grant program and subsidy payments authorized in this section.

The State Board, through this new bureaucracy, had just given itself, *by regulation,* powers beyond what it had before. It could initiate in future years all sorts of procedures and mandates (*"prescribe such further procedures as are needed"*) under the cover of "educational choice," eligibility for which may or may not be related to low income.

"Do you realize what you just passed?" an exasperated Anita Hoge asked a jubilant group of education activists. Their faces fell.

Fortunately, the Pennsylvania House of Representatives later said the measure was unconstitutional.

January 1992

So far the Pennsylvania Department of Education had failed in every attempt since 1989 to reinstate EQA, under whatever name. The federal bureaucracy had been forced to involve itself directly in Pennsylvania affairs — to demand state budgets, audits, and other accounts because of increasing complaints on the part of Pennsylvania citizens. The purpose of the state education agencies was to run interference for the federal Department of Education, and now here was a state agency not only dragging the federal government into its problems but getting egg on both their faces as well.

Anita considered that the move to revise Pennsylvania's testing and curriculum regulations might be about damage control as much as passage of the actual regulations. The old waiting game — waiting for someone to sue, waiting for the opposition to make a first move — suddenly may have become less attractive. Perhaps Pennsylvania (and federal?) officials wanted to know just exactly where their opposition was coming from, other than from Anita Hoge; how well this opposition was organized, and what cards it held. Then again, perhaps they felt bound to mount an offensive — ready or not — before the opposition became strong enough to resist in earnest, in which case they might have decided to take their chances on passage of the revisions. Either way, the hearings gave behaviorists and officials time to sit back and take a good look at their opposition.

Anita Hoge, meanwhile, had become to many parents what Rosa Parks was to the Civil Rights movement. Too many parents for too long — liberals, conservatives, and moderates — had watched a decadent educational system take their hard-earned dollars and undermine their efforts at home. Word of documentation to support charges of educational fraud and other skulduggery had become increasingly believable, and Anita Hoge was a much-requested speaker on the lecture circuit. She and her cohorts, which included by now some local officials, continued to challenge education authorities who skirted the law with illegal requests for social security numbers, covert efforts to use tests that had been pulled for investigation and criterion-referenced scores that went to national computer banks instead of to local schools. Anita Hoge had set off a small earthquake, and the "shock waves" were beginning to be felt nationwide.

For that reason, among others, Anita Hoge decided there was nothing to be gained by her testifying at the hearings. Others whom she had groomed were doing a more than adequate job of it. She was politically sophisticated enough now to know that if she appeared at the hearings, she would be doing precisely what her opposition expected and, perhaps, wanted.

Instead, she decided to go with Peg Luksik, Chairman of the 22,000-plus-member Pennsylvania Parents Commission, to the Independent Regulatory Review Commission (the IRRC). Luksik, who had lost narrowly in a bid for governor in the last election and still had huge grassroots support, had been keeping abreast of developments inside the Pennsylvania Group for some three years. She didn't know just how much clout the IRRC had, but concluded it was time to put all the cards on the table, to show Commission members how they — and Pennsylvania citizens in general — were being defrauded. Peg Luksik also thought it was time to show that the education scam in Pennsylvania was part of something much larger.

So on January 8, 1992, Peg Luksik and Anita Hoge met for two hours with regulatory analysts Kimberly Trammell and Kim Pizzingrilli at the IRRC headquarters in Harrisburg. Anita knew that the presentation would have to be laid out so as to avoid overwhelming the analysts with evidence, yet say enough to ensure that they understood the magnitude of illegality, fraud, and manipulation. She started with the historical background of EQA.

Anita placed the proposed new regulations beside documents defining and outlining the so-called "higher order thinking skills." She showed the analysts how these "skills" were the same as the psycho-behavioral Quality Goals of Education, only broken up into smaller components. She and Peg Luksik presented multiple evidence of federal ties, both to the EQA test itself and to the curricular programs, and then demonstrated how the learning programs were not really local at all but, rather, emanated from a national databank. Anita presented documentation from the Council of Chief State School Officers which outlined the plan to achieve federal control over the state education agencies. She then pulled out the letter describing how "a policy was issued" to "resolve" her complaint.

Anita also showed the letter written to Mrs. Virginia Fischer by Dr. Kohr, which defined behavior modification and denied that officials advocated the technique. Beside it, she laid out the page where he was given credit for his attitude scale developed to test psycho-behavioral responses on the EQA.

"This is how parents are lied to and manipulated," Anita said. "This is how our opponents are buying time to get their programs through, by wasting the time of those who complain and throwing them off course when they tried to locate the "proper" authorities to complain to."

Trammel and Pizzingrilli literally gasped when they saw the documents given them by Hoge and Luksik. They could hardly believe the audacity of the State Board and the PDE.

Then the subject of the missing student outcomes for the proposed regulations came up. Trammell and Pizzingrilli responded that the State Board couldn't get away with the excuse about the "new" learning outcomes still being rewritten. If there was anything "new," they said, then the State Board should have waited until they had it to present at the hearing. No, the Commission would go by last year's outcomes since that was what it had in hand.

This provided Anita Hoge and Peg Luksik still another opportunity to point out the magnitude of the education scam. Look at these outcomes from Michigan, Missouri, and other states, they offered. Michigan's outcomes included: a person capable of learning over a lifetime; a person who makes decisions for successful living; a creative and innovative person; and so on. Keep in mind, they said, that these "desired student outcomes" must match up with the educational goals. The August 1991 ASCD High School of the Futures Planning Consortium in Traverse City, Michigan, described "A Vision of a Preferred Curriculum for the 21st Century" as the goals: "change and adaptability,' "self-actualization," "global interdependence," "cultural diversity," and "technology." The trend was repeated to a greater or lesser degree in other states around the country, the culprits consistently being well-known behaviorist educators.

"Don't you think you ought to take a look at these assessments?" suggested Anita Hoge. "No one is ever allowed to see them. But on what grounds could the State Board refuse to allow *you* to see them?" A good question, indeed, agreed analysts Trammell and Pizzingrilli.

In the end, the evidence was clear that the State Board and the Pennsylvania Department of Education would be violating state laws with the new regulations, and indeed with testing itself as long as it continued to be EQA-based.

As for the elusive policy that was issued between the U.S. Department of Education and the PDE — a carbon copy of which had been sent to state Education Secretary Don Carroll, Jr. — it was clearer than ever that it had been issued for the purpose of getting Anita Hoge out of the way. Leroy Rooker had stated in his final letter that "Pennsylvania did not substantiate its position" about the EQA not being a psychological test and not using federal funding. This meant that the federal government was implicated in wrongdoing as well as the state. If the press ever got wind of it and made bad publicity for the state education agency, the PDE would have only two choices: to take the heat and be the goats, or to say it wasn't their fault because the federal government made them write behavioral goals and initiate behavioral testing.

The PDE apparently decided on the latter option; they were going to yell "federal funds" very loudly, to cover themselves if the whole business ever came out in the press. Officials there may not have thought of it as threatening to blackmail the federal government, but that, in effect, was what it appeared they were going to do! So a "policy was issued" and Pennsylvania "entered into extensive negotiations" with the federal government. In other words, they cut a deal to close Anita Hoge's case, and fast.

The two analysts took all this to their boss, Frank Ertz, Executive Director of the IRRC. They showed him how the various pieces of the education puzzle fit together and explained how Pennsylvania's testing program clearly came under the Protection of Pupil Rights Amendment (PPRA) because of federal funding. They offered, too, that the State Board probably already had written the "new" student learning outcomes, if there were any. And the place where the "planned curriculum" should have gone, where the State Board had instead inserted the word *"reserved"* 58 times ... well, that was the last straw.

Anita Hoge was exhausted when she finally pulled in her driveway late on the evening of January 9. The drive to and from Harrisburg had taken four hours each way. Anita had even missed her own birthday party the day before because she had been busy preparing her presentation for the IRRC analysts. When she walked in the house, she saw that her answering machine was blinking. She flipped it on as she reached for the refrigerator door. It was Nancy Staible, regional state coordinator of one of the organizations Anita networked with. Staible had just received word that somebody named Frank Ertz at the Independent Regulatory Review Commission had issued a directive to the State Board of Education saying that "they would have to start over from scratch" on the regulations. This meant, among other things, that EQA-based testing was probably stopped for at least another year, perhaps permanently.

"This time you've *really* won," said Staible.

A few days later, Anita received a copy of the letter the IRRC sent to the State Board formally rejecting every one of the proposed revisions.

The Mexican standoff was over. The Pennsylvania Department of Education, the State Board, and the behaviorists at the federal level: all of them had miscalculated. They didn't expect Anita to know about the court of last resort, the IRRC. They didn't count on her missing the hearings or having backing from Peg Luksik and her 22,000 supporters. Instead, the State Board had sent out "instructional support/collaborative teams" to implement the "new" regulations throughout Pennsylvania even before the hearings were over. So confident and arrogant were the promoters of behavioral testing and programming, that they had forged ahead with their plans without bothering to wait for the measure to pass. Now they'd been caught red-handed. At least three state officials, including the Pennsylvania Secretary of Education, were implicated directly in engineering a coverup of the State Board's plan to ignore state law as well as PPRA regulations. Even now, the State Board was hastily calling an emergency meeting of superintendents to say that implementation of the new regulations was "off." Finally, there was court-admissible proof of foreknowledge and deliberate intent at the state level, which directly implicated the federal government (because of PPRA).

Of course, when they found out who had gone to the IRRC, and that it was she who had been responsible for Ertz's directive, they would be furious. And no doubt they would try to discredit her. But for now it was enough that she had thrown the ball back in their court, that they had risked all on a tremendous gamble, and lost. It was the best Christmas present she could have hoped for.

The irony of it was beyond anything Anita could have imagined. Pennsylvania education officials and their behaviorist helpmates in the federal government had thought if they could get testing and behavioral programming thoroughly entrenched in the key state of Pennsylvania, where they were facing their toughest resistance, they could get it through anywhere. What they had not considered was that if Anita Hoge could stop them in Pennsylvania — the state where Carnegie big-wig, Taba-coached, world renowned behaviorist Ralph Tyler had carefully crafted his first "state" assessment — then they could be stopped anywhere.

———————

Debbie Nalepa was carrying laundry as she walked down the hall of her middle-class Michigan home. She still couldn't help looking in when she passed by Stephen's bedroom. She kept half-expecting her little dynamo to come bursting out from behind the bed.

"Ha! I fooled you. I was hiding!" she would pretend to hear him say.

But there was no sound, of course. And there never would be again.

It had been nearly two years since that awful, dreadful day. She still wanted to scream "No!!" whenever she thought of it. A horrible dream. Impossible. Yet it had happened. And in an instant he was gone.

To make matters worse, she and her family were being harassed by school officials, who understandably, perhaps, wanted to avoid responsibility for what had happened. What was not understandable is how they could lie. Couldn't they feel her pain? How could they tell deliberate falsehoods about a relationship they knew nothing about, a relationship between a little boy and his mother. Officials had made innuendos about possible sexual abuse. Absurd. They had said the child was hyperactive. Well, so what? He was her little bundle of energy: bristling, curious, eager, smart. Too bad parents couldn't sell back all that energy when their children reached the age of 40.

But Stephen would never be 40.

Debbie dropped the laundry on the living room sofa. Oh, Lord, did the pain ever end? Was taking school officials to task worth the anger, the constant reminders of her loss, the anguish of not being able to fight back? She was just a parent after all. She and her husband. They had no clout.

Fighting back. That's just what the lawyer told her she shouldn't do. The case could take years. Probably never would be resolved. Hard to prove negligence in a case like this.

But Debbie Nalepa knew now that it was more than mere negligence.

Can't fight back. Just a parent. No clout . . . No Stephen.

Fighting back the tears that had welled up still again, she made her way toward the kitchen with her laundry. She had to get on with things, she told herself. Then her eye fell on a piece of paper lying on an end table. It had been there for days. Maybe weeks, who knew at this point? One day was the same as another. She squinted, dropped the laundry again, and picked up the torn scrap with writing on it.

Debbie Nalepa looked at the writing for a long time, as if to digest the few words that were scribbled there. She spent another five minutes just standing and staring into the empty gloom that had once been filled with laughter, and bustle, and the sound of refrigerator doors forever opening and closing.

Debbie walked disinterestedly past the laundry on the floor and over to the telephone on her kitchen wall. She picked up the receiver and dialed the number written on the scrap of paper. Shakily, she waited through four rings.

"Hello. This is Anita Hoge," said the voice on the other end of the line.

Notes

1 R.I.S.E. stands for Research Information Sources in Education.

2 Values clarification is a potentially dangerous psychological technique that has caused an uproar among many professionals as well as parents. Nevertheless, most teachers have whole books of these strategies on their desks. The term, *values clarification*, however, has fallen into some disrepute and tends not to be as blatantly advertised. See *Chapter 11* for more on this.

3 March 22, 1989.

4 from *Getting Inside the EQA Inventory*, "Questions and Answers about the EQA," Pennsylvania Dept. of Education, grade 11 test, page 20.

5 U.S. Dept. of Education figure for 1989 was almost $48 billion; projected total expenditure for 1990 is $50 billion (Source: Education Information Branch, Office of Educational Research and Improvement (OERI), July 1990.). This does not account, however, for the government's total annual expenditures for education, which is estimated at about $370 billion. This sum reflects education expenditures that go through other agencies, such as Defense, Labor, Agriculture, Housing, and even NASA. Although staffing for these education-related positions and curriculum development are usually done through the U.S. Dept. of Education, by temporarily "detailing" personnel to the agency in question so that only candidates with many graduate hours of opinion-molding education courses (as opposed to coursework in hard subject areas, such as math or science) have any chance at these positions, the Department does not add to its budget figures the amount of money they spend on such activity for elementary and secondary schools, public and private, as well as for colleges and universities. In 1989, this conglomerate figure was $353 billion. (Source: Educational Research Associates, Portland, Oregon.) Another probable reason for not counting these expenditures as part of the Education Department budget is because it might leave itself open to charges of establishing curriculum, which, of course, is against federal law.

6 Chris Pipho, Director, ECS Information Clearinghouse, Education Commission of the States, Denver, Colorado, in a telephone interview.

7 from *Crucial Issues in Testing*, ed. Ralph W. Tyler (Center for Advanced Study in Behavioral Sciences) and Richard M. Wolf (Assoc. Professor of Psychology and Education, Teachers College, Columbia University), McCrutchen Publishing Corp., Berkeley, Calif., 1974, p. 128. This book is one of four titles in a 1974 Series on Contemporary Educational Issues published under the auspices of the National Society for the Study of Education. Various individuals in the field contributed articles and essays for this book.

8 *Ibid.*, "Assessing Education at the State Level," by Henry S. Dyer and Elsa Rosenthal, Educational Testing Service, p. 105.

9 *Ibid.*, pp. 112-113.

10 Grayson later became an official at the U.S. Dept. of Education's National Institute of Education, where he wrote an important paper questioning the amassing of personal and private information on children into non-secure databanks: "Education, Technology and Individual Privacy," Lawrence P. Grayson, National Institute of Education, delivered to IEEE, 1978. See *Chapter 8* for more on this paper.

11 Originally the title of the test was "Teaching for Essential Learning and Literacy Skills (TELLS)." In 1980, one of the "L"s was dropped — "Literacy" — thus making the title "Teaching for Essential Learning Skills." But there was such a public outcry about this change that last year the word "Literacy" was reinstated.

12 *The Dynamics of Education*, published in London; *School Culture: Studies of Participation and Leadership*; *A Teacher's Handbook to Elementary Social Studies: An Inductive Approach*; and *Thinking In Elementary School Children* are among the credits to Taba.

13 In *Chapter 11*, it will be shown that this type of questioning increasingly is being used by employers to find the "honesty quotient" of prospective employees. A wrong guess at the more obscure or redundant questions can mean a job-seeker will be turned down. The practice is currently being challenged, and the OTA is reviewing these tests. Reviewer's conclusions may end them — at least in the workplace. Unfortunately, schools seem to be exempt from legal statutes that bind other institutions. Despite the evidence at OTA on schools indulging in this practice, little about it has been said since the 1978 Grayson paper.

14 James P. Shaver, "National Assessment of Values and Attitudes for Social Studies," published through *The Nation's Report Card*, U.S. Dept. of Education (Office of Educational Research and Improvement), Aug., 1986, p.24. He discusses how to use essays and writing samples to obtain affective-attitudinal information. This is exactly what was done in Maryland. *The Washington Post* reported the resulting furor that erupted: "Maryland Board Votes To Delay Writing Test Requirement," May 1, 1986, p. B1. The test, which was scored for opinions, "not for punctuation or grammar," was being made a requirement for graduation. Someone let the cat out of the bag, sending the information on scoring to the *Post* reporter. A similar writing test in Texas was later found to be scored by the same source as the Maryland test — in North Carolina. Other writing sample methods include student diaries and journals, kept in the school by the teacher or counselor.

15 It is worth noting that on page 72 of the teachers' guide of the citizenship curriculum examined by Anita Hoge, values clarification is described in the computer printout not only as a major teaching strategy, but as "one of the most popular in-school approaches to come out of the *humanistic education movement*." Values clarification is taken from Dr. Carl Rogers' non-directive therapy. In any case, while the term "humanistic" (or "humanism") along with its teaching methodologies, of which values clarification is one, are frequently said to be the bugaboos of overzealous Christian Fundamentalists, or the "lunatic fringe," the fact remains that a large

humanistic movement does exist, along with its own magazine and doctrinal code, and that certain curricula carry the label. More on this in Chapter 11.

16 from "Goals for Death Education," by Audrey Gordon and Dennis Klass, *The School Counselor*, Vol. 24, No. 5, May 1977, p. 346.

17 Robert Muller was with the United Nations for 37 years. He was Secretary of the U.N. Economic & Social Council and coordinated 32 specialized U.N. agencies.

18 The NIE was part of the U.S. Department of Education, but it came under a lot of fire in the early 1980s. It was supposedly "abolished" — in actuality absorbed by OERI, another division within the Department of Education. Thus, in reality the same work has been transferred to OERI — an organization which turns out to have a most interesting background. More on this later, in Chapter 24.

19 The same approach is used to disseminate special education material at the Bureau for the Education of the Handicapped.

20 This document did not have numbered pages, thus none can be given. In the first sentence of the quotation, *Title IV-C* refers to the ESEA legislation — the same designation Anita Hoge found on the cover of the citizenship curriculum guide.

21 *Getting Inside the EQA Inventory*, "Questions and Answers About the EQA," Pennsylvania Dept. of Education, grade 11 test, page 20.

22 Many of the ESEA titles under the designations (I, II, III, etc.) were switched around as the legislation expanded over the years. "Basic Education" provisions, for example, became the new Title II in 1983, which spurred the development of tests like TELS in Pennsylvania; a "gifted and talented" provision was added to Title I in 1973, as were portions of the old National Defense Education Act and other, previous legislations. Major changes were again made when Title I was recast as "Chapter 1."

23 published Dec. 1975 in *Elementary School Guidance and Counseling*.

24 Charles W. Sherrer and Ronald A. Roston, *Federal Bar Journal*, Vol. 30, No. 2, Spring 1971.

25 "Education, Technology and Individual Privacy," Lawrence P. Grayson, National Institute of Education, to IEEE, 1978.

26 The paper also makes clear that the NAEP is legislated and that regulations exist designed to assure its use in American schools. The appendix to his paper even includes the relevant sections of these laws: Public Laws 95-561 and 98-511.

27 NIE is now part of another division, OERI, as noted earlier.

28 Moreno was written up May 4, 1957, in the *New York Times* as "discoverer of phsychodrama, group therapy and sociometric techniques in psychotherapy." He came to the United States from Austria (where he served as Officer of Health) in 1935. Once in this country, he lectured extensively on his research and eventually founded the Moreno Institute in New York. In a leaflet describing the Institute, there is a quotation from him that provides insight into his thinking and method:
"...whatever happens in the mind of patients in the course of group therapy and psychodrama sessions, in the physician's mind, in connection with the patient's

ailments ... we should not keep anything secret from each other. We should divulge freely whatever we think, perceive or feel ... we should act out the fears and hopes ... and purge ourselves of them." He went on to apply the idea vigorously to the teaching profession. He became a frequent lecturer on the subject at Teachers' College, Columbia Univ., and detailed its use for the classroom in his book *Who Shall Survive*. John Dewey, father of modern education, was the first to accept the idea; the psychiatric community, oddly enough, was among the last. It was a more conservative bunch back then.

29 *Motivation and Personality*, Harper and Row, 1954.

30 Frank G. Goble, *The Third Force: The Psychology of Abraham Maslow,* Grossman Publishers Inc., 1970, Chapter 10.

31 For more about Sherrer and Roston's article, see *Chapter 8.*

32 from "Invasion of Privacy in Research and Testing," by Bernard Berelson, Spring 1967, page 123, reprinted in *Critical Issues in Testing*

33 Harper and Row, New York, 1970.

34 As told to *Parade Magazine.* Test publishers: Lousig-Nont & Assoc., Las Vegas; London House, Park Ridge, Ill., and E.F. Wonderlic Personnel Test Inc., Northfield, Ill. Creators of tests include ETS people.

35 from an interview by Bernard Gavzer, published in the same *Parade* issue, May 27, 1990.

36 See Chapter 8.

37 Joe Coors is founder and primary funder of the conservative Heritage Foundation in Washington, D.C.

38 presented at a federally sponsored education workshop in Washington, D.C., June 15-17, 1971. Hall represented Savannah State College, Savannah, Georgia.

39 Teacher training was completely revamped between 1967 and 1974 to reflect behavioral teaching goals and strategies. That's why so much of the change agent work was contracted to people out of the University of Michigan: It was the Office of Education's official Center for Teacher Education Research, created under the ESEA of 1965. Most teachers of that period, including this writer, thought that the deemphasis on subject matter meant that they were learning to be relevant. They were led to believe that "coping skills" were more important than subject matter and would, in the end, help students to learn better. The National Teachers Exam reinforced this belief. More about this later.

40 from: "Not Just Another Test" by Carmen J. Finley, *Critical Issues in Testing*, ed. Ralph W. Tyler (Center for Advanced Study in Behavioral Sciences) and Richard M. Wolf (Assoc. Professor of Psychology and Education, Teacher's College, Columbia University), McCrutchen Publishing Corp., Berkeley, Calif., 1974, p. 96. This book is one of four titles in a 1974 Series on Contemporary Educational Issues published under the auspices of the National Society for the Study of Education. Various individuals in the field contributed articles and essays for this book.

41 from *The Power Game* by Hedrick Smith, Ballantine Books, p. 10.

42 *The Long-Range Planning Guide* for McGuffey School District, which Anita Hoge and her colleagues found, indicated the District had been "impacted." Numbers on several pages had been crossed out, switched around, and generally made to conform to funding specifications. Furthermore, community leaders already had a pretty good idea how many handicapped and disadvantaged children there were prior to Long-Range Planning.

43 See *Chapter 9.*

44 op cit., *Critical Issues in Testing*, p. 127.

45 ref. Title I ESEA: *Participation of Private School Children: A Handbook for State and Local Officials,* DHEW, 1971.

46 *Handbook on the Performance Objectives Title I, ESEA of 1965*, U.S. DHEW/OE, 1973. Pub. no. OE-73-07103.

47 Although many learning programs, or "strands," come through the NDN, the counselor's office, the IU, and the Labs and Centers, still other monies for curriculum may be buried somewhere in unrelated legislation. A Senator might, for example, add a provision to a bill that would allow school districts to use block grants to fund alcohol-abuse curricula or death education courses. Legislation sometimes is introduced to fund pilot projects for controversial courses ($1 million in 1988, for example, was proposed for death education). The Senator or Representative who proposes the funding or adds the line to an unrelated bill is probably acting on the "suggestion" of a "constituent group" — one that is wealthy enough to affect his or her upcoming campaign. In other words, such suggestions can be used as a form of blackmail. Ironically, it is "against the law" for the government to fund specific academic programs. The reasoning goes like this: The federal and state government can fund learning programs that are *in the public interest* — anti-smoking information, alcoholism and drug programs. But *academic* programs are not in that category; they are subject to strictures about imposing curriculum and are, therefore, "local issues."

48 A memo from Donald Senese, Assistant Undersecretary of Education in 1982, claims that the education research function brings the federal share of education to 90 percent. The CCSSO's definition of "research" tends to confirm this.

49 Ramsey Seldon, remember, was Director of the Center for Coordination of Educational Assessment and Evaluation, at the federal level, the man who stated in his October 1985 speech that CCSSO would henceforth be working to promote the agenda of the federal government with regard to computerization and data collection.

50 See *Chapter 18* for some background on ECS.

51 "A Plan for the Redesign of the Elementary and Secondary Data Collection Program," Center for Education Statistics, Office of Educational Research and Improvement, March 7, 1986. More on this working paper later.

52 This issue was Volume 13, No. 5.

53 Memorandum control no. 0399401, completed April 26, 1989.

54 *op. cit.*, Dyer and Rosenthal, "Assessment of Noncognitive Development," *Critical Issues in Testing,*p. 115.

55 from *An Historical/Evaluative Analysis of: The Lancaster, Pennsylvania Student Skills Project*, for the Pennsylvania Dept. of Education and American Telephone and Telegraph Company, R.I.S.E. document 02845. Communication Technology Corp., June 30, 1975, p. vii.

56 Lay researchers in the Pennsylvania Group got hold of several booklets listing the grants from CFAT to and from other organizations and groups dating from 1964. One of the largest recipients of CFAT grants turned out to be none other than the United States Department of Education, and before that the old Office of Education under Health, Education and Welfare. Millions of dollars for every sort of program, including testing and databanking, emanated from this one organization's generosity. Thus it is unsurprising that new funding for testing, at both the state and national levels, is frequently sought first from government sources, and if that doesn't work, as occasionally is the case when state legislators or governors balk at the large capital outlay, then the Carnegie organization comes through with dollars.

57 See Chapter 9.

58 See Chapter 25. The *Washington Post* carried a long story on June 19, 1974, detailing the late Sam J. Ervin, Jr.'s then-released results of a four-year study on "Federal Data Banks and Constitutional Rights." He and former Attorney General Elliot Richardson were the first to key in on the potential of abusing the social security number.

59 Conversion of testing programs became typical. Old tests everywhere — even such excellent substantive tests as the California Achievement Test — were by 1988 being replaced or redefined using behavioral goals. Some were already utilizing the social security number.

60 According to some documents, such as *The Nation's Report Card*, the word "Integrated" is changed to "Information." But the working papers use the former term, as do most people in the education business.

61 Ed. by Project Director Edgar L. Morphet and Assistant Director David L. Jesser, Citation Press, 1967.

62 Proof of this is found in several documents; among them, the McGuffey School District's initial *Long-Range Plan*, Section 9, page 2.

63 See Chapter 7.

64 As an interesting aside here, Hopewell District authorities balked at the idea of the parent in question hiring a private math tutor for her child in lieu of the girl being put in a remedial class. In fact, the woman was threatened with legal action if she tried to keep her child out of a remedial class. But eventually Dr. Terry Mack, Curriculum Supervisor at Hopewell, got wind of what was going on, and there is an effort now to stop testing in the District and get out of the Intermediate Unit program. Repercussions are expected and it may well be a test case for local control. The District may well lose its federal funding.

65 excerpted from the testimony of Orrin Hatch, August 23, 1978.

66 World Institute for Computer-Assisted Teaching Systems, based in Utah.

67 OERI is part of the U.S. Dept. of Education, but it also has international connections and appears to be the link to international data-trafficking of education statistics. In fact, it appears to be the counterpart of the European OERI, where the "I" stands for "Innovation" instead of "Improvement." The U.S. version of Office of Educational Research and Improvement is connected to the Organization for Economic Cooperation and Development (OECD)'s Centre for Educational Research and Innovation (CERI), based in Paris, and it is primarily on the basis of economic cooperation and development that data transfer and comparison is justified. OECD was created under the Marshall Plan to aid the economies of war-torn Europe. No one ever dreamed at the time that OECD would become so heavily involved in education. The extent of international cooperation is revealed in an August 1982 "restricted circulation" document, "Strategies for School Improvement," in which the concept of "external change agents" is shown to "exist in most member countries," with the interesting caveat that "the term 'consultant' is frequently used to describe them." The term "facilitator" is also used, and Havelock's change agent texts are frequently referenced in the discussion. With the publication of "Strategies," the timetable to get all U.S. schools involved in the NAEP accelerated. It is also interesting to note that OECD papers refer to workers in the professions as "units." A country is spoken of as having so many "engineering units" or "medical units." OECD works to ascertain how many "units" produce what in each country — and how many it takes to strike a world balance.

68 "Alternatives for a National Data System of Elementary and Secondary Education," by George Hall, Richard M. Jaeger, C. Philip Kearney, and David E. Wiley (the latter formerly of WICAT in Utah), OERI, U.S. Dept. of Education, 1985.

69 "Educational Evaluation and Assessment in the United States," a Position Paper and Recommendations for Action, Nov. 13, 1984, Wilmington, Delaware, Annual Meeting of the CCSSO. See Chapter 18.

70 It was an inventory at the end of the citizenship curriculum that listed the 1969 book by Walcott Beatty. Anita located the book in a R.I.S.E. reference library. The book describes a NAEP committee being formed that would collect all non-cognitive tests. This book listed under "Behavioral Objectives-Affective Domain:" an EQA-based "Understanding Others" Resource packet. The book lists the objectives and the "committee" that formed them — the Educational Testing Service.

71 op cit., "Making Data Work" Critical Issues in Testing, p. 104.

72 from Appendix A, The Nation's Report Card, under "Costs," p. 68.

73 One of the best popular, non-technical pieces ever written on the subject is "Watching Me, Watching You" by Pete Earley that appeared in the Washington Post Magazine on May 11, 1986. A more technical look at the issue, from a domestic and international viewpoint, is Wilson Dizard's The Coming Information Wars, Longman, Inc., New York and London, 1982.

74 See Chapter 11.

75 "Peering Into Private Lives," by staff writers Daniel Mendel-Black and Evelyn Richards, *Washington Post,* January 20, 1991, pp. H1, H4.

76 "Keeping Tabs on Card Holders," by staff writer Albert B. Crenshaw, the *Wahington Post,* January 20, 1991, pp. H1, H4.

77 ref. ED-77/WS/133, Paris, Nov. 1977.

78 The following chapter presents a more thorough look at the route private and group computerized data travel.

79 Iran, in particular, has a sophisticated system of computers, put in place by the millionaire Texan Ross Perot's company, Electronic Data Systems Corporation, to build a modern social security system from scratch. Readers may remember Perot's daring rescue of his company executives, who were taken hostage there in 1979, shortly after the Shah fell.

80 Given the changing events inside the Soviet Union, it is unclear where the line should be drawn on transborder data flow and computer technology. Should Mikhail Gorbachev be replaced by a hard-liner, it might be less than comforting to know, for example, that "Soviet scientists have publicly confirmed that they regularly gain access to U.S. computer databases through overseas telephone hookups...." and that "Soviet researchers [have] used data networks in Canada, Europe and elsewhere to gain access to commercial and government data bases in the United States...These data base systems, employing sophisticated computers, enable users to retrieve in seconds reams of important...data...." This was reported in the *Washington Post,* May 26, 1986, by Michael Schrage under the headline "U.S. Seeking to Limit Access of Soviets to Computer Data," pp. A-1, 18. Since that time, of course, *glasnost* has made Americans less fussy — but our data systems, according to GAO reports, are no more secure now than then.

81 His latest attempt was defeated in 1989 thanks in part to an astute Senator Dan Coats (R-Ind.).

82 It may be rather startling to realize that already the U.N. Charter supersedes, in some cases, the U.S. Constitution in matters directly related to our foreign policy decisions. For example, although President Bush had the go-ahead to use force in the Persian Gulf to oust Saddam Hussein from Kuwait, the United States never did declare war. The reason was that according to the U.N. Charter, the President *couldn't* declare war as long as he was invoking the U.N. Resolutions and U.N. approval to move against Hussein. This situation, however, technically compromised our position with regard to the treatment of prisoners of war. Since there was technically no declaration of war, did Saddam Hussein have to abide by the Geneva Conventions in his treatment of our prisoners? That not a single journalist or commentator thought to bring up this awkward situation shows how giving away our national prerogatives can sneak up on people, until before they know it, they have given up more than they ever dreamed possible.

83 Both organizations were departments of the National Education Association at the time of the study in question, which took place at the Pocono conference January 18-20, 1947. The book discussed above was published by the NEA in 1948. The two departments, the ASCD and the NCSS, later became organizations in their own

right. Both, however, continued to maintain the same thrust and viewpoint. Chronological history was changed to "social studies" across the nation, and a tremendous output of educational materials, as well as a well-coordinated lobbying effort on education and political issues, continue today to emanate from their Washington offices. Their aim in education, they say, is a "world core curriculum" to help ensure the peace goals outlined in *Education for International Understanding*. Toward that end, a large conference was held in 1988 in Talloires, France. CFAT was well-represented along with other big-wigs of the education establishment, from this country and around the globe.

84 Pavlov, the reader may remember, was the Russian psychologist who pioneered "the conditioned response," or "programmed learning," as it applies to humans. Pavlov is best remembered for the conditioning experiments he conducted with his dog, which he conditioned to salivate in response to a non-food stimulus.

85 B-STEP is a landmark document that will be discussed in detail in the next chapter. Teacher training began nearly a century ago at the Michigan State Normal School, Eastern Michigan University. Thus Eastern Michigan evolved into the launching pad for new teacher instruction methodologies. The National Center for Research on Teacher Education at Michigan State University is one of those federally funded education Centers discussed earlier. It was a pilot for education reform in teaching methods. CFAT and other behaviorist groups were, and still are, the dominating influence for that reform. The B-STEP paper outlines the teaching "reforms" which took place after 1967. On June 3, 1990, the *Washington Post* reported a new five-year plan for teaching reform ["Teacher Training: Slow Changes"]. Taxpayers will fund this new project whether they want to or not.

86 From the Introduction to the Behavioral Teacher Education Project (B-STEP), 1967. More details next chapter.

87 Project no. 320424, U.S. Office of Education contract no. OEC-0-9-320424-4042 (010).

88 publisher: Longmans, Green, New York, 1956.

89 excerpted from "Education for A Global Society," *Phi Delta Kappa Educational Journal*, 1973, p.10. On page 16, he seeks to "reduce the strength of nationalism."

90 Bloom, *Taxonomy of Educational Objectives, Handbook II*. McKay Publishers, 1956.

91 from "The Responsibility of Psychiatry," by G.B. Chisolm, *Psychiatry — Journal of the Biology and Pathology of Interpersonal Relations*, Vol. 9, No. 1, Feb. 1946. The William Alanson White Psychiatric Foundation, Inc.

92 The American Association of Suicidology prepares a number of programs for the classroom.

93 The July 1986 issue of *Family Planning Perspectives* (a publication of the Allen Guttmacher Institute, which is the research arm of Planned Parenthood) stated that youngsters who go through sex education courses have a 40 percent increased likelihood of experimenting with sex than if they had never taken the course. Sex education courses tend to legitimize teenage sexual activity by implying, under the

authority of the school, that "everybody is doing it." Yet, the same publication quoted an Ohio State University study, based on interviews with 6,000 young women in a national representative sample in which it was found that only 6.6 percent had had sex by age 15. Another study, put out by "Who's Who Among American High School Students," found that among 1987's top senior year students — those with straight A's and B's — a full 70 percent had never had sex and 82 percent had never tried marijuana.

94 Wesleyan Univ. Press, 1983 (distributed by Harper & Row).

95 The following Lagemann quotations are taken from the book's Preface, pp. xi-xiii.

96 The appointment by President Nixon of Pifer brings up an interesting set of circumstances stemming from Nixon's long and apparently friendly association — save one exception — with Carnegie men. That exception was the infamous Hiss case, which involved a high-level Carnegie man, Alger Hiss himself, who, as may be remembered, was disgraced. Hiss' colleagues in the Carnegie Endowment for International Peace repeatedly attempted to come to his aid until, at last, the evidence appeared to be too overwhelming against him. Nevertheless, the three Carnegie organizations continued to enjoy nothing but praise from Nixon. For example, Nixon's close friend, former Secretary of State John Foster Dulles, also a Carnegie man, is heartily praised by Nixon in his presidential memoirs. Moreover, given Nixon's penchant for Carnegie advisors, he appears never to have had the least suspicion that a Carnegie kingpin may have had reasons for wanting to do him in. (See Nixon's memoirs and Stephen Ambrose's comprehensive work about Nixon, *The Education of a Politician*). The Hiss affair could not have pleased colleagues at the Carnegie Endowment for International Peace, and as a matter of fact, Nixon claims he received at the time many anonymous threats, including promises to get even. One cannot help but wonder, in light of subsequent events, whether Nixon had somehow gotten on a "hit list." Could he have been encouraged to follow "advice" which subsequently led to his downfall? Clearly, Carnegie organization leaders are expert manipulators, of Presidents and the public. Whether one approves or disapproves of either Nixon's policies or his actions in office — some of which Nixon insists were not his ideas, or even good ideas but, rather, the ideas of "trusted" advisors — one has to wonder whether the President had become a liability to one or more of the Carnegie organizations; whether one or more of his "advisors" eventually carried out the ultimate vendetta — promised anonymously many years prior — for his nailing the Hiss affair. The identity of "Deep Throat," for example, was never determined. Who or what were the sources of the leaks Nixon tried to stop with his "plumbers"? And Nixon apparently never did find out why his men broke into the Watergate; Nixon was way ahead of McGovern in the polls anyway. This and other incidents during Nixon's years in office to this day, he writes, continue to puzzle him — as well they might.

97 from *Today's Education*, Nov./Dec. 1978, p. 70.

98 See chapters 22 and 28 for discussion of this 1978 government investigation.

99 U.S. Dept. of Education cost-per-pupil figures for 1988 totaled $4,243 for public schools. Private day school figures were about the same. A few states differ, of course. Alabama and Tennesssee, for example, spend far less per pupil in public

schools, but private schools there — what few there are — also are lower. New York schools, public and private, are higher. On the whole, however, the figures are amazingly consistent, and parents who send their children to private facilities are, in effect, paying twice.

100 Joe Clark is an ex-Marine who turned around a crime-ridden, failing inner-city school and won the admiration and respect of the students.

101 All three incidents reported in the *Washington Post,* June 3, 1990, "Business Goes Back to the Three Rs," by Cindy Skrzycki.

102 Section 98.9a and b was the "Investigation of Findings" clause stating that the "office must provide to the complainant written notice of its findings and the basis for those findings" and that it could not ignore the letters of complainants. See Chapter 21, p. 167.

103 Thomas had denied Anita access to her own initiated audit (see Chapter 21).

104 See Chapter 28.

105 Rutherford Institute's International Headquarters are located in Charlottesville, Virginia

106 "America 2000" is the name given to President George Bush's Education Plan.

Reference List of Acronyms

ACLU — American Civil Liberties Union

ACT — American College Testing program

BEH — Bureau of Education of the Handicapped

CAEP — Connecticut Assessment of Educational Progress (the state test in Connecticut)

CAP — Cooperative Accountability Project: the seven state project headed by first Education Secretary Terrel Bell

CCSSO — Council of Chief State School Officers

CEIR — Coordinating Educational Information and Research

CEO — chief executive officer

CES — Center for Education Statistics (formerly National Center for Education Statistics)

CFAT — Carnegie Foundation for the Advancement of Teaching

ECS — Education Commission of the States (headquarters in Denver, Colorado)

EQA — Educational Quality Assessment (Pennsylvania's state assessment test)

ERIC — Educational Resource and Information Center (federal database)

ESEA — Elementary and Secondary Education Act of 1965

ESIDS — Elementary and Secondary Integrated Data System

ETS — Educational Testing Service (headquarters in Princeton, New Jersey)

HEW — old Dept. of Health, Education, and Welfare (now broken up into separate agencies)

IEA — International Education Achievement Organization

IRA — International Reading Association

IU — Intermediate Unit (the repository of educational materials, often disseminated by van)

JDRP — Joint Dissemination Review Panel

LEA — Local Education Agency (applies to any school district)

MMPI — Minnesota Multiphasic Personality Inventory

NAEP — National Assessment of Educational Progress (also referred to as the National Assessment

NCER — National Council on Educational Research (under President Reagan only)

NDN — National Diffusion Network (federal data bank containing curricular programs approved by a federally appointed review board)

NIE — National Institute of Education (now absorbed by OERI, also a part of the U.S. Dept. of Education)

OE — old Office of Education under HEW

OECD — Organization of Economic Cooperation and Development

OERI — Office of Educational Research and Improvement (under the U.S. Dept. of Education). Its Eurpoean counterpart, OERI, stands for Organization of Educational Research and Innovation

OTA — Office of Technology Assessment

PAS — Pennsylvania Assessment System (newest version of the EQA)

PPBS — planning-programming-budgeting system (launched in California)

PPRA — Protection of Pupil Rights Amendment

R & D — research and development

R.I.S.E. — Research Information Sources in Education (Pennsylvania's regional computer)

SAT — Scholastic Aptitude Test

SEA — State Education Agency (applies to any state); also known as a State Department of Education

SEAR — State Education Assessment Repository

TAP — Texas Assessment of Progress (Texas version of EQA)

TELS — Test for Essential Literacy Skills ("basic skills" test in Pennsylvania)

UNESCO — United Nations Education, Scientific, and Cultural Organization

WICAT — World Institute for Computer-Assisted Technology (based in Utah)

Index

National Institute of Education 34, 50, 61, 186, 210
National Teachers' Exam 35, 223
National Training Laboratory 223 - 224
Nationalism 64 - 65, 212 - 214
Nebraska 51, 102, 142, 144, 147 - 149, 154, 198
Nebraska Data Advisory Committee 149
Nebraska Education Data Center 143
New Model Me 82
New World Information Order 64
New York Times 186
Newman, Larry 151, 250
Newmann, Frank 142
Nightmare on Elm Street 11
Nixon, Richard M. 126, 232
Non-directive therapy 72, 78
Noriega, Manuel 214
Norman, David 84
North Carolina 59, 61
Northwest Regional Laboratory 240

O

Office of Educational Research and Improvement 188
Office of Technology Assessment 40, 91, 182
Ohio Bell Telephone Company 155
Olmstead v. United States 86
Omsbudsman 82
Operant conditioning 230
Organization of Economic Cooperation and Development 205

P

Parents Who Care 181
Pearson v. Dodd 86
Pell, Claiborne, Sen. 208
Pennsylvania Assessment System 162, 251, 253
Pennsylvania Assessment Test 161
Pennsylvania Bureau of Planning and Evaluation 33
Pennsylvania Department of Education 246, 249, 251, 261 - 262, 267
Pennsylvania Division of Testing 161, 248
Pennsylvania Group, the 2 - 3, 5, 22, 34 - 35, 40 - 41, 49, 51 - 52, 115, 118 - 119, 131, 138 - 140, 151 - 152, 154, 156 - 157, 163, 201, 264
Pennsylvania Parents Commission 263
Pennsylvania School System of Assessment 252 - 253, 257
Pennsylvania Senate Education Committee 28
Pentagon Papers 63

Pepperman, C.W. 86
Petrov, Sergei 236
Philadelphia Inquirer 253
Phonics 106, 108 - 110, 210, 228
Piaget, Jean 30, 72, 171
Pierce, Chester M., Dr. 218
Pifer, Alan 126
Pizzingrilli, Kim 264
Planning-programming-budgeting system 186
Pritchett, Henry Smith 231
Privacy Act of 1974 xi, 168 - 169
Privacy Office, Social Security Administration 168
Privacy Times 202 - 203
Private Power for the Public Good 231
Project '81 155
Project Charlie 82
Project on Information Technology and Education 240
Prometheus Books 79
Protection of Pupil Rights Amendment 1 - 3, 6, 88, 103, 140, 157 - 158, 165, 167, 169, 183, 247 - 249, 267
Psychiatry 225
Psycho-behavior 111
Psycho-behavioral education 68, 86 - 87, 97, 120, 128, 158, 162, 170, 177, 206, 218 - 219, 225, 235, 241 - 242
Psycholinguistics 105
Pumroy, Donald K. 170

Q

Quest 82

R

R.I.S.E. 18, 249, 282
Rand Corporation 118, 121
Reagan, Ronald, President 126
Research Council on Ethnopsychology 77
Research Information Sources in Education 18, 20, 22, 47, 156, 282
Richardson, Charles M. 104, 109
Richardson, Elliot 180
Riley, Bill 140
Robert Muller School 49
Rockefeller Foundation 50
Rogers, Carl R., Dr. 72, 76 - 77, 80, 82, 159
Rogers, Mary 157, 164
Rooker, Leroy 139, 157, 163, 247 - 248
Rosenthal, Elsa 38 - 39
Roston, Ronald A. 60, 86
Ruffner, Lee 252 - 253
Rutherford Institute 258

About the Author

Beverly K. Eakman

A NATIVE OF Washington, D.C., Beverly Eakman has a distinguished career in politics, education, and public affairs. She has served as chief speech writer for such eminent figures as Richard W. Carlson, Director of the Voice of America, and Chief Justice Warren E. Burger, Chairman of the Bicentennial Commission. She has penned numerous articles for these, and other, public figures; among them, Representative Lindy Boggs (D-La.), Thomas H. O'Connor, Bicentennial Commissioner and professor of history at Boston College; and Robert T. Barry, U.S. Ambassador to Bulgaria and former Deputy Director of Voice of America. Her ghosted pieces have appeared in *Education Today, Newsday, State Legislatures Magazine, the Philadelphia Enquirer, Human Events,* the *Washington Times,* and *Vital Speeches of the Day.* Her own byline has appeared in the *Washington Times, Education Week, USIA World,* in NASA publications, and elsewhere.

Eakman launched her career in 1968 as a secondary school English teacher in California (and briefly in Texas). Over the course of ten years she taught a variety of subjects, including debate and creative writing, to students ranging from "remedial" to "gifted." In the early 1970s, she wrote an English grammar curriculum designed for Vietnamese immigrants and a unique spelling curriculum for remedial students. Both were successful and adopted district-wide. Her latest curriculum, written in 1987, is a political science text for high school students: *The Strategy of Defense.* It has been used in many schools, particularly in Texas and Colorado.

In the late 1970s, Eakman took her skills to the Johnson Space Center, where she began writing and editing technical and scientific documents (as a NASA contractor) for engineers and scientists. She was soon asked to join the public affairs and education divisions, where she began to produce layman-oriented brochures, pamphlets, texts, and tour guide manuals on the U.S. space program. In the process, Eakman became well-versed in space medicine, lunar geology, and other technical subjects. In 1977, she became editor-in-chief of NASA's official news publication, *Roundup*, where she again worked to bring technical concepts to the layman's level. Her most notable story, "David, the Bubble Baby," in 1978, was picked up by the popular press and received national attention.

In 1984, Eakman returned to Washington and turned her attention to politics. She did a brief stint with a then-new education foundation, as Director of Research and Publications. It was during this period that she started ghosting articles and speeches, brochures, and monographs. Her work brought her to the attention of the Deputy Director of the Commission on the Bicentennial of the U.S. Constitution. Her work at the Commission brought her to the attention of the Director of Voice of America. Eakman has been a consultant to the Office of Juvenile Justice and Delinquency Prevention, the Institute of Comparative Social and Cultural Studies, and other clients. Today, Eakman is a writer and research consultant for the U.S. Department of Justice.

Eakman spent her formative years at an old and respected international academy, Maret School, in Washington, D.C., where she became multi-lingual. She earned her Bachelor's degree in Education from Texas Tech University and went on to do graduate work in education at the University of California, then in political science at the University of Houston. She lives in a Maryland suburb of Washington with her husband, Dave, an aerospace engineer.

If additional copies of this book are not available through your local bookstore, you may order direct from the publisher:

Educating for the New World Order (# 344100, ISBN 0-89420-278-2, Library of Congress Catalog Card # 91-73096, $21.95 (postpaid)

Ask for information about other Halcyon House books, including

House for Sale! (#344044, ISBN 0-89420-282-0, © 1991, $19.95 postpaid), an exposé of the U.S. House of Representatives

Decline and Fall of American Education (#440050, ISBN 0-89420-283-9, L.C. 91-73097, © 1991, $19.95 postpaid)

War Against Academic Child Abuse (#342110, ISBN 0-89420-287-1, available June 1992, $19.95 postpaid)

Both of the last two books deal with the failure of vision and leadership and further misdeeds in our school systems.

Send Check or Money Order to :

Halcyon House
PO Box 8795
Portland OR 97207-8795

VISA, MasterCard, American Express, or Discover:
Call (800) 827-2499 to order

Purchase orders:
accepted from Libraries, other educational institutions,
and qualified resellers